Simala Prasad is an Indian Police Service (IPS) officer from the 2011 batch. Her academic grounding in the social sciences deeply informs her approach to policing and her commitment to community upliftment.

Born to distinguished parents—her father, Dr Bhagirath Prasad, an Indian Administrative Service (IAS) officer and former Parliamentarian, and her mother, Padma Shri awardee Mehrunnisa Parvez, a celebrated Hindi writer—Simala inherited a blend of administrative insight and literary sensibility.

Her work in films reflects the same purpose that drives her public service: to convey profound social messages and inspire reflection and reform. Through her writings and creative pursuits, she seeks to awaken sensitivity, provoke thought, and encourage lasting social change.

SHE Goes

MISSING

Broken Childhoods, Fractured Systems, and the Pursuit of Justice in India

FOREWORD BY
DR KIRAN BEDI

SIMALA PRASAD

Om Books International

First published in 2026 by

Om Books International

Corporate & Editorial Office
A-12, Sector 64, Noida 201 301
Uttar Pradesh, India
Phone: +91 120 477 4100
Email: editorial@ombooks.com
Website: www.ombooksinternational.com

Sales Office
107, Ansari Road, Darya Ganj,
New Delhi 110 002, India
Phone: +91 11 4000 9000
Email: sales@ombooks.com
Website: www.ombooks.com

ISBN: 978-93-6395-133-4

Printed in India

10 9 8 7 6 5 4 3 2 1

To my mother, who keeps reminding me that
I have wings!

CONTENTS

FOREWORD

She Goes Missing is not merely a book of cases or procedures; it is a moral lens held up to society and an appeal to our collective conscience. The phenomenon of missing girls is among the most troubling indicators of social health. A missing girl is not simply absent—she is erased from the attention of the very society that should protect her. Each disappearance is a world undone: a future interrupted, a home left searching, and a trust betrayed.

Contrary to comforting assumptions, these cases are neither rare nor accidental. They arise across regions, classes, and cultures—from villages to cities, from poor households to educated families. Girls go missing due to domestic violence, false promises of love or work, trafficking networks, or the silent burden of neglect. Beneath every story lies gender inequality, loss of dignity, and the denial of voice. The author writes not from theory but from lived experience as a police officer, revealing the vulnerability, courage, and human truth behind every case.

This crisis is cultivated over years of conditioning that teaches girls to be silent and boys to be entitled. True safety comes not from restriction but from dignity, respect, and freedom. The book urges society to move from judgement to understanding—every missing report deserves urgency, every rescued girl deserves dignity. Sensitivity in policing is not weakness; it is strength rooted in empathy, purpose, and justice.

Rescue is only the beginning. Rehabilitation must involve emotional, social, and institutional support so girls are not returned to the same environments that harmed them. A survivor must receive acceptance without stigma, and opportunity without condition.

The issue of missing girls is not solely a policing challenge but a societal and ethical one. It demands coordinated action among law enforcement, families, communities, schools, and welfare institutions. Awareness, prevention, and early identification of vulnerability are essential. When a child goes missing, we lose a fragment of our collective humanity.

This book is a call to conscience—an invitation to rebuild systems with compassion and to recognize that reform is a shared responsibility. Let this work guide institutions, students, and citizens towards a future where every girl is seen, heard, and safe. For the true measure of a society lies not in its achievements, but in how it protects its most vulnerable.

Dr Kiran Bedi
IPS (Retd) & Former Lieutenant Governor of Puducherry

PREFACE

In every society, there are unspoken truths, hidden under layers of social norms and guarded by age-old traditions. The stories of missing children, particularly missing girls, are often among those truths—shrouded in misconceptions and overlooked pain. This book is written with a purpose: to bring these hidden narratives to light, to inspire empathy, and to encourage collective action.

The reasons why girls go missing are numerous and complex, ranging from societal pressure, exploitation, and family constraints to issues of self-identity and belonging. Often, these cases are misunderstood or minimized, allowing the cycle of disappearance to continue silently. In many instances, the response to missing girls has been shaped more by stereotype than by understanding, which not only fails the victims but also limits our society's ability to address the root causes of this problem.

It is my sincere hope that this book serves as a call to action—urging us to look beyond mere statistics and into the lives and futures of these young individuals. By illuminating the factors that contribute to girls going missing and exploring avenues for rehabilitation, I aim to equip readers with knowledge and insight to approach these issues with sensitivity and informed compassion. This book was conceived not just as an exploration of missing girls but as a catalyst for change—aimed at deepening the sensitivity that already exists within our institutions, particularly within the police force. It strives to elevate our understanding and compassion for the young lives affected by this harrowing reality. For those of us who serve in the public arena, there is a duty not only to respond to crimes but also to recognize the hidden layers of trauma and social injustices that lead to these disappearances.

The issue of missing girls is not simply a matter of numbers or isolated cases; it is a grave problem with far-reaching implications that intersect with many other crimes, including trafficking, abuse, and exploitation. Each girl who goes missing is a story of vulnerability, shaped by a complex interplay of social, economic, and cultural pressures. And while our existing systems have made strides, there remains a pressing need for a more profound, empathetic approach that can only come from truly understanding why these young girls vanish.

This book is, therefore, a call to action—to look beyond the obvious and fully grasp the severity of this issue and its devastating impact on families, communities, and society as a whole. My hope is that, in reading these pages, both the public and those in positions of authority will feel compelled to amplify their efforts in protecting and rehabilitating these girls. Let this work serve as a reminder that each child deserves safety and a future—and it is our shared responsibility to make that future possible.

At the heart of the issue of missing girls lies a deeper, systemic challenge: the entrenched nature of crimes against women and the long-standing inequalities that undermine their position in our society. The tragedy of missing girls is not an isolated phenomenon; it is part of a broader struggle that women face every day—a struggle for dignity, respect, and equality. This book aims to bring attention to these underlying issues, to highlight that the safety and empowerment of women are not just matters of individual well-being but essential for the growth and progress of our society as a whole.

Crimes against women are not only attacks on individuals but reflections of societal attitudes and long-held biases that see women as vulnerable and secondary. Addressing these crimes requires more than immediate action; it demands a transformative approach that changes how we view women's roles, capabilities, and rights. By confronting the reality of violence, exploitation, and systemic disregard for women's safety, we pave the way for a society that values every individual equally.

Empowering women is not merely a means of ensuring their personal security or autonomy; it is a powerful tool for societal advancement. When we lift up our women, we strengthen the foundation of our families, communities, and institutions. An empowered woman contributes to a society that is more resilient, inclusive, and progressive. By addressing these critical issues, we ensure that each girl has the opportunity to grow up in a society where her worth is recognized, her voice is heard, and her future is secured. Through this book, I hope to underscore the pressing need for change and inspire a renewed commitment to supporting and uplifting women and girls at every level.

Throughout my ongoing journey as an IPS officer, I have encountered numerous cases of missing children and girls, each of which has left a lasting impact on my understanding of the importance of a responsive and empathetic approach to such issues. While these situations have been challenging, they have also reinforced the urgency and potential for meaningful change in how we address crimes involving women and children. In this book, I share real-life examples from my service—not to dwell on the difficulties, but to illustrate the resilience of our systems and the power of informed action in tackling these cases.

The experiences I've had have shown me that, while the problem of missing girls is significant, there are also countless opportunities for intervention, support, and recovery. With the right measures in place, we can protect our children and ensure their safe return. These examples serve to highlight the dedicated efforts of law enforcement, the invaluable role of community involvement, and the need for society to actively collaborate in safeguarding its most vulnerable members.

By sharing these stories, I aim to demonstrate how, with collective commitment and a sensitive, informed approach, we can effectively prevent these tragedies and create a society where every child and girl is empowered to live with dignity, safety, and opportunity. The focus here is on hope, progress, and the potential to make lasting positive change for all.

It is often assumed that civil servants, after retirement or at the end of their tenure, take the time to reflect on their experiences and share their thoughts with the world. However, I consider myself fortunate to have had the opportunity to write about this critical issue while still in active service. In the midst of a demanding career, I felt it was essential to address the issue of missing girls and the broader concerns related to women's safety and well-being without delay. For me, there was no time to waste. We can't miss out on our missing girls.

The challenges faced by minor girls and women in our society are urgent and require immediate action. Each day that passes without tackling these issues represents a missed opportunity to create a safer, more supportive environment for those who are most vulnerable. As a civil servant committed to making a positive impact, I have always believed that every day matters. Our ability to address the concerns of missing girls, to protect them, and to help them rebuild their lives cannot wait for the future—it must begin today, in real time.

I am deeply humbled and profoundly grateful to Dr Kiran Bedi, whose life and work have been a guiding light for many of us in the service. It was through a simple message that I reached out to her, and with characteristic warmth and generosity, she readily agreed to write the foreword for this book.

For a personality of her stature—a trailblazer who has redefined courage, integrity, and compassion in policing—to acknowledge my work is both an honour and an encouragement. Her gracious acceptance and kind words have added immense strength and meaning to this endeavor. I remain sincerely thankful to her for lending her voice and presence to this cause, which seeks to bring attention to the most vulnerable among us—our missing girls.

This book would not have taken the shape it has without the constant support and inspiration of my fellow officers—the men and women who stand each day on the frontlines of duty. Their sincerity, empathy, and unyielding commitment toward the cause of missing girls have profoundly influenced my thoughts and helped me shape my understanding of this complex issue. Each conversation with them—whether in moments of challenge or reflection—strengthened my belief that policing, at its core, is a service to humanity.

I am equally indebted to the many remarkable individuals outside the service who have walked with me through this journey—friends, social workers, writers, and thinkers—whose perspectives have enriched my vision and lent depth to my reflections. Their unwavering belief in the importance of this subject, and their encouragement through the long and often emotional process of writing, have been invaluable.

Through this book, I hope to inspire a sense of urgency within society at large. We cannot afford to postpone meaningful action. Every moment we delay, we risk allowing another child to fall through the cracks. Therefore, it is my firm belief that we must act decisively and immediately to safeguard our children and empower women—ensuring that no day is lost in this crucial battle.

This is my first book, and as I put these words on paper, I request readers to understand the underlying message—perhaps even beyond what is written. In my limited capacity, I have made an effort to express, with real-life examples, the ways in which we can collectively work toward a better society. While I may have missed certain points or failed to fully capture every aspect of this complex issue, I want to emphasize that the core message is much larger than the words on these pages.

There might be gaps in my expression, and I acknowledge that I could have refined my thoughts further. However, as my father always says, "Better is the enemy of good". I have chosen not to delay my work in constant pursuit of perfection, but rather to focus on communicating the importance of addressing the issue of missing girls and women's safety. The idea of endlessly improving might mean losing precious time that could be spent taking action. The better may be yet to come—but for now, this effort is meaningful in itself, and the message I hope to share is clear: we must act now to protect our children and empower our women.

I believe that in sharing these thoughts, we take a significant step forward—one that will, in time, be refined and expanded upon. But for now, I am content knowing that the words shared here are part of a larger movement toward change. I trust that, as you read, you will find deeper connections, insights, and inspiration that go beyond what I have written.

Chapter 1

BREAKING THE BUBBLE

"No one is born believing in harmful stereotypes. They are learned over time. The good news is that they can be unlearned."

- Kevin Faulconer

Stereotypes are the presumptions made by the powerful few. These presumptions are often disguised as the will of all. There exists a pervasive and persistent human tendency that stems from a basic cognitive need to categorize, simplify and process the complex world. Stereotypes are an exaggerated or distorted generalizations about an entire category of people. They dislodge the belief that there exists an individual variation. Subsequently, they form the basis for prejudice and discrimination. It creates barriers in an empirical mind, which in turn results in oversimplified ideas about people and problems. We invariably come up with generalized solutions for specific issues under the influence of these stereotypes.

These stereotypical underpinnings obfuscate the reality and subterfuge the real issues. The different perspectives in the realm of social sciences like the phenomenological sociology, symbolic interactionism, ethnomethodology, accentuate the fact that the mundane world is the outcome of human synthesis, which has boundless possible interpretations. These connotations cannot be exhaustively explained by the rational methods of natural science. The ethnomethodologist, Harold Garfinkel, recapitulated in his study, human actions and communication are based on a shared set of 'background understandings' which are never, and can never be, fully spelt out. Exchange of symbols, expressions and gestures are an indispensable part of human communication. It is derived from the social knowledge one acquires without being taught. Stereotypes, by their very nature, fail to grasp the intricate nuances that define a person's life. They offer a reductionist view, stripping away the layers of complexity that shape human experiences. Life, with all its unpredictability and depth, cannot be captured by mere categorization. Individuals are not static; they are continuously evolving, shaped by a myriad of influences—cultural, emotional, intellectual and spiritual.

To confine someone within the boundaries of a label is to ignore the fluidity of their existence. It overlooks the subtle shifts in thought, the quiet revolutions of the mind, and the personal transformations that occur over time. Labels, in their rigidity, are inadequate to represent the diversity of human experience. Each person carries within them an ever-changing narrative, rich with contradictions, growth, and untold stories—elements that no label can ever fully encapsulate.

In reducing someone to a single dimension, we deny the fullness of their humanity, for life itself is not a static condition but an ongoing process of becoming. To truly understand a person, one must see beyond the labels and recognize the depth, the texture, and the evolution that defines their journey.

While serving as the superintendent of police (SP) in many different districts and continuing with the same to this date; I have received piles of missing girl cases, in each district I was posted to. Same is the case with other SPs as well. Probably, these case files wait for their turn to come. These case diaries compete consistently with the other cases registered under other different sections, which keeps the police preoccupied. If one turns the pages of these missing girl case diaries, each page unravels a sad story. When asked why these cases were kept pending for years, the investigating officers usually come up with quite calm conclusions to these flaming cauldrons of heinous offences—she voluntarily eloped with the boy of her choice; her parents know her whereabouts but are not willing to cooperate with the police; parents have probably received the bride price. Each of these gratuitous reasons seems to be pitching against each other. The complete investigation process boils down to the same story. We feel rather comfortable in arriving at these stereotypical conclusions.

These stated presumptions that cloud the analytical mind of an investigating officer manifests in the fact that police is also the part of the same sociological milieu from where these stereotypes originate. Police cannot be viewed as isolated or individual identities. When members of the society join the police force, they carry their experiences, beliefs, biases and prejudices with them. This is perhaps, the reason why crime against women, if we exclude the cases of rape and murder, are not taken up that imperatively when it is compared with other heinous offences. Each case is unique but this uniqueness often obliviates into a generalized stereotype that the police has developed through all these years, as a member of the society. The major challenge that confronted me as the superintendent of police, in every district, was not so much, solving these cases but to change this stereotyped mindset towards crime against women, especially the missing girl cases. Every task in police requires teamwork. It is important to get each member of the team on the same platform to get the desired result. In policing—whether it is a routine patrol, a high-stakes investigation, or crisis management—success depends on seamless collaboration. No action is carried out in isolation; it needs synchronized efforts of officers across different roles and hierarchies. The success of any operation hinges on precise coordination, with every team member aligned to a shared objective and strategy.

When a person, tightly clenched by the norms of the society, dons the uniform, he or she needs to unlearn the prejudices, discrimination and the stereotypes that one has learnt through all these years as a member of the society. One needs to become more rational in opinion, more neutral in conduct and more sensitive to all. This unlearning happens at a glacial pace. Few months of training can only sublimate these entrenched sociological ideologies—not eradicate them. Each day requires a conscious personal effort to overcome these barriers. Notwithstanding the fact that the police are adept at solving even the most hard-bitten cases, their investigative prowess is often overwhelmed by the force of the majoritarian wave.

There is no paradox lurking within the department nor any enigma within individual officers that compels a harmony between self and cognitive dissonance. It is merely the cliche of convenience, echoing the prevailing social sanctions. Therefore, it is important to keep reminding the mind and the conscience that one has joined the service to make this society better. One cannot afford to flow with the existing norms, which eventually defeats the very purpose of joining the civil services.

Over a period of time, when stereotypes become stringent, it culminates into alienation. Alienation, as a concept rooted in sociology and psychology, refers to a sense of estrangement or disconnection an individual feels from their environment, society, or even their own identity. When linked to the existing stereotypes around missing girls or crimes against women, alienation can manifest in multiple ways, impacting how officers perceive and handle such cases.

Officers get alienated from the reality of the victims. Officers often work within an institutional framework where stereotypes are embedded into the culture. For instance, the preconceived notion that girls who run away do so for romantic reasons alienates the officers from the real, often complex, socio-psychological factors at play, such as abuse, forced marriages, or human trafficking. These stereotypes lead to the officer's disconnection from the victim's lived experiences, making it difficult for them to empathize with or understand the nuanced circumstances of each case. The alienation here prevents rational, case-specific thinking and reduces the likelihood of seeing beyond the superficial labels assigned to the girls.

Professional socialization often leads to alienation. The professional socialization of police officers tends to reinforce rigid hierarchies, legal frameworks, and crime categorizations. This creates a divide between their personal rationality and the institutionalized mindset. Officers, especially in environments where stereotypes prevail, may feel an internal conflict between what they might personally sense is just or empathetic and what they are expected to think within the force. Over time, the repeated exposure to biased perspectives can result in deep alienation from their own capacity to think critically or challenge these stereotypes.

Cultural norms prompt the process of alienation. Societal stereotypes around women, particularly around "honour" and "shame", create alienation between officers and the very concept of justice for women. For instance, if a missing girl is automatically labeled as "having brought it on herself" due to her behaviour (running away, interacting with boys), the officer's judgment is clouded by these cultural biases. Alienation from the core values of justice, such as fairness and human dignity, gets replaced instead by a cultural reinforcement of gender stereotypes that skews the investigation. In essence, the officer becomes alienated from their own rational duty to protect and serve all citizens equally.

Gender bias in police culture often alienates officers from understanding the broader systemic and patriarchal structures that lead to crimes against women and girls. Male officers, in particular, may struggle with preconceived notions about gender roles, making it harder to acknowledge the depth of suffering experienced by missing girls. Their alienation from these experiences creates a barrier to seeing victims as human, instead reducing them to mere subjects of stereotyped scenarios like "rebellious minors" or "troublemakers".

To break this cycle of alienation, institutional reforms and focused training on gender sensitivity, emotional intelligence and psychological understanding are a desideratum. Officers need to reconnect with their humanistic duty, seeing victims as individuals beyond labels and recognizing the socio-psychological depth of each case. Sensitization efforts need to focus more on reducing the disconnect between the officers' professional role and their rational, empathetic judgment. Empowering officers to challenge stereotypes through structured reflection can help dismantle these internal barriers and allow for more rational and humane decision-making. The alienation exacerbates an officer's inability to see beyond ingrained stereotypes, and without conscious effort to bridge this disconnect, rational and impartial decision-making is hindered.

It took me an average of two to three months in each district to overcome this challenge. Allow me to make a candid confession here. The challenges become more challenging as a woman. As the stereotypes in question are less pliable and more pellucid. As a woman police officer, one has to prove the calibre in all the respective outlined aspects of policing a little more than one's male counterpart to navigate one's way as a leader of the team. Inadvertently, there exists rigid frameworks within which one has to perform and within these configurations one is assessed and evaluated. Equality of gender still remains to be a subjective entity. Women today are representing themselves in almost all fields and yet being professionally ambitious makes a woman feel guilty towards the role ascribed to her by society. The reflection of her image in the social mirror continues to be in contrast with what she wants to see.

A woman's social conditioning often leads her to seek validation from the men around her for the decisions she makes or tasks she accomplishes. From the vast territory, women are allotted only a small island as part of their share, unobtrusively identified by the society and silently accepted by all. Women are made to compete with each other within the confines of this identified category. Consequently, she fails to see the complete territory. Her vision is bridled by stereotypes, which refrains her from seeing things in the correct light. Here, I would like to share few questions that often keep confronting me. I keep questioning the very existence of these questions but surprisingly they keep coming. These questions originate from the unbroken stereotypes, that still exist in society. Why are women compelled to compete only with women? Why does she fail to compete with women and men alike? Why is she instigated to react to the issues instead of augmenting her confidence to face them? With so much mental baggage, will she be able to grab this equality of opportunity? Why despite all the efforts, her confidence and self-esteem so low? Why is she so scared of failing? As and when the inner strength of a woman is put to test, these questions invariably pop up. The idea that women are often conditioned to compete against each other, rather than alongside or against both men and women, arises from deeply entrenched social norms that serve to maintain patriarchal control. For centuries, women have been relegated to roles that prioritize their relationship to men, whether as objects of desire, caretakers, or symbols of virtue. Within these confines, competition has often been encouraged along narrow lines, with women being pitted against each other in superficial arenas, such as beauty, domesticity, or perceived social worth.

These dynamics create a false scarcity, where women are led to believe that their value is relative, not intrinsic, that there is only so much success, attention, or validation to be had, and that it must be won at the expense of other women. The result is a form of rivalry that perpetuates the status quo, distracting from the larger structures of inequality that constrain women collectively. Instead of questioning why the opportunities available to them are so limited, women are often socially trained to internalize competition with their peers as a way of securing approval or advancement within a male-dominated framework. The reality is that competition should not be a gendered concept. True competition is about merit, intellect, skill and talent, and these traits transcend gender. When women are allowed to compete equally, both with men and women, it pushes society towards a more just and equitable landscape, one where individuals are measured by their capabilities rather than their conformity to outdated roles.

The ideal is not to eliminate competition, but to redefine its terms. Competition, in its healthiest form, inspires growth and innovation, and it should reflect the broad spectrum of human potential. By shifting the narrative away from rivalry towards mutual empowerment, women can challenge not only each other but also the societal structures that limit all of us, fostering a more inclusive and dynamic society in the process.

Empowerment flourishes when women unite, not as competitors for limited validation, but as collaborators in the pursuit of shared ambitions and collective progress.

Women and men need to work together to break this stereotype to build a just and equal world for both genders. I would like to mention an interesting Harvard study in this context. The study mentions the paradoxes that one needs to command in a professional setting as a woman: demanding yet caring, authoritative yet participative, advocating for themselves yet serving others, maintaining distance yet being approachable. It appears to be difficult and a bit confusing at the same time, but it appears closer to reality. In a practical professional setting, I found these set of paradoxes to be relevant. Every woman is expected to excel in these paradoxes if she expects to be a leader. Qualifying an exam provides one with an authority, a progressive administrative setup in the state gives an opportunity to hold that authority. But as a woman, one needs to win that authority to command it.

There was no exemption for me from this stereotype as well. I wanted to lead my team. To start with, I started with all the other pending heinous cases registered under various sections of the Indian Penal Code and the Bhartiya Nyaya Sanhita. It was a herculean task for me and my team. In police work, the possibility of solving a case becomes bleaker with each passing day. One needs to bank upon the available evidence only. As time passes, new evidence becomes too sparse to be collected, identified or correlated with the crime. Some of the old evidence stay relevant, some fade away with time. Nevertheless, we kept working relentlessly with whatever was available with us. Once success was achieved in these cases, a point was put forth for the long pending missing cases as well. Without this warm-up, my concern for these missing girl cases would have been fabled as just a feminist furore.

After the Supreme Court's landmark judgement and directions, every missing girl report is registered under the section 363 of the IPC (as per the directions of the Hon'ble Supreme Court of India in *Bachpan Bachao Andolan vs. Union of India* { WP[Civil] 75 of 2012 } on 10 May 2013—upon receipt of a complaint regarding a missing child, an FIR should be registered forthwith as a case of trafficking or abduction). The Ministry of Home Affairs also issued a detailed advisory on missing children and steps to be taken for tracing these children. As a result of this judgement registration of the cases regarding a missing minor child, is a battle already won. But investigating these cases and finding the missing child in these cases still remains an unfought battle.

Missing child cases registered under the section 363 of the Indian Penal Code, now 137 BNS, is a heinous offence. But the attitude to consider this as heinous is at times, abjected by our stereotypes. The heinous nature of these cases and the insincerity generated, which is usually backed by the existing stereotypes in solving these cases, often coexists. This dichotomy is treacherous to the concern of finding the missing girls. I was confronted with this anomaly every time I joined a new district. With limited personnel and a growing backlog of cases, it becomes difficult to send a team to other states or to a distant district when a missing girl's whereabouts are found or reported by her parents. Apart from the documents leading to the confirmation of her age, rarely any pains are taken to collect evidence in the case. The police is usually engaged in logically discrete and incommensurable duties, which are a normative mismatch with the responsibility of finding a missing girl. The police investigation in such cases is mainly contained with inquiring the parents of the missing girl, whether she came back home or whether they received any information about her. Taking a few statements from her neighbourhood, her schoolmates (in case she was enrolled in some school), or from her friends. These statements are taken from time to time to simply update the case diary. This procedure can never solve a case or help in anyway, to find the missing girl. We fail to enquire about the pressure she went through, or the myriad influences she was exposed to when she was present. Most of the times, the police in such cases has a habit of conveniently concluding rather than inquiring. We usually get stuck with our stereotypes and fail to assess the urgency to address these cases. It remains interruptedly difficult to understand how an officer could justify discriminating against a victim solely on the basis of gender. Being neutral is the premier quality we seek in a civil servant, irrespective of rank. The barriers of caste or creed, religion or region, rich or poor, female or male, are considered to be oblivious to a civil servant's vision for the society. A victim is only a victim. Whenever I interact with women complainants, I often hear this from them: Aap to mahila hain, aap zyada ache se samajh sakti hain (You are a woman, you can understand our plight better). This in turn, raises many questions. Why is there so much insecurity in the minds of female victims? Why should they feel that male officers cannot empathize with them? On the contrary to this assumption, I have experienced that many female officers are also not as sensitive towards female victims as they are expected to be. This reveals that sensitivity can never be gender specific. It often happens when the social conditioning of a person takes place through the gender stereotypes which exist in the society. A person conditioned in such a manner, when exposed to the reality, feels scared to digress from the existing norms. They lack the confidence to hold an individual opinion. The concept of masculinity in policing has undergone a profound transformation, driven not only by the changing nature of crime but also by the growing representation of women in law enforcement. In the past, policing was seen as a bastion of masculinity, where physical strength, authority and toughness were the defining traits of a successful officer. This perception was so deeply ingrained that women who joined the force often felt compelled to adopt a more "masculine" appearance and demeanor. They used to cut their hair short, dressed in ways that minimized their femininity, and even mirrored the aggressive, hardened persona expected of their male counterparts, all in an effort to fit into a system that equated policing with manliness.

However, as crime patterns have evolved and as the role of the police has expanded to address more complex and sensitive issues, such as domestic violence, child abuse, and human trafficking, the narrow definition of masculinity in policing has gradually diminished. These modern challenges demand not only physical presence but also emotional intelligence, empathy, and nuanced communication. The rise in the number of women officers has played a crucial role in reshaping the expectations of what it means to be an effective police officer. Today, femininity and policing are no longer seen as contradictory. The presence of women in the police force has demonstrated that qualities traditionally associated with femininity—such as patience, empathy, and the ability to de-escalate situations without force, are just as essential in policing as physical strength. Women officers have shown that they can bring a different, but equally valuable, approach to law enforcement, one that balances authority with care, and firmness with compassion.

This shift marks a broader acceptance of diverse forms of leadership and problem solving within the force. The rigid, hyper-masculine ideals of the past have given way to a more inclusive understanding of policing, where both men and women can succeed without conforming to outdated gender norms. As a result, policing today is seen less as a domain of "tough men" and more as a profession that requires a wide range of skills, many of which transcend traditional gender roles. This balance of masculinity and femininity in policing has strengthened the force, allowing it to serve better diverse communities with a deeper understanding of the complexities of modern society. True strength in policing lies not in the absence of vulnerability, but in the ability to blend authority with empathy, recognizing that both masculinity and femininity bring essential qualities to the pursuit of justice.

I referred to this antiquated pattern here to highlight that the fear of being considered as a persona non grata with the group is so grave that compliance to the existing norms becomes sine qua non. This simply connotes the reason why a woman feels hesitant in standing up for another woman. This is the disadvantage of living with the stereotypes. Majoritarianism can carve out the power parameters that encourage a herd mentality. This in turn deepens the existing stereotypes. But, time has witnessed that the ultimate power lies only in individual professional competence. Now, taking this reference in policing explains the existing incongruity. Listening to a victim empathetically, being sensitive to their concern is not feminine but humane. Probably, the impact of stereotypes is so deep that even after many years of sensitization sprees carried on in letter and spirit, we are still left with a few more miles to go in making the civil servants gender neutral. These questions need to be answered if we are really concerned with dealing crime against women. Many forums come up with solutions such as more women should be inducted into the police force to address this issue. But what about the existing male force? Why is only a female officer expected to understand a female victim? Why do we need to compartmentalize the qualities of a female and male officer differently? Why cannot we have a common set of parameters for both? Why cannot a male officer inculcate the sensitivity required to address the grievance and appreciate the concern of a female victim? If we view victims through the prism of gender, then we will continue to view officers through the same prism as well. We will require different officers to handle different victims based on gender lines. Isn't this a dangerous divide? These questions appear to be strange, awkward, perplexing but surprisingly, in the real world, they do exist.

As a woman victim stands before the police station, she feels a profound mix of emotions swirling within her. The building looms large, a symbol of authority and a potential ally, yet it also represents fear and vulnerability. She takes a deep breath, her heart racing as the reality of her situation sinks in. There's a flicker of courage inside her, ignited by the thought of finally stepping forward. She reflects on the countless moments she has spent in silence, burdened by her experiences. The idea of voicing her pain feels like a release, a way to reclaim her narrative. This could be a turning point, she thinks, imagining the relief that might come from being believed and validated. Yet, as quickly as that courage rises, it is overshadowed by fear. Memories flood her mind, instances where she was dismissed or belittled, where her experiences were downplayed. What if the officers don't take her seriously? What if they see her as just another statistic, another case to file away? The thought sends a shiver down her spine, leaving her feeling small and powerless. She fears becoming a voice lost in a sea of indifference. The societal judgment that often accompanies reports of abuse weighs heavily on her. She can almost hear the whispers, the assumptions that might follow her. What will people say? She worries about how others might perceive her, how they might label her. The fear of ridicule feels like a noose tightening around her neck, constricting her ability to act. Will they think she's exaggerating? Will they pity her? Her thoughts drift to her family. How will they react? Will they stand by her or turn away? She knows that cultural and familial expectations often dictate silence, especially regarding sensitive matters. The prospect of being ostracized by those she loves fills her with dread. If she chooses to report, will she be seen as a traitor to her family? The weight of potential shame feels unbearable. But then, amid the chaos of her thoughts, a glimmer of empowerment emerges. What if this decision leads to healing? She considers the strength it takes to confront her past and the possibility that by taking this step, she might inspire others to do the same. The notion of becoming an agent of change, not just for herself but for others who have suffered in silence, brings a glimmer of hope. Yet the weight of her choice feels monumental. If she steps inside, what will that mean for her future? Will she be able to return home and look her family in the eye? Or will her decision mark a point of no return, a path that leads to isolation? The duality of empowerment and fear creates a tumultuous storm within her, leaving her feeling torn between the desire for justice and the instinct for self-preservation. As she stands at the threshold, each second stretches into eternity. The noise of the world around her fades, leaving only her internal struggle. She feels the weight of societal expectations, her own vulnerabilities, and the longing for justice merging into a potent mix.

In this moment of reckoning, she realizes that her decision could redefine her entire narrative. It could propel her toward empowerment or further entrapment. With each breath, she contemplates the possibility of change, the hope that she can reclaim her story, that stepping forward might inspire others and perhaps shift the very narrative that has kept so many silent.

The decision to enter the police station or retreat to the safety of silence is not just about her, it's a reflection of her fight for her own dignity, her voice, and her place in a world that has often tried to silence her. In this pivotal moment, she knows she stands not only at the entrance of the police station but at the crossroads of her life, ready to make a choice that could echo far beyond these walls. Now, the climax of the situation is whether the person sitting in uniform inside the police station, will comprehend this onerous journey of her from the main gate of the police station to the complaint table.

If we view the other side of the social continuum, the lack of acknowledgment by women, of crimes committed against them is often rooted in a complex interplay of social and psychological factors. Some of the primary reasons include fear, societal pressure, internalized norms, and emotional distress. For many women, acknowledging the crime is a second battle, one fought against the disbelief and stigma that linger long after the incident itself. Several social and psychological features help in comprehending this phenomenon:

The theory of Learned Helplessness, as suggested by Martin Seligman, enumerates that when individuals are repeatedly exposed to adverse situations in which they feel they have no control, they may develop a sense of helplessness. Women who have experienced abuse or discrimination over time may believe they cannot change their circumstances, leading them to accept or downplay the crime committed against them. In the echo of her silence, there's a story of resilience, a narrative woven from pain, hope, and the courage it takes to keep moving forward in a world that often fails to listen.

According to the process of socialization, from a young age, women are often associated with certain roles and behaviours, which includes tolerance for violence or abuse. This socialization may teach them that acknowledging a crime could lead to shame, dishonour, or family breakdown, discouraging them from reporting or even recognizing it as a crime. In a world where her worth is often measured by her scars, a woman may choose silence, fearing that speaking her truth will only deepen her wounds.

A woman may feel conflicted between the knowledge that she is a victim of a crime and the societal norms that tell her to stay silent or bear the pain. When an individual holds two conflicting thoughts or beliefs, they experience psychological discomfort or internal dissent. To reduce this discomfort, she may rationalize or minimize the crime. When society places the burden of proof on the victim, she learns to carry her pain alone, guarding her story like a fragile secret in a hostile world.

The Rape Myth Acceptance concept involves the internalization of false beliefs or stereotypes about rape and sexual violence, such as "it was the victim's fault" or "the victim was asking for it". These myths can lead women to question whether what happened to them qualifies as a crime, inhibiting acknowledgment. When a woman chooses silence, it is rarely out of weakness. It's often a survival tactic in a world that blames her for her scars and dismisses her truths as exaggerations or mistakes.

Stockholm Syndrome suggests that women who experience prolonged periods of abuse, especially in intimate relationships or captivity, may develop positive feelings towards their abuser. This can distort their perception of the crime, leading them to justify or excuse the behaviour, making it harder for them to acknowledge the harm done to them. A woman's voice can feel like a whisper in a storm, drowned out by blame and disbelief.

So, she learns to keep her pain hidden, hoping that if she buries it deep enough, it might one day be forgotten.

The existence of cultural and societal shame is profoundly entrenched in society. In many cultures, the concept of "honour" is tied to a woman's behaviour, leading to a fear of public humiliation or ostracization if they report a crime. Crimes like domestic violence or sexual assault are often associated with stigma, making it difficult for women to admit to being victims due to the social consequences. The shame of the crime too often rests on the shoulders of the victim, as if her suffering is her own to bear alone. In quietude, she seeks to protect herself not just from the pain of the crime, but from the cruelty of a world quick to judge and slow to understand.

The Trauma Theory explains that the psychological impact of trauma can affect how women process and acknowledge their experiences. Trauma may lead to dissociation, repression of memories, or avoidance of confronting the reality of the crime due to the emotional pain it invokes. She fears that speaking up might mean reliving every detail, only to be questioned, doubted, and criticized. So, she locks her pain away, not because she forgives, but because she's too tired to fight. This internalization of trauma can manifest in various ways—she may struggle to form trusting relationships, experience hypervigilance, or feel detached from her own emotions. The trauma shapes not only her perception of the crime but also her interactions with the world, making even supportive environments feel unsafe. Understanding trauma in this context emphasizes the need for sensitive, patient engagement rather than immediate demands for disclosure or action.

The traditional gender roles often portray women as passive, submissive, or weaker than men. These roles can reinforce a belief that women are meant to endure hardship and abuse without complaint, leading to their silence about crimes committed against them. Society teaches women to carry the burden of shame, not just for their actions but for the actions inflicted upon them. So, they carry silent wounds, hidden beneath layers of resilience that no one cares to unravel. These socially prescribed roles are reinforced from childhood through education, family expectations, and cultural narratives, creating a feedback loop where endurance of hardship becomes valorized in women. Over time, this can erode their sense of agency, convincing them that speaking up is selfish or inappropriate.

The concept of Victim Blaming elucidates that when society places responsibility for the crime on the victim rather than the perpetrator, women may internalize these beliefs and blame themselves. This leads to self-doubt and prevents them from acknowledging the crime as something that was done *to* them, rather than something they caused. Her silence isn't a sign that she's unscathed; it's a silent scream, one that echoes with the unspoken understanding that in a world quick to blame, it's safer to stay unheard. The consequences of victim blaming extend beyond silence. It can lead to anxiety, depression, and long-term psychological distress, reinforcing a cycle where women anticipate judgment and thus avoid seeking justice. By shifting the focus from blame to support and accountability, society can validate the victim's experience and encourage reporting, making silence less necessary for survival.

By understanding these social and psychological factors, we can see that a woman's failure to acknowledge a crime against her is not a sign of weakness or ignorance, but rather the result of deep-seated societal norms and psychological coping mechanisms.

The acknowledgement of pain and trauma can be understood in the light of these existing frameworks in the society. It needs to be acknowledged and comprehended by all, irrespective of gender. Trust in law enforcement is built on the foundation of assurance that all officers, regardless of gender, are allies in the pursuit of justice. By cultivating an environment where victims feel empowered to approach any officer in uniform, we strengthen the relationship between law enforcement and community. This fosters a culture of inclusivity within the force, where all officers are trained to recognize and address the complexities of gender-based violence effectively. True empathy knows no gender; it is the ability to listen, understand, and support, which transcends the uniform worn. All officers, regardless of gender, can be champions of justice and healing for those in need. Sometimes, the silence of a woman is not a lack of strength, but a shield built from fear, shame, and the haunting question of whether her truth will ever be believed. In a world that too often holds her responsible for the crimes against her, she learns to bury her voice deep, hoping that in hiding her pain, she can escape the judgment that follows.

Coming back to my experience, we started with a sensitization workshop before taking up these missing girl cases. Both policewomen and policemen were called to attend this workshop. Majority of them had already attended similar workshops many times. Honestly, it was nothing new for them. I wanted this workshop to be gender neutral. I wanted a common team, with a few of the sessions led by men, and a few by women. A common team always yields better understanding of the problem, meticulous examination of the available facts, provides better observations of things, better analysis of the available data and finally better results. I did not want to prove a point in front of my team, but I definitely wanted to make a point. I wanted a sensitive start, a more empathetic effort than usual.

We started. As we moved forward, the dust settled on these missing girls diaries and on our attitude towards these cases started dwindling away. We readdressed the statements recorded in the diaries, recollected and revisited every piece of information from all the possible sources. Teams were sent in the same manner as is done in case of any other heinous offence. In a few cases, we achieved the desired results. This little success enthused in us huge amount of confidence and recharged us with new enthusiasm. More sensitivity towards these cases arose when the rescued girls told us their stories. Once the signals were set in the right direction, results started coming in. Now, when we received any new missing girl cases, we were punctilious in asking questions that gave us information on the minutest of details. Teams were sent on every frangible piece of information. Even after so much of unlearning sessions and exercises there were a few members in the team with stubborn stereotypes who required a constant push. They were the demotivated lot, with a fossilized mindset. But they did the work assigned to them as their opinion faded in the motivated spree of the majority.

With this team, it was possible to achieve a gratifying number of successful cases. The team kept marching ahead. Parents were overwhelmed to finally reunite with their missing daughters. It was not less than a miracle for them. The rescued girls felt safe and secure after years of their fortuitous expatriation. Some of them were missing for more than a decade. Few of them got married, had kids but felt ashamed of coming back to their own village. With the help of the police, they found a way back home.

In the quiet of a shattered home, where the echoes of laughter once danced through the halls, a mother's heart had learned to live with a haunting absence. Each day felt like a heavy weight, laden with the memories of a daughter who had vanished, leaving behind a void that echoed with unanswered questions. The relentless ache of uncertainty gnawed at her spirit, filling her nights with restless worry and her days with a dull, persistent dread. Then, one fateful day, the air shifted. The police arrived, and with them, the glint of hope, a small flame in the all-encompassing darkness. As they stepped in through the door, her heart raced, caught between disbelief and yearning. "Is it possible?" she wondered, her breath hitching in her throat. The officers, with their solemn faces, carried both the burden of sorrow and the promise of the new. When the door opened, and there stood her daughter, trembling, yet unmistakably her, time seemed to freeze. In that moment, the world blurred around her, and all that mattered was the sight of her child, safe and alive. Waves of emotion crashed over her, relief flooding her veins like cool water after a long drought, followed by a tide of joy that threatened to overwhelm her. The mother rushed forward, arms wide open, a desperate embrace that spoke of all the days and nights spent longing for this moment. Tears streamed down her face, mingling with laughter, the sound of both sorrow and joy intertwined. She held her daughter tightly, as if afraid that letting go might cause her to disappear once again. Years of worry and pain transformed into profound gratitude, the weight of despair lifted by the sheer presence of the girl who had once seemed so far away.

As they stood together, their heartbeats synchronized in a rhythm of renewed love, the mother felt hope rekindle within her. It was as if every fear had been chased away by the light of her daughter's return, and in that embrace, a promise was forged, to never take for granted the simple act of being together, to cherish every moment that lay ahead, free from the shadows of the past. In that fleeting instant, she understood the depths of love, the kind that endures, withstands the darkest nights, and emerges, brilliant and resilient, into the dawn of a new beginning. In the embrace of her daughter, lost but found, a mother discovered that love is not only the bond that endures but also the light that transforms shadows into dawn.

As we moved ahead with high spirits, out of the total pending missing girl cases, we rescued 92% of the girls in District Betul, 89% in District Dindori and 94% in District Rajgarh. All these districts shared boundaries with other states. Two of these districts were predominantly tribal in their demographic constitution. All these girls were rescued in first year of my joining as Superintendent of Police in these districts. We succeeded in making a consolidated team with different ranks, different genders but with no ideological differences. No one was more, no one was less; we all were on an equal threshold, sharing a common objective. We kept motivating each other and continued with our task in the months that followed. Girls were rescued—some from within the state, some from far away—each one of them with a unique story to share.

Success never comes easy. A few eyebrows were also raised in doubt, and some furrowed their brows in distress. How could a district that once ranked last in the entire state for the rescue of missing girls suddenly rise to the top? One of my supervising seniors concluded, in front of a few media persons, that we were finding the girls before we registered the offence. Well, my team was swift enough in the investigation procedure to find the missing girls, but we were not competent enough to anticipate which girl will go missing. Moreover, this logic couldn't suffice to explain the rescue of those girls who had been missing for years. To add fuel to this tarnishing conspiracy, a discontented subordinate invited a media team from outside the district to interview the parents of the missing girls. This media team was sent to confirm whether the girls who went missing were actually rescued, or whether it was a mere false projection. The rescue figures appeared too good to be true, too real to be believed.

These episodes made me realize that doing good can be a big threat to people who believe in doing nothing at all. As a matter of habit, I never start to stop. I always start to finish. In the realm of creativity and ambition, the shadows of criticism often loom large, casting doubt and uncertainty upon our endeavors. It is a peculiar paradox—the very act of pursuing our passions invites scrutiny from those who dwell in the safety of the sidelines. They murmur their doubts, voicing their judgments behind our backs, as if our efforts were mere fodder for their skepticism. Yet, in this tumult lies an opportunity—a chance to transform negativity into fuel for our journey. To navigate these turbulent waters, one must first anchor oneself in purpose. Like a ship braving the storm, our commitment to our craft must remain steadfast, regardless of the waves of discontent that threaten to capsize us. We must remind ourselves that the essence of our work holds intrinsic value—a light that can pierce through the fog of doubt.

Criticism, though often delivered with biting words, can carry whispers of truth. Rather than allowing it to sting, we can receive it with curiosity, sifting through the noise for constructive feedback that may illuminate paths for growth. It is a delicate dance, balancing the weight of others' opinions with the strength of our convictions. As we journey onward, it is essential to gather the treasures of our accomplishments. Each milestone reached, each positive comment received, becomes a shield against the arrows of negativity. In moments of doubt, we can revisit these tokens, reminding ourselves of the impact we have made and the lives we have touched. Our work, after all, is a testament to our dedication, a story that speaks volumes beyond the whispers of critique. Emotional resilience becomes our armor, allowing us to weather the storms of dissent with grace. We must cultivate the ability to respond rather than react, to rise above the cacophony of negativity with dignity. It is a skill that requires practice, but in mastering it, we reclaim our narrative, refusing to be defined by others' judgments.

Invariably, every police action is critically scrutinized by the public at large. While we cannot entirely evade the shadows of criticism, we can control our exposure to its darkness. Surrounding ourselves with those who uplift and inspire becomes imperative. Their support acts as a beacon, guiding us through murky waters and reminding us of the light within. In the alchemy of our experiences, we find the power to transform criticism into motivation. Each disparaging remark can serve as a catalyst, igniting a fire within us to rise higher, persevere against the odds, and prove—through our continued success—that their doubts were misplaced. Ultimately, it is our work that must speak for itself. The fruits of our labour, when nurtured with passion and dedication, become the eloquent response to all who doubt.

In the end, the narratives we weave through our endeavours are far more compelling than any whispers behind our backs. Thus, let us march forward, undeterred by negativity, armed with purpose, resilience, and the knowledge that every shadow only serves to enhance the brilliance of our light.

As I had mentioned earlier, each case was unique and case raised a plethora of issues that needed to be addressed. One such case I encountered was in the district of Dindori, a small tribal district sharing its borders with Chhattisgarh. Because migration was high in this area, we initiated a campaign named *Prawas* with the intention of ensuring that every citizen leaving the district for work outside the state informed the local police station. This campaign was designed to address the many challenges faced by migrant labourers—most notably when they failed to return within the expected time, leaving their families without information about their whereabouts. Other concerns included unfair wages, poor working conditions, and several related hardships. To counter this, a register was maintained in every police station, recording key details such as the worker's destination, the contractor's name, duration of stay, and contact numbers of associates. The initiative relied heavily on community support, particularly from village *kotwars* (kotwars are the village officers who keep a watch and ward over the houses and properties of the villagers under MPLRC) and the members of gram raksha samiti (members enrolled in each village who work in close coordination with the police under the community police initiatives, covered under the MP Gram Tatha Nagar Raksha Samiti Adhiniyam 1999).

One fine morning, I was running later than usual in reaching the office. I had to attend a crime scene in a remote village near Bajag block. Tribal districts have a vast geographical expanse, which often turns travel into long, winding journeys. Yet, this also offers an opportunity to enjoy the exhilarating forest rides I always look forward to. The district, known for its breathtaking natural beauty, unfolds like a vibrant tapestry. Serpentine roads wind gracefully through the terrain, inviting travelers to explore the rich scenery. Often bordered by lush fields, these roads offer a feast for the eyes, where patches of green sway gently in the breeze as farmers toil diligently, cultivating crops that reflect their deep connection to the land.

As one ventures along these winding paths, small hamlets emerge like hidden gems, each with its own distinct charm. The houses, crafted from local materials, blend seamlessly into the environment, showcasing the architectural traditions of the tribal communities. The warmth of the people radiates through their smiles and welcoming gestures, embodying a way of life deeply rooted in cultural heritage.

Towering trees, some standing for centuries, provide a majestic backdrop to this picturesque setting. Their branches stretch wide, forming a natural canopy that filters sunlight into shifting patterns of light and shadow on the ground below. These trees not only enrich the beauty of the landscape but also stand as silent witnesses to the stories and traditions that have shaped tribal life for generations.

The harmony between the serpentine roads, fields, hamlets, and towering trees paints a serene picture of life in the tribal district. It was a place where nature and humanity coexisted, offering a glimpse into a world where time seemed to stand still and simplicity was celebrated amidst the splendour of the surroundings. What I was witnessing was what I once used to paint on canvas as a child—absolutely mesmerizing.

Although it often took considerable time to reach a crime scene, the journey was always worth it. At times, it became exhausting, especially when long distances had to be covered on foot. Yet, as a matter of habit, I always visited the crime scene myself. I believe it makes the work both easier and clearer. These visits answer many questions during an investigation; they help in assessing the case, correlating evidence, and preventing people from misleading or concealing the truth.

Since my training days, I had often heard the phrase, "the scene of crime speaks". And indeed, it does—if only one listens.

That day, it took me three hours to return to the district headquarters. By the time I reached my office, it was already 12:30 in the afternoon. A long queue of visitors was waiting outside. In these tribal districts, people often have to travel great distances, forgo their daily wages, leave behind household chores, and spend a significant portion of their hard-earned money on bus fares just to reach the headquarters. Many struggle even to locate the office and then wait patiently for hours in the hope of meeting an officer. I find it nothing short of criminal to delegate such people to a subordinate after they have gone through so much effort to see me in person.

As I stepped out of my vehicle I gave an assured gesture towards them, and swiftly entered my chamber. As I placed my feet on the footrest, my middle-aged stickman entered with a cup of black coffee as part of his routine. Each wrinkle on his face embodied his experience in the department, which he proudly wore every day as a medal. His observations used to surprise me often. Out of the heap of visitor slips, he took out a slip and insisted that I should call this person first, as he had some information to share. I always trusted his suggestions. This shortlisted visitor was ushered in. A young man, in his denims and a striped shirt, rushed in. Before I could ask him anything, he grabbed a chair and started speaking like a whirlwind. He was a sincere citizen of the district, well aware about the campaign Prawas. He informed me that one person from the nearby village was taking five minor girls of the same village along with him in a jeep. They would be boarding the train from Jabalpur railway station to Coimbatore. After noting down the basic details, teams were dispatched. The road from Dindori to Jabalpur was a single serpentine stretch. Iron stoppers were put in place on the road for intercepting vehicles. Within no time, there was a long queue of vehicles. The team was afraid that the suspect might take a bypass route after seeing that the police was checking vehicles. We sped up the checking process. Backup teams were sent from the district headquarters to cover these bypass points. We were not very sure about the type of vehicle. In police work, the information received is usually not very precise; due to its amorphous nature we in police need to sieve this information through our police acuity. Finally, the vehicle was stopped.

The jeep was intercepted by my team in the jurisdiction of Shahpur police station, which bordered Jabalpur district. Five girls were sitting on the rear seat of the jeep, surrounded by luggage. The person occupying the front seat wore a fluorescent yellow scarf around his neck, a checked shirt and grey pants. His complexion contrasted sharply with the bright scarf, and his mouth was stained red from gutka he was chewing. He was a local resident of the district and had been working in a factory at Coimbatore for the past five years. Sanguinely, he pulled out his I-card and employee badge from his wallet and presented them to the police. With polished sophistry, he tried to convince them that he was doing a noble job by providing employment to his fellow villagers. From his bag, he produced the Aadhaar cards and appointment letters of the five girls seated inside the vehicle. The sub-inspector from Shahpur police station, who had intercepted the vehicle, informed me that according to the Aadhaar cards, all the girls were shown as majors, and each carried an appointment letter from a factory in Coimbatore.

The argument at the check post quickly took a demented turn. I instructed the sub-inspector to bring them to the police station and make the necessary entries in the migrant labour register. In the heat of the moment, this was the only advice that came to mind. He protested, saying they would miss their train, and kept arguing, but we remained firm. Eventually, the jeep, along with all its passengers, was redirected to the police station.

Once there, we verified the Aadhaar cards with the local authorities. Every single one turned out to be fake. The five girls were in fact minors. The fraudulent identity cards had been crudely manufactured in a local printing and photocopy shop.

We uncovered a long chain of people involved in the case. Documents recovered from the shop revealed that this illegal business was flourishing in many parts of the district. What began as a routine interception eventually led to the busting of an interstate trafficking racket. In total, eleven minor girls were rescued from Coimbatore in Tamil Nadu over the course of the investigation. Several accused were arrested, most of them residents of Dindori district. They had lured the girls and their families with false promises of jobs outside Madhya Pradesh and the hope of a better livelihood opportunities.

In cases like these, parents or guardians often remain mute spectators, burdened by the responsibility of feeding many young mouths at home. A few years later, these younger members too may face the same fate. Sometimes, we fall prey to our own cocooned concepts and fail to comprehend the social milieu that endangers these young lives and leads them to such vulnerable situations.

In the pursuit of unfulfilled dreams and aspirations, these young souls fall into traps laid by cunning middlemen—the kingpins of the exploitation chain—who must be identified if we are to break it. They are shrewd enough to convince vulnerable families in villages, and girls become the easiest targets.

In agricultural fields, girls are rarely considered assets, where survival demands relentless toil. But in big cities, they promise better prospects for the middlemen. Most of these girls, often school dropouts, become their prime victims. On the skeletal framework of the flesh trade, the traffickers erect the scaffolding of false opportunities, deceiving innocent girls and their helpless parents.

These middlemen usually belong to the local community. With impressive command over the local dialect and the striking personality of a practiced charlatan, they stand out in the village. Slightly better off than the rest, they wield influence with ease. Behind them operates a caucus of village agents who quietly identify vulnerable targets. Together, they skillfully exploit local aspirations for their own gain. In the rural heartlands, life follows the rhythm of the earth's cycles—marked by simplicity, trust, and deep-rooted innocence. It is precisely this innocence that becomes the fertile ground for manipulation.

Here, people move through the world with a quiet confidence in the goodwill of their neighbours and the timeless bonds that have sustained their communities for generations. Life is woven from kinship, shared traditions, and a reverence for the natural world—lessons in resilience, humility, and above all, trust. In their eyes, deception is not just a wrongdoing but an aberration, a rupture in the invisible thread that binds society together. Their worlds may be small, but they are rich with a sense of shared destiny, where every face carries familiarity, every name holds a story, and every heart beats with loyalty.

But, in this very fabric of trust lies their vulnerability, a doorway that shadowy figures exploit. Middlemen, sometimes even those once seen as friends, find ways to entrench themselves in these communities. These agents often operate as if they are protectors and providers, speaking the language of familiarity and promise. With gentle words and persuasive actions, they weave themselves into the fabric of rural life, creating a semblance of kinship while concealing darker motives.

These middlemen often belong to larger criminal networks, whose ambitions reach far beyond the fields and villages. To such networks, the trust and innocence of rural people become opportunities, open doors to further their agendas, to exploit without suspicion, and commit acts unimaginable to the rural folk. The villagers, often with limited access to formal education and isolated from the world of deceit, place a childlike faith in these intermediaries. The villagers' lives, steeped in honour and loyalty, become pawns in a game with rules they can hardly grasp, let alone combat.

The rural world, rich in tradition and noble simplicity, quietly faces its most tragic irony. The very qualities that elevate their lives to something gentle and true are also those that expose them to cruelty and betrayal. They live unaware, continuing to uphold a faith in humanity that, ironically, makes them vulnerable. This fragility reminds us of the deep tragedy beneath rural life's noble surface, a reminder that the power of trust, left unguarded, can also be the power that betrays.

In such cases, there exists an extended network of stakeholders. The parents are convinced that one of the members of the family will become the earning member of the family. One of the fortunate family members will get a job in the city. On the continuum, they will shift from more mouths to more bread earners in the family. They are also exposed to some successful examples in the near vicinity to believe in this hope. It becomes an unavoidable trap. The innocent girls move towards this trap with all her expectations and dreams for a better future for her and her family back in the village. They all end up in the same place. The vulnerable feel that they have become victims of their own fate. Her name and identity are altered. Fresh identity cards are issued with a fancy name, a fake address, and a false age stating that she is an adult. The adolescent girl who came to work disappears. A new woman is born, left with no route of return. Back home, parents receive a regular amount credited to their accounts. Sometimes, advance payments are made by the trafficker to the parents. This further entangles the matter, turning it into bonded labour.

Everyone was made to believe that all was well. Parents thought their daughters were working, the girls were convinced this was their destiny, and the middlemen thrived on this false balance. Earlier, as I admitted, we had been working on these cases at a very superficial level, limited to her parents, friends, and a few schoolmates.

But after interacting with the rescued girls, we realized the crime ran much deeper. We needed to dig further to uncover the real picture. We stepped outside the walls of the police station, spoke with villagers, and built trust with the local community. These efforts helped us identify the middlemen and their associates. It was a tightly knit web that stretched across the entire area. Based on information gathered from locals, we traced the crime channels, nabbed frequent commuters, and identified vulnerable hotspots. These proactive measures enabled us to find and rescue girls who were not listed as missing in official records but were, in reality, missing from their very existence.

Creating an efficient information network in rural areas demands a nuanced, strategic approach that is both inclusive and sensitive to the community's unique social fabric. To effectively gather intelligence on heinous crimes, especially those disguised under less suspicious facades. Police should aim to embed themselves within existing community frameworks by collaborating with key figures such as village heads, religious leaders, teachers, and health workers. These individuals naturally hold influence, and fostering their trust ensures access to vital grassroot information. By formalizing these ties through periodic meetings and consultations, police can receive a steady flow of insights that may not be immediately available through conventional means. Specialized rural liaison officers, trained in both cultural sensitivity and intelligence gathering, can serve as a bridge between the community and law enforcement.

These officers, stationed within the villages, can gain firsthand knowledge of local issues, assess patterns that may signify hidden crimes, and develop a rapport with villagers that facilitates the sharing of sensitive information without fear of reprisal. Introducing secure, anonymous reporting channels within the village, such as discrete reporting apps, community phone lines, and secure drop-boxes, can empower individuals to report potential crimes without compromising their safety or social standing. These channels should be integrated with protective policies that reinforce the community's trust in the system's confidentiality. Implementing awareness campaigns that resonate culturally with the rural population is essential for changing perceptions around certain taboo crimes, such as trafficking or gender-based violence. By tailoring messages through local dialects, symbols, and media, the police can make it easier for the community to recognize and report covert crimes. Training programmes can be created for both community members and officers to ensure these crimes are not mistakenly overlooked as mere 'family matters' or 'domestic issues'. Establishing intelligence cells within the villages in coordination with local authorities, like panchayat bodies and district officials, can help identify crime patterns masked by benign fronts, such as certain businesses, migration schemes, or social gatherings. Through regular briefings and data sharing, the police can analyze and trace suspicious activities with more accuracy and local context. Given the sensitivity of certain crimes, especially those impacting women and minors, empowering female-led networks within villages is crucial.

Women are often more attuned to the subtle signs of exploitation or abuse but may hesitate to share these concerns with police officers. By enlisting local resource persons in information gathering, the police can gain insights into crimes that might otherwise be silenced due to social stigma. For crimes that are not directly reported but suspected, employing undercover surveillance in cooperation with the village network can help substantiate leads without disrupting community life. This involves using intelligence resources to monitor movement patterns, suspicious gatherings, or financial transactions that may suggest the presence of hidden criminal activities. Through these interconnected strategies, the police can construct an inclusive, multilayered intelligence framework that addresses the complexities of rural crime. This approach ensures that intelligence gathering is respectful, strategic, and sensitive to the vulnerabilities within these communities, ultimately making it difficult for heinous crimes to go unnoticed or unaddressed.

There is nothing more satisfying and fulfilling than reaching out to a missing girl as a police officer. A person who is psychologically broken, betrayed by the most trustworthy people in her life, monetarily dependent on the criminal for her survival. Returning home is rarely an option—the burden of shame is too heavy to bear. She worries about the repercussions her family might face, the stigma that will follow them, and the uncertain future of her younger siblings. These are just a few of the many barriers blocking her path back home. She is someone who feels as though she is dying a little each day yet is compelled by her circumstances to keep living.

Reporting a case to the police and getting it registered is still a missing link. The mind of a victim remains chained by sociological pressures. Legs tremble when one tries to take a stand. Fear of falling keeps them from standing at all, and hesitation prevents them from taking the first step. But how can the change we expect as a society ever be achieved if cases are not reported to the police, if voices are not raised in a court of law? Confidence in the police and in legal procedures is still lacking. This raises many questions: What exactly is missing? How do we recover what has been lost? Where are we falling short? Is the problem rooted in cumbersome procedures, or in flawed methodology? How can synergy between the people and the system be built? Over the years, the system has grown, developed, and been redesigned, yet it still seems disconnected from the realities of society. During my training days, one senior officer remarked that the police exist to regulate society, not to reform it. But then, who carries the responsibility of reform? The answer to that question often feels diffused.

Civil servants within the system have become more effective responders, but we still lag behind in developing ourselves as true changemakers. While we have advanced significantly in managing crises and addressing immediate needs, the real challenge lies in evolving from responders to genuine agents of societal transformation. Our current approach tends to focus on enforcing laws through compliance and immediate action. Yet, the deeper potential of these laws is to instill lasting change—to reshape attitudes, behaviours, and the cultural narratives that underpin them.

For instance, preventive laws aimed at protecting vulnerable communities—such as those safeguarding women and children—must go beyond mere regulatory oversight. Our goal should be to cultivate an environment where these laws are not just enforced from the outside but are internalized within communities as part of the social fabric. This requires leveraging the law not only as a response to crimes or violations but also as a tool to educate communities about their rights, empowering them with the knowledge and agency to protect themselves. A preventive approach builds a stronger foundation—one where communities become self-reliant and actively participate in sustaining social harmony, rather than remaining passive recipients of state protection.

Our existing legal frameworks also hold the potential to empower rather than merely control. Laws on domestic violence or child protection, for example, were crafted not only to penalize perpetrators but also to uplift survivors—offering them avenues for safety, rehabilitation, and growth. If we actively invest in promoting legal literacy, with equal emphasis on rights and responsibilities, individuals can begin to view the law not as a distant enforcer but as a trusted ally in their daily lives. This proactive engagement fosters resilience, as people learn to rely on their own knowledge and agency rather than waiting for authorities in moments of crisis. A genuine shift toward change-making requires us to see law enforcement through the lens of restorative justice. Many legal provisions—particularly those concerning juveniles or minor offenders—already allow for rehabilitation and reintegration, breaking cycles of marginalization. By embracing these rehabilitative approaches, we disrupt patterns of criminality and victimization, demonstrating that laws serve not only to punish but also to reform and heal. Prioritizing restorative justice helps us confront the root causes that drive individuals into conflict with the law, creating a society that values second chances and supports reintegration. To achieve this, we must adopt a mindset that transcends compliance and moves toward transformative engagement. Only then can the law evolve from a reactive instrument into a catalyst for progressive, society-wide change. This shift demands consistency, inclusivity, and an unwavering commitment to building trust, resilience, and empowerment across all levels of society.

When a crime is committed against a woman, an instinctive silence often envelops her, growing heavier with each moment she hesitates to speak. This silence is not born from weakness; it is a shield of survival, woven from generations of fear, mistrust, and the harsh lessons of a world that punishes women who dare to raise their voices..

To break this silence and report the crime is to confront the world that too often shifts blame from the perpetrator to the woman herself, scrutinizing her every choice, every word, every movement, as if searching for reasons to hold her accountable for the violence inflicted upon her. Speaking out is not a mere act of declaration; it is stepping into the storm, knowing that, more often than not, the question will not be, "What happened to you?" but rather, "What did you do to make this happen?"

There is the fear of not being believed, of seeing her truth diluted, her pain dismissed. It's a brutal gamble, one where she stands to lose more than what was already taken from her. Many women learn to tread lightly around the shame that society drapes over them in the aftermath of violence, as if it's they—and not the criminals, who should feel stained by it. When she hesitates, it's because she knows that once her story is out, it is no longer hers alone; it becomes subject to the eyes and voices of others, ready to dissect, question, and sometimes, cruelly twist it.

The voices around her only add to the weight. There are whispers that speaking out will disrupt her family, tarnish her name, and invite questions that may stay with her for years. She knows that too often, justice doesn't arrive as swiftly as judgment. Her words may echo unanswered, or worse, be met with indifference from those entrusted with the law.

Yet, within her hesitation lies a profound resilience, a knowing that once she speaks, she reclaims her story. She steps out of the shadows, not because the world is ready to listen, but because she refuses silence to validate her suffering. For every woman who hesitates, there's a part of her that longs to be heard, to be respected and to reclaim the dignity that violence tried to strip away.

In this tension, in this hesitation, lies the battle of her inner world against the outer one, a fragile balance between silence and survival, truth and protection. And when she finally speaks, her voice isn't merely a complaint; it is a flame, a testament to the strength it takes to make her story heard in a world all too ready to turn away.

When I was serving as Superintendent of Police in Betul district, one Sunday afternoon I was sitting in my bungalow garden, admiring the colourful birds that often visited. It was a feeling of absolute bliss. As a police officer, one rarely gets a true Sunday, since crime never takes a break for the weekend. This was one of those rare days that gave me the chance to simply sit quietly and observe the world around me. Betul was a beautiful district, with nature at its best. I noticed a tiny yellow bird walking across the lawn, as if searching for something. Perhaps it had picked up this habit from its frequent visits to the SP bungalow. With a smile on my face, I kept following its movements in complete amazement. Suddenly, my phone rang. The screen displayed an anonymous number. I always make it a point to pick up such calls. It takes a great deal of courage for someone to dial anonymously and admit that he or she is going through something wrong. Often, it may be an important piece of information, shared after gathering much confidence, before finally dialing the SP's number. That courage must never go unanswered.

I never take a chance with anonymity; I always embrace it. I picked up the phone. What the caller narrated to me, sent chills down my spine. In a remote village, a twelve-year-old was raped and consequentially became pregnant. She went through an abortion procedure and the foetus was buried in a dried bore well in the village. The team was dispatched to the village immediately. By the time they arrived, night had already fallen. After a careful search, they identified the borewell in question. Inside, we found the foetus, wrapped in a cloth, lodged in the dry pipe of an abandoned borewell located in an isolated part of the village. The mouth of the pipe had been sealed with a heavy stone in the middle of a barren field. With great difficulty, we finally managed to retrieve the foetus from the pipe. The victim revealed to us that she had been raped by her tuition teacher. Earlier, when the girl had informed her mother about the incident, the mother asked her to remain silent. A few weeks later, when the pregnancy began to show, she took her daughter to a private clinic where the foetus was aborted. They paid fifty thousand rupees for the procedure. This clinic, located in a densely populated area, usually handed over the aborted foetus to patients for disposal. In this case, we were fortunate—the same practice was followed, which meant the police were able to preserve crucial evidence. Clinics like these are often hubs of criminal activity, quietly harbouring offenders. They thrive in small towns where crime ferments in silence, feeding many hands, each satisfied with its share of the spoils. Such crimes seldom surface. This is why the administration must be proactive, vigilant, and, above all, accessible. Only then can these deeply entrenched practices be dismantled. In this case, the disposal procedure turned into an unexpected breakthrough for the police.

When the investigation began, we discovered that many other minor girls had suffered the same fate. Beyond conducting illegal sex determination and abortions for married women, this doctor had also erased vital evidence of rape. Examination of the sonography machine data revealed a chilling truth—countless girls had gone missing from the womb itself. They were denied the very chance to be born. Their absence benefits no one. It is the same old stereotype, the same cycle we have been hearing, seeing, and witnessing for generations—yet we have been unable to break it. This incident shook the entire district. The doctor, along with her medical staff, was arrested, and the three-storied clinic was sealed. A heinous offence like rape had been silently buried without a trace. This district is often described as peaceful—but here, peace is not maintained through the rule of law. Instead, it is enforced by the might of a few who silence the weak. A district can only be truly peaceful when cases are registered, investigated swiftly, and those who misuse power are put behind bars. Perhaps these powerful few had begun to believe they owned the system. But this incident exposed a larger truth. Why should a female victim be punished for life for a crime committed by a man? Why is it a matter of shame for her, and not for the criminal? Why do we fail, even today, to break this stereotype rooted in an age-old, chauvinistic mindset? Why is the victim branded as polluted? Why is she denied the chance to marry, to live with dignity?

The data we recovered from the clinic gave a record of many minor girls who had undergone abortion procedures. These were potentially rape victims. Yet, from the long list, only five came forward to register a case. I was instructed to restrict my investigation to these few. The inquiry was soon wound up. Out of nearly 240 minor patients on record, only five cases of rape were registered, as no other girl came forward.

Many of the perpetrators still roam scot-free. Society tends to treat such criminals as if they have committed a small mistake. It refuses to acknowledge rape as the heinous crime it is. Often, it is dismissed as a "mutual affair," or the blame is shifted onto the victim, as if she lured the offender. These are the sociological distortions we have nurtured for generations—distortions that shield criminals and isolate victims.

A victim rarely finds the support system she needs to stand up for herself and approach the police. Instead, what we see are defensive reactions, not genuine answers to these anomalies. Such reactions surface only when a crime makes headlines: streets roar with cries for justice, slogans rise, candles are lit—and then they melt away. But what about the countless other cases silently brushed under society's carpet?

My team was shaken by this reality. Despite relentless community outreach programmes, interactive sessions in schools and colleges, role-plays, and awareness drives, we still struggle to instill confidence in young victims to say, "Yes, I was wronged". When will women come out of this enforced denial? Regardless of the gravity of the crime, they are silenced.

This deafening silence haunts us as police officers. Perhaps our efforts are still not enough to break it. Society must evolve beyond these stereotypes and face reality. The responsibility cannot lie solely on the victim's shoulders. It is the collective duty of society. Awareness efforts must be more intensive, more inclusive, and more gender-sensitive if we are to break these chains and dismantle the stereotype once and for all.

This case was widely reported and extensively discussed, yet no new cases surfaced. No girl came forward with her story. No victim could gather the confidence to put the man who wronged her behind bars.

For a police officer, each day brings a new challenge. The way we address these challenges changes everything. The promptness and sincerity with which we face them inspire public confidence in the police.

Crimes against women in India are more than just legal matters; they are deeply rooted sociological challenges. Our society lives in several centuries at once. On the one hand, we are moving progressively towards a more victim-friendly environment. Women's desks have been set up in all police stations. Women staff have been recruited and deployed. Male officers are regularly sensitized. Yet, on the other side, both those sitting behind the desk and those sitting in front of it remain exposed to the parochial, ideological mindset we have inherited. This mindset views women as weak and dependent.

We are constantly caught in this dichotomy. It blurs the image of the modern, independent woman. Sacrifice, forgiveness, and self-blame are often glorified as virtues for women. But the police are entrusted with the responsibility of stripping away this misleading palette of colors and presenting the truth in black and white, ensuring crimes are not hidden in society's grey areas.

Women endure cruelty silently, navigating through daily outbursts of violence, yet fail to identify themselves as victims. But acknowledging a problem is the first step toward eradicating it. Denying its existence only makes it worse.

In a quiet corner of a bustling neighbourhood, a woman named Anjali wakes up each day to a life shrouded in shadows. The morning light filters through her window, illuminating a space that feels more like a prison than a home. The walls echo with memories of harsh words and violent encounters, constant reminders of the torment she endures at the hands of her husband. Yet, Anjali remains trapped in a cycle of fear and shame.

Each day unfolds with the same grim routine. Her husband, once charming and affectionate, has become a figure of terror. He lashes out not just with his hands but with words that cut deeper than any physical blow. Anjali has learned to tiptoe around him, careful not to provoke the storm within. She wears a smile, masks her pain, and clings to fleeting hope, only to be met with disappointment time and again.

The torment seeps beyond the physical; it corrodes her spirit. Anjali struggles with crushing isolation. She longs to share her suffering, to seek comfort from friends or family, yet societal expectations silence her. The fear of judgment looms: What would her husband's family say? Would her own family blame her for not being a "good" wife? These questions torment her, swirling endlessly in her mind, leaving her consumed by anxiety and utterly alone.

At night, when the house falls silent, Anjali's trauma resurfaces. She lies awake, staring at the ceiling, wrestling with the ghosts of her reality. The mental anguish is relentless; she feels as if she is losing herself bit by bit. Memories of laughter and joy are overshadowed by the specter of abuse. With every bruise, every insult, she is stripped of her identity, reduced to a mere shadow of the woman she once was.

Yet the most profound agony lies in her inability to voice her pain. The silence suffocates her. Each day, she dons a façade of normalcy, greeting the world with a smile that belies the chaos within. When friends ask how she is, she responds with practiced cheerfulness, afraid to reveal the truth. The fear of retribution, of being further ostracized or blamed, keeps her chained to her suffering.

In moments of solitude, Anjali grapples with her worth. She questions whether she deserves better or if this is her fate. The battle rages within her: a desire for freedom clashes with the chains of fear and obligation. Each tear she sheds is a silent plea for help, a cry lost in a world that often turns a blind eye to the plight of women in her position.

Despite the darkness, a stint of hope resides deep within Anjali. The yearning for a life free from fear, filled with love and respect, ignites a small flame. It whispers that she deserves happiness, that she can break free from the shackles of abuse. Yet the journey is fraught with challenges, and the path to liberation is steeped in uncertainty.

As the sun rises each day, so does Anjali's resolve. She knows that one day, she may find the courage to speak her truth, to break the silence that has bound her for too long. Until then, she endures, a warrior in her own right, navigating the treacherous waters of domestic violence with grace and resilience.

A woman, who is a victim will only move ahead if she is convinced that something wrong has been done to her. The persistence of crimes against women in India, despite a robust legal framework, reveals deeper systemic issues beyond merely the existence of laws. To understand why strong laws and legal procedures fail to bring about the expected societal change, we must explore the multifaceted interaction among law, society, and institutional structures.

Cultural and social conditioning in India is deeply patriarchal, where women's roles and identities are still largely defined by rigid norms and stereotypes. This cultural conditioning continues to overshadow the effectiveness of legal frameworks. Even though the laws may provide for gender equality, societal values often subvert them. For instance, in many parts of India, domestic violence, dowry harassment, and other forms of gender-based abuse are normalized and justified by cultural or familial expectations. Laws like the Domestic Violence Act or Dowry Prohibition Act exist, but they are rendered ineffective because society perceives such crimes as private, not warranting legal intervention. Many crimes against women, such as honour killings or forced marriages, are rooted in concepts of family honour. Legal provisions against such crimes exist, but they are undermined by strong social support for maintaining family "reputation" over individual rights. This reduces the likelihood of reporting, prosecuting, or even acknowledging these crimes.

Victim blaming and social stigma is a critical barrier to the effective implementation of laws is the persistent victim-blaming culture. This phenomenon is more than just a psychological response; it is a social tool to protect patriarchal structures. When women report crimes such as rape, sexual harassment, or trafficking, they are often subjected to scrutiny and judgment, making them reluctant to seek legal recourse. Social ostracization, the fear of being labeled "impure" or "dishonoured" is enough to deter many victims from pursuing justice, especially in cases of sexual violence. The legal process itself can become traumatic, as victims are often questioned about their character, past behaviour, or clothing, which disincentivizes them from coming forward.

Weak implementation of laws, even with strong laws on paper, remains a significant challenge in India. The legal and judicial process is often bogged down by inefficiency, corruption, and delay. Legal procedures often take years to be resolved, if at all, during which the victims and their families lose faith in the justice system. A delayed trial diminishes the deterrent effect of the law. In many cases, especially in rural areas, families and community leaders may pressure victims to "settle" cases outside of court, often leading to perpetrators escaping punishment. This is particularly common in cases of rape, abduction, or honour crimes, where social prestige is placed above legal justice.

Law enforcement agencies and even parts of the judiciary are not immune to the pervasive patriarchal mindset that exists within Indian society. Despite formal education and training, police officers, judges, and other legal practitioners may still harbour biases against women, which can severely impact the enforcement of laws. Police officers, particularly in conservative areas, often view crimes against women through the lens of traditional gender roles. For instance, when a minor girl elopes, police may treat it as a consensual act or a family matter rather than investigating possible coercion or trafficking, despite laws against child marriage and abduction. Court rulings may sometimes reflect gender biases, where judges might deliver verdicts based on personal or societal perceptions of women's morality or behaviour. This was evident in cases where rape survivors were asked why they didn't "resist more" or why they were out at night.

India's legal framework is largely modelled on Western jurisprudence, emphasizing individual rights and equality. However, the societal structure in many parts of India remains feudal and collective, where the interests of the family, community, or caste outweigh individual rights. This clash between the progressive ideals of the law and the conservative realities of Indian society creates a void between legal procedures and real-world outcomes. Laws such as the prohibition of child marriage or dowry often meet resistance from communities that view them as outside interference in their traditions. This resistance is compounded by the legal illiteracy prevalent in rural and semi-urban areas, where people may not even be aware of the laws protecting women's rights.

Many women do not report crimes due to the fear of retaliation from their families, communities, or even the perpetrators. The protection mechanisms provided by the legal system are often insufficient to shield victims from further harm, especially in cases involving powerful individuals or entrenched social hierarchies. In many cases, perpetrators of gender-based crimes belong to powerful political or economic classes, making it difficult for victims—particularly those from marginalized communities—to pursue justice. Fear of violence, social exclusion, or economic deprivation often prevents women from seeking legal redress.

India lacks a comprehensive support system for women who wish to escape abusive environments. Shelter homes, rehabilitation centres, and counselling services are often underfunded, understaffed, and inaccessible, especially in rural areas. Many women remain trapped due to financial dependence on their families or spouses. While laws such as the Maintenance and Welfare of Parents and Senior Citizens Act, 2007, exist, they do not address the broader economic vulnerabilities of women who lack access to employment or financial independence. The incongruity between strong laws and societal outcomes in India arises from a complex web of cultural conditioning, social stigmas, systemic biases, and institutional inefficiencies. While legal frameworks are essential in curbing crimes against women, they alone cannot bring about change. Deep-seated societal attitudes, patriarchal norms, and weak implementation remain significant obstacles. Real change requires a holistic approach, where legal reforms are accompanied by societal education, institutional accountability, and grassroots efforts to dismantle patriarchal structures that perpetuate violence against women.

Despite numerous legislative efforts, Indian society often resists social and legal reforms due to a complex interplay of historical, cultural, and structural factors. To understand why reforms fail to produce visible change, it is crucial to examine deeper sociological dynamics and institutional limitations that create inertia in societal evolution. Indian society is shaped by cultural and social norms historically legitimized over centuries. This hegemony functions as a powerful force, maintaining the status quo and resisting reforms that challenge long-held beliefs. Gender roles, caste hierarchies, and concepts of family honour are deeply institutionalized, influencing individual and collective behaviour. The persistence of these norms often creates a disjunction between the formal structures of law and informal societal practices. Even progressive reforms appear alien or incompatible with entrenched worldviews, encountering resistance at both micro (family) and macro (community) levels. Structural domination and subjugation maintain inequality and discrimination not through explicit coercion, but through everyday practices. The socialization of individuals, especially women, into subordinate roles, and the normalization of male dominance, hinder the impact of legal reforms on issues such as women's rights, domestic violence, and inheritance laws. The cognitive dissonance between progressive legal frameworks and patriarchal conditioning makes it difficult for reforms to penetrate daily life. Traditional institutions—families, caste councils (khap panchayats), and religious bodies—retain symbolic authority that frequently operates parallel to, or in defiance of, state law. Practices such as honour killings or child marriages illustrate the power of these institutions over legal mandates. Legal reforms are often perceived as peripheral or threatening to the social fabric, where allegiance to cultural practices supersedes adherence to state regulations. Many reforms in India are introduced top-down, without adequate grassroots engagement. While legislation may reflect progressive ideals, it often lacks contextualization within the lived experiences of diverse populations. India's sociocultural heterogeneity means state-enacted reforms do not always resonate with local realities, where customs and traditions vary widely. A lack of participatory governance mechanisms that involve communities in the law-making process results in alienation and resistance to reforms. The disconnection between legislative intent and ground-level realities diminishes the transformative potential of these reforms. Reforms, particularly those addressing deeply ingrained issues such as caste or gender, demand a fundamental shift in societal consciousness. Societal change is evolutionary rather than revolutionary and often occurs incrementally over generations. India exhibits strong social inertia, where legal reforms are viewed as impositions on a collective consciousness that has yet to internalize fully the ethical imperatives of equality, justice, and individual rights. For instance, while caste-based discrimination is outlawed, social mobility for marginalized communities remains constrained by informal caste networks influencing economic and social opportunities. Reforms are often selectively applied based on political or economic considerations, diluting their impact. Bureaucratic structures, entrenched in traditional hierarchies, may resist reforms that threaten their power. The disconnect between law and enforcement fosters perceptions of state ineffectiveness, reducing reforms to symbolic gestures rather than instruments of real change. At the heart of societal resistance lies a reluctance to challenge normative power structures that have historically governed Indian society.

Whether it is the caste system, patriarchy, or religious orthodoxy, these power structures maintain dominance by framing themselves as essential to social order and cohesion. Reforms that challenge them—such as promoting inter-caste marriages, women's autonomy, or religious freedom—are often seen as destabilizing forces. This reluctance to confront entrenched hierarchies ensures that reforms remain superficial, failing to disrupt the deeper social fabric.

Resistance to social and legal reforms is frequently justified through a lens of cultural relativism, where practices such as dowry, child marriage, or caste distinctions are defended as culturally specific and deserving of respect. This moral exceptionalism allows regressive practices to persist under the guise of preserving tradition, undermining the universality of human rights and legal reforms. Efforts to modernize or liberalize society are often cast as external or Western impositions, threatening the authenticity of Indian culture and fostering defensive attitudes that stifle progressive change.

The slow pace of social transformation in India, despite substantial legal reforms, reflects a complex interplay between legislation, entrenched social norms, and institutionalized power structures. Real change requires not only legislative interventions but a multifaceted approach that includes grassroots mobilization, education, and a shift in societal values. Reform must go beyond legal frameworks to engage with the cultural and ideological foundations of Indian society, fostering a long-term process of social re-education that bridges the gap between legal mandates and lived realities.

Historically, stereotypes were shaped by the practical demands of survival in societies contingent on strict divisions of labour. In agrarian economies, roles had to be specialized: men as labourers and defenders, women confined to domestic spaces focused on caregiving and home management. Over generations, these roles hardened into stereotypes, portraying men as natural providers and women as inherently nurturing. Similarly, during colonial rule, racial and cultural stereotypes were deliberately constructed to reinforce hierarchies. Indigenous populations were depicted as "backward" or "primitive," while colonizers positioned themselves as "civilizers," justifying exploitation and leaving a legacy of enduring biases.

Religious and cultural narratives added further layers, idealizing behaviours and roles that became normative expectations. While these norms were functional historically, they became limiting as societies evolved. The transition from agrarian to industrial and later to knowledge-based economies challenged these roles. Women's increasing participation in the workforce, for example, contested the notion that they were best suited for domestic responsibilities, yet societal expectations have been slow to adjust, creating friction between tradition and modern reality.

Moreover, stereotypes have historically acted as powerful tools for controlling behaviour and maintaining social order. By reinforcing certain traits in specific groups, societies could control those who were deemed "other" or "inferior", discouraging them from aspiring beyond prescribed roles. Today, however, these stereotypes no longer serve any pragmatic function and, instead, impede growth and progress. They cast unfair limitations on people's capabilities, reducing them to preordained labels rather than allowing them the freedom to define their own identities. For instance, the stereotype that men are "natural" leaders, while women are "nurturers", circumscribe the leadership opportunities available to women in professional spheres, even though countless women have demonstrated remarkable leadership qualities.

In the digital, globally interconnected world, these stereotypes are more than just antiquated ideas, they are barriers to inclusive growth. Studies show that diverse perspectives enhance innovation and creativity, yet stereotypes that label certain groups as "unsuitable" for specific roles continue to restrict collaboration and inclusivity. Understanding the historical roots of these stereotypes reveals that they were often practical or politically motivated at one time but now have no place in a world that values individuality, equality, and mutual respect. Breaking these matrixes is more than a societal shift; it's a liberation of human potential, allowing people to be seen as individuals rather than representatives of a label, which is essential in building a society that fosters equity and embraces diverse contributions.

Challenging stereotypes can provide inspiration and underscore the value of breaking free from outmoded norms. There are several impactful case studies, where people have challenged the old norms and embraced the new. In Pakistan's Swat Valley, stereotypes around women's roles were entrenched, particularly in education.

Girls' education was restricted, with many believing a woman's place was solely in the home. Malala Yousafzai, however, defied these norms, advocating for girls' right to learn even under the threat of violence from the Taliban. Despite facing pestilential consequences, her voice led to a global movement for girls' education, challenging stereotypes that limited women's opportunities. Malala's work inspired millions and redefined expectations around girls' rights, creating a global dialogue that encouraged acceptance of gender equality in education and beyond.

In the aftermath of the 1994 genocide, Rwanda faced the challenge of rebuilding a society with a severely skewed gender ratio, as many men had been lost to the conflict. Women were called upon to step into roles traditionally dominated by men, taking on leadership positions in the government, the workforce, and even in rebuilding the economy. In 2003, Rwanda established one of the world's most progressive constitutions on gender equality, including a quota mandating that 30% of parliament seats be held by women (though women now make up over 60% of Rwanda's parliament). This shift challenged deeply rooted gender stereotypes and fostered a model of gender inclusivity that serves as a global afflatus, demonstrating that embracing equality can transform societies.

Stereotypes around caste have long persisted in India, with entrenched ideas about "untouchable" castes (Dalits) historically limiting social, economic, and educational opportunities. Activists such as Dr. B.R. Ambedkar, and more recently grassroots organizations like the Dalit Rights Collective, have worked to dismantle these biases through awareness campaigns, empowerment programmes, and social mobilization. One notable example is the village of Hiware Bazar in Maharashtra, where community-led efforts to promote equality spurred significant economic growth. As locals witnessed the tangible benefits of social inclusion, caste-based discrimination began to decline, and equality became a shared community value, allowing individuals to contribute based on ability rather than birth.

Similarly, Japanese society has historically framed disability as a weakness or source of shame. Organizations like the Nippon Foundation's Para-Sports Movement have challenged these perceptions by using sports as a vehicle for inclusion. The Tokyo 2020 Paralympic Games marked a turning point, generating national pride and respect for athletes with disabilities and helping reshape public attitudes. Awareness campaigns highlighted the diverse capabilities of individuals with disabilities, leading to greater accessibility in infrastructure and workplaces. This movement fostered a broader cultural acceptance and appreciation of inclusivity, encouraging recognition of a wider spectrum of abilities.

Brazil, too, has a complex racial history, with Afro-Brazilian communities long marginalized by deeply entrenched racial stereotypes. Initiatives like the Black Awareness Movement and Afro-Brazilian festivals have aimed to reclaim cultural pride, celebrate African heritage, and counteract racial stereotypes. Over time, initiatives such as affirmative action policies in education and job opportunities have improved socio-economic conditions for Afro-Brazilians, challenging the stereotype of limited roles for certain racial groups. By celebrating Afro-Brazilian culture and contributions, their society has gradually moved toward a more inclusive narrative, creating space for new generations to view racial diversity as a national strength. Ireland traditionally held conservative views on family and marriage, but the 2015 referendum legalizing same-sex marriage marked a historic turning point. Campaigns emphasized empathy and understanding, using personal stories to highlight that LGBTQIA+ individuals were not distant 'others' but family members, colleagues, and friends. The vote passed with a decisive majority, demonstrating the power of visibility and human connection to reshape public opinion. This landmark moment not only redefined norms around family and love but also proved that deeply ingrained stereotypes and biases can evolve when a society engages in open dialogue rooted in compassion.

These case studies reveal that dismantling stereotypes often requires persistence, community involvement, and narratives that resonate on a deeply human level. Through campaigns, activism, and policy changes, these examples show that societies can learn to embrace inclusivity, empathy, and understanding while breaking free from restrictive beliefs. Such shifts, once internalized, do more than challenge norms—they enrich communities, foster equality, and empower individuals to participate fully and authentically in shaping a more just society.

Building empathy and fostering open dialogue are essential strategies for challenging and dismantling stereotypes. Empathy allows individuals to see their shared humanity with those who may appear different, reducing reliance on dehumanizing or marginalizing narratives. Storytelling initiatives—such as community forums and workshops where people share personal experiences—can bridge divides, foster connection and understanding. Educational campaigns that emphasize emotional intelligence further shape perception, with schools and organizations offering training programmes that encourage participants to step into others' shoes, engage in role-playing scenarios, and confront their own biases.

Art and media are powerful tools for cultivating empathy, as films, literature, theatre, and visual arts can portray the complex realities of marginalized communities. Documentaries and storytelling projects featuring individuals who defy stereotypes often challenge ingrained assumptions and inspire reflection.

Equally important is creating safe environments where individuals feel comfortable expressing their views without fear of ridicule or backlash. Active listening—focusing on truly understanding another's perspective—can help people feel valued and respected. Facilitated discussions, led by trained moderators, allow difficult conversations to remain constructive, while diverse participation ensures a richer exchange of perspectives. By bringing together individuals across cultures, genders, ages, and socioeconomic backgrounds, communities can nurture critical thinking, challenge monolithic views, and build relationships grounded in mutual respect and understanding.

By examining common misconceptions and their origins, individuals can begin to question the validity of stereotypes and understand the harm they cause. Encouraging participants to share their personal experiences—whether as targets or as those who have perpetuated stereotypes—can promote accountability and inspire collective action against discriminatory beliefs. When empathy and open dialogue are prioritized, they create a ripple effect across communities, prompting people to reflect on their own biases and recognize the shared humanity of those they may have once seen through a narrow lens. As conversations that challenge stereotypes become more common, they foster a culture of acceptance and inclusivity. These approaches also strengthen resilience against prejudice, empowering individuals to speak out against discrimination.

Communities that embrace empathy and open dialogue can form supportive networks that not only dismantle harmful stereotypes but also actively cultivate a fairer and more harmonious society. Ultimately, empathy and dialogue are not just strategies for challenging bias; they are foundations for building a culture of understanding, respect, and equality. Through these efforts, individuals and communities can work together to replace harmful beliefs with compassion and justice.

As we reflect on the intricate web of stereotypes that pervade our society, it becomes clear that breaking these barriers is not merely an act of defiance but a necessary step toward creating a world where every individual—especially girls—can thrive, free from outdated expectations. These stereotypes, subtly woven into the fabric of daily life, cultivate fear and limitation, suppressing the aspirations and potential of countless young girls. If we are to make meaningful progress in addressing the issue of missing girls, dismantling these deeply rooted beliefs is essential.

The path to transformation begins with acknowledging the powerful influence of socialization and cultural narratives that dictate how girls should behave, dress, and dream. By challenging these narratives, we open the door to fresh perspectives and innovative solutions. Breaking stereotypes means redefining what is possible for girls and women, giving them permission to pursue their ambitions without the weight of societal judgment. This mission demands a collective commitment from every sector of society. Families must nurture environments of open communication and unwavering support, empowering daughters to voice their needs and aspirations. Educators hold a unique responsibility to shape young minds, designing curricula that celebrate diversity, encourage critical thinking, and dismantle harmful gender myths. Policymakers and law enforcement must prioritize the safety and empowerment of girls, advancing legislation and initiatives that challenge systemic inequality and discriminatory practices.

Moreover, the media holds immense power in shaping public perception. By amplifying diverse narratives that celebrate the strength and resilience of girls, it can dismantle harmful stereotypes and inspire a generation to challenge the status quo. Community leaders and activists also play a critical role in sparking dialogue, creating platforms where marginalized voices are heard, validated, and empowered.

Ultimately, progress demands the courage to confront uncomfortable truths. Building a culture of inclusion and respect for every individual's dignity is essential to dismantling the systemic barriers fueling the crisis of missing girls. Safety and freedom must be recognized as fundamental rights for all—not privileges reserved for a select few.

These uncomfortable truths often unsettle the very foundations of our beliefs, values, and identities. From systemic inequality and gender-based violence to racial discrimination and economic disparity, these realities expose a world rife with contradictions. Many struggle to acknowledge them, fearing that doing so could disrupt their worldview, demand accountability, or dismantle long-held narratives. Socialization and cultural conditioning often reinforce these beliefs, creating echo chambers that marginalize dissenting voices and make it even harder to embrace complexity.

Moreover, systems of power and privilege can perpetuate denial, as those who benefit from existing hierarchies may lack incentive to confront injustice. This disconnect silences the lived experiences of marginalized groups and fosters narratives that are easier to accept but far removed from reality. Yet, engaging with these uncomfortable truths is essential. They hold the key to empathy, dialogue, and lasting transformation. By recognizing systemic injustice and personal bias, society can deepen its understanding of the human experience, creating space for healing and inclusivity. Acknowledging these truths is not merely a moral responsibility but a vital step toward building a just and equitable world—one where every girl has the freedom and safety to thrive.

In this pursuit, it is crucial to recognize that each action, no matter how small, contributes to a larger movement toward change. By challenging and reshaping societal norms, we empower not only the current generation but also future ones to rise above the limitations that have long constrained them. Together, by breaking these stereotypes, we can build a future where every girl can thrive—transforming the crisis of missing girls into a chapter of history rather than an ongoing reality. When a person steps into a bubble, they find themselves encased within an invisible yet unyielding boundary, one that reduces the entire world to a limited, repetitive echo of the same thoughts, fears, and rigid beliefs. Inside, the air grows stagnant with negativity, clouding vision and narrowing the possibilities beyond. This bubble becomes a prison of the mind, distorting perception and anchoring a person in a space where growth feels impossible, and the freedom to think differently is lost.

To move forward, one must summon the courage to pierce this self-imposed cocoon, shattering its walls and scattering the negativity that has accumulated within. Breaking free is not merely a step forward—it is a profound metamorphosis: a shedding of limitations, biases, and the deceptive comforts of restriction. Only by confronting and dismantling this barrier can we open ourselves to a world enriched with new perspectives, expansive ideas, and boundless potential. Let us break free from the bubbles that confine us to truly comprehend the journey of missing girls.

Chapter 2

THE PAPER WINGS

"I started running away when I was five years old.
It wasn't until I was an adult
That I realized what I really wanted was
Somebody to come after me when I was running
away."

- Willie Aames

Morning crime briefings are perhaps the sanctum sanctorum of policing. As an IPS probationer, I was appointed as the station in-charge of a rural police station, Hatod, located on the outskirts of Indore city in Madhya Pradesh. Being on probation, I was required to report daily to the Superintendent of Police about registered cases and the overall law and order situation within my jurisdiction, alongside the SDOP (Sub-Divisional Officer) who supervised my work.

Briefings about heinous crimes typically required a detailed account of the case, covering even the smallest details. Two days after I joined, a woman was stabbed to death in a remote village. The entire police station mobilized to investigate. It was a sensational case for a rural setting, prominently covered by both local print and electronic media, with every step of the investigation being closely followed and highlighted on social media. I was deeply immersed in the case, able to recall every detail at my fingertips. After all, it was a heinous offence. I felt confident during the daily briefings as I updated senior officers on the progress.

It took us two days and one night to solve the case and arrest the culprit, who turned out to be the woman's husband. He confessed to killing his pregnant wife because he suspected her of being in an illicit relationship. Ironically, evidence suggested he himself was involved with his sister-in-law. Society, it seemed, imposed very different standards of loyalty on men and women.

Nevertheless, every officer in our team—practically the entire strength of the police station worked tirelessly, minute by minute, to crack the case. The department rewarded us for our success, and the local media and public showered the police with admiration and respect. For me, it was a moment of immense pride and a valuable lesson on how deeply teamwork is ingrained in the police force.

A week later, a 15-year-old girl went missing. This too was categorized as a heinous crime. The next morning, I confidently briefed: a 15-year-old girl had gone to school, attended her classes, but never returned home. That was all I knew. I concluded my briefing with that single statement.

Then, my SP began asking questions: Had she had any arguments at home? Did anything unusual happen at school? Did she walk to school alone, or was she accompanied back? Was it a co-educational school or all-girls? What conversations had she had with her friends that day? I had no answers to any of these questions.

This case was as important as the murder case. A young life was missing. Yet this heinous offence failed to spark even a faint sense of emergency among the police station staff and I, too, responded in the same manner. Not a single crease of worry appeared on anyone's forehead. Not an eyebrow was raised. No headlines were written. No words were spoken. The media remained silent, and social media was utterly oblivious to the fact that a young girl was missing.

I was flummoxed by this stark dichotomy: the case was heinous, yet it was not treated as heinous. We failed to acknowledge its gravity. And by "we," I mean every stakeholder—myself included—the police, and society at large. How had this happened? Why had it happened? How could I, after months of training, behave with such complacency just days into my posting? How could socialization in the field be so powerful that it eclipsed everything I had learned at the academy? How had certain crimes become stereotyped, one commanding urgency and another dismissed as ordinary?

These questions gnawed at me, making me feel complicit in the very crime I was meant to solve. That morning briefing shook me to the core. The questions my SP asked were not mere inquiries; they were a wake-up call, a lesson meant to jolt me into seeing the true weight of the situation. Perhaps it was expected of me to carry this realization back to my colleagues, to shift their perception as well.

I rushed back to my desk and opened the missing girl's case diary. As I turned each page, seeking answers to the SP's questions, more questions rose up instead. It felt as though I had opened some arcane box of secrets, and from it poured a torrent of accusations. They circled me like predators, mocking my ignorance, laughing at my lack of comprehension. The silence and indifference that had surrounded the case now felt perfidiously, suffocating. I was submerged in a deep sense of guilt and iniquity, as if the absence of urgency itself was a crime I had become a part of.

Suddenly, the HCM (Head Constable Moharrir) walked in with a glass of water, breaking the mystical spell that had gripped me. In the cool month of February, I was experiencing a heated rush of blood flooding my face, tiny droplets of sweat glistened on my forehead. I closed the diary that seemed to scream for help. Perhaps this was why these missing-girl diaries were left untouched, allowed to gather dust, left to find their own quiet, tragic conclusions. No one dared to open them, for doing so was like unleashing a monster. Each question scrawled in those pages was a mirror reflecting our inadequacies as police officers, a painful reminder that what we were doing was just not enough. The HCM, his years of experience etched into every line of his face, placed the glass of water in front of me with a quiet grace. He tried to console me, perhaps to ease the tension he could clearly see building. "Don't worry, sir," he said, his voice steady with unwarranted confidence. "Girls go missing, but they come back on their own after some time".

I looked at him, my eyes silently questioning the casual certainty in his words. His gaze, calm yet firm, seemed to challenge me. "What if she never returns?" I asked. He smiled—a smug, hubristic smile—as he balanced the tray in his hand. That smile was enough to harden my resolve. I knew then that this case would not be treated as routine, not under my watch.

How many girls have gone missing? We all know the numbers. With a single click, we can access data in every permutation and combination, curated to suit our needs. But numbers are cold. They tell you nothing of the fear in a child's eyes, the desperation of parents, the vacuum left behind by a missing girl. If we truly seek solutions, we must look beyond arithmetic equations. We must search for the stories buried beneath those numbers—the stories that hold the real answers. Seeing only what is obvious is merely half the story. Anything incomplete can never be true, and truth always lies in its fullness. We cannot sit comfortably with these closed case diaries, clinging to the hope that one day a missing girl will reappear on her own.

Historically, the very notion of missing children only entered public consciousness in 2004, when the National Human Rights Commission (NHRC) Action Research first established a link between missing children and trafficking (Sen & Nair, 2004). Until then, the term carried no precise meaning in public or administrative discourse. It was not until January 31, 2012, that the Ministry of Home Affairs (MHA) issued an advisory formally defining missing children.

Most of these children—often but not exclusively from impoverished families—remain at high risk of being drawn into exploitative and criminal networks, including bonded labour, domestic servitude, trafficking, forced begging, sexual exploitation, and illegal organ trade (Ghosh, 2014; Mishra, 2000; Malhotra & Malhotra, 2012; Mamidi & Mamidi, 2015; Sen & Nair, 2004; Sarkar, 2014; Bhattacharya, 2015). Research shows that some children, both in urban and rural poor households, also run away from home in an attempt to escape poverty, neglect, or physical abuse (Mathur, 2009).

The umbrella term "missing" extends beyond children, encompassing the deeply entrenched tragedy of missing women (Anderson & Ray, 2012; Balan & Mahalingam, 2014; Bhattacharya, 2014; Hu & Schlosser, 2015). As highlighted by Rituparna Bhattacharya in her seminal paper Sociologies of India's Missing Children, the concept of "missing women" was introduced into academic discourse by Nobel Laureate Amartya Sen, who used it to describe the alarming gender imbalances—primarily due to female foeticide—across parts of Asia and North Africa, with a sharp focus on India (Sen, 1990, 1992, 2003; also Anderson & Ray, 2012).Indubitably, this was an important lesson taught to me by my SP during my probation. He wanted me to understand that one needs to practice the change to witness the change we expect to happen. The transformation we seek in society cannot manifest unless we actively embody and practice that change in our own lives. Change, in its essence, is not simply a matter of discourse or advocacy; it demands conscious effort and a deliberate shift in our behaviours, decisions, and interactions. When we aspire to challenge entrenched norms or dismantle outdated systems, the first step lies in internalizing those values ourselves. It is through consistent action, no matter how subtle or profound. We become catalysts for larger societal shifts.

By practicing the change we wish to see, we do more than just influence our immediate surroundings; we create a visible, living example of the ideals we espouse. This personal commitment acts as a powerful catalyst, slowly chipping away at the resistance of entrenched norms. When individuals collectively adopt this mindset, they create a ripple effect that expands exponentially, turning isolated acts of courage into a unified movement that can reshape societal structures. True change is never passive, but an active, lived experience that begins with individual choices and radiates outward, transforming the world one step at a time.

During the probation period, one learns not just through personal experience but through the wisdom and actions of others—by observing, questioning, and absorbing. It is understood by everyone that a probationer has come to learn, and those around them take on the role of teachers, explaining, narrating, and demonstrating. As a probationer, one encounters people of different ranks and generations, each with their own evolved way of doing things. Yet learning does not simply mean adopting these ways as gospel. The "best" method developed over years by others is not always the right method; part of the probationer's journey is discerning that difference.

The quote by Willie Aames, mentioned at the beginning of this chapter, offers multiple interpretations. First, running away—like many behaviours—may conceal complex motivations beneath the surface. Second, Aames suggests that the act of running away is a form of communication, one that often goes unrecognized. Third, he reflects that this understanding came to him only years later, illustrating how our conscious interpretations often lag behind our experiences.

Patrick Tomlinson, in *Reasons a Traumatized Child Runs Away*, notes that most children eventually reach a stage where they realize they can run away. This awareness may stem from healthy curiosity about the wider world. The child begins to see herself as capable of stepping beyond her parents' domain, experimenting with boundaries—at first in her imagination and fantasies, even if never acted upon. Could this urge to run be a sign of a child's growing independence? It may well be part of the natural process of individuation, as a child becomes disillusioned with parental authority and begins to define herself apart from it. Child psychotherapist Adam Phillips explores this tension in his article *In Praise of Difficult Children* (2009):

"A truant mind has to have something to truant from and something to truant for. The adults provide something to truant from, and the adolescents have to discover something to truant for. In straightforward psychoanalytic terms, adolescents truant from parents as forbidden objects of desire, as the people who have deprived them; they truant for accessible objects of desire, for the possibility of making up for the inevitable deprivations they have suffered growing up with their parents. Truancy has something utopian about it, and not truanting something unduly stoical or defeated. The truant mind matters because it is the part of us that always wants something better; and it also needs to come up against resistance to ensure that the something better is real, not merely a fantasy".

After more than a decade of fieldwork as an IPS officer, I often find myself reflecting on why someone—especially a child—would choose to leave what accounts to be their comfort zone. I call it a comfort zone because it is familiar, known, tied to identity, and, ideally, a place of belonging. Yet something happens to turn that comfort into discomfort, even danger. A comfort zone is more than physical space; it is an emotional and psychological sphere where a person feels safe and in control. For a minor girl, this zone is often her home, surrounded by family and the life she knows.

Gradually, this "comfort" isn't always genuine. It can be a fragile illusion, often concealing feelings of emotional repression, suffocation, or psychological distress caused by rigid family expectations, societal norms, or even abusive situations.

When a girl chooses to leave this comfort zone, especially at a young age, it reflects an inner struggle far deeper than mere rebellion or a thirst for adventure. More often, it is driven by a profound desire for self-liberation—a need to escape the emotional and psychological confines of her environment. The outside world, though uncertain and full of risks, may represent freedom, possibility, and the hope of redefining herself beyond the stifling constraints of home.

Psychologically, this decision is layered with complexity. She may grapple with cognitive dissonance; torn between her inner desires and the life she is expected to lead. The pull of autonomy—the urge to assert her identity, make independent choices, and claim her own path—can become stronger than the fear of the unknown. In many cases, the pain of staying in a restrictive environment outweighs the risks of stepping into a world she scarcely knows.

Sociologically, her decision resonates with theories like reactance theory, which explains how individuals push back against perceived threats to their freedom. For a young girl, the weight of societal expectations—traditional gender roles, fear of judgment, and the burden of maintaining family honour—can feel suffocating. Leaving becomes an act of resistance, a rejection of a life scripted for her, and a refusal to remain bound by expectations she never agreed to.

This internal conflict—between remaining in a "safe" but oppressive environment and venturing into an unknown yet potentially liberating world—is a deeply psychological journey. It is not merely about leaving home; it is about leaving behind an identity imposed upon her, in search of one she can claim as her own.

The reflections and refractions arising from the empirical assessment of the registered cases of missing girls lead us into a riveting socio-psychological paradigm. The concept of a comfort zone stands as a delicate equilibrium on the continuum of attraction and repulsion—an emotional and psychological balance that, when disrupted, can propel an individual away from the norm. This imbalance manifests as both attraction towards the new and repulsion from the old.

Patrick Tomlinson, elaborates on this tension, noting that people may feel both relieved and angry simultaneously. Even if a child's decision to run away reflects a healthy aspect of development, those being run away from are rarely inclined to view it positively. A central question, often posed, is whether the individual is running away from something or towards something. The American novelist Sherwood Anderson (2012, p. 220) captured this duality when he wrote, "I wanted to run away from everything, but I wanted to run towards something too".

The person could be running away from something external, internal, or both—from herself or toward someone else. A runaway, as Phillips (2009) suggests, could be "someone who is trying to evacuate himself from his own home because there is a war going on". Yet this "war" may not always be external; it may just as easily be internal. When a child struggles with violent or overwhelming emotions, running away may feel like a way to protect both herself and others from the consequences of those feelings.

Patrick Tomlinson expands on this, reminding us that flight is one of the instinctive responses to threat, often perceived as safer than fight. For example: is she fleeing bullying? Has someone lured her away? Are there unsafe, frightening circumstances from which she is escaping—or toward which she is being drawn? Does she feel safer, freer, or more in control when distanced from people? Could she be running from the vulnerability of forming a meaningful relationship, or is there something positive she is actively seeking?

The definition of "runaways" captures this complexity; it refers to decisions made independently by girls, without parental consent, who—after leaving—may find refuge with relatives, neighbours, or attempt to live on their own.

An adolescent mind, when exposed to a myriad of hedonistic existentialities, often aspires for the unknown. These aspirations leave these young lives vulnerable and impressionable. In their pursuit for the unseen, they may fall prey to human predicaments and exploitation. Based on an analysis of the missing girls' cases, we can broadly categorize these compelling circumstances into the following socio-psychological configurations.

For the moon

A young girl struggling to meet academic expectations, navigating parental pressures, or striving to live up to the standards set by her surroundings may feel trapped by these demands. Perhaps she dreams of pursuing something she loves, something at odds with her family's expectations. Her desire to soar freely is stifled by the only world she knows, pushing her to believe that the unseen and unknown might be more welcoming, understanding, and comfortable than her current reality. Over time, this belief transforms her so-called "comfort zone" into a zone of conflict.

An examination of missing girls' case data—specifically those who left home alone in search of their own definition of comfort—reveals that the reasons behind their decisions are often startlingly simple:

- She was scolded by her mother, father, or elder sibling for not doing household chores.
- She struggled to perform well in her studies.
- She was unhappy with the responsibility of caring for younger siblings.
- Her parents restricted her from using a mobile phone or watching television.
- She did not receive a gift she had been asking for.
- She was not allowed to visit or stay at a friend's house.
- Her academic performance was constantly compared with that of others.
- She wanted to pursue an interest or passion her family did not approve of.

These examples, drawn from an analysis of real cases, reflect the seemingly "trivial" yet deeply impactful triggers that can drive a young girl to leave her home in search of freedom or understanding.

At this impressionable age, the desire to follow one's own thoughts and dreams often overshadows the risks involved. A flash of lightning in the darkest cloud feels magical, and the world seems wide open—ready to be conquered. Data analysis reveals that the socio-economic background of a child's family plays a significant role in influencing her decision to run away.

When a 13-year-old girl was rescued in Betul district, she confessed: "My parents are farmers, so they spent all their time working in the fields. As the eldest daughter, I was left with all the household responsibilities in their absence. I felt overworked. I used to cook, fetch water, tend our herd of oxen, and take care of my younger siblings and grandmother at home. At times, I also helped my parents in the fields when there was too much work".

Similarly, broken families have a profound effect on the lives of adolescent girls. Another girl, around 11 years old, told the police after being rescued that she had always been more comfortable confiding in her mother. After her mother's death, she had no one to share her feelings and thoughts with. She felt frightened to speak openly with her father and hesitant to share her emotions with her siblings. At such a tender age, simply being heard and understood is of paramount importance. Without this emotional support, even a familiar home can begin to feel alien, leading a child to seek comfort elsewhere.

A minor girl who decides to run away from home experiences an emotional whirlwind, marked by a profound internal conflict. Initially, she may feel a surge of relief, the kind that comes from breaking free from an environment that has stifled or hurt her. This relief could give way to a fleeting sense of exhilaration, the heady rush of seizing control over her own fate, something she might have believed impossible within the confines of her home. For a brief, perhaps naive moment, she may feel empowered, believing that by running away, she is claiming her right to autonomy, safety, or happiness.

Yet, beneath this initial surge of freedom lies a deep undercurrent of fear. The unknown world beyond her home is daunting, and she is painfully aware of her vulnerability. As the reality of her situation sets in, fear could begin to creep in, overwhelming her thoughts. The imagined freedom that beckoned her away starts to blur with anxiety, she may not know where to go, whom to trust, or how to survive on her own. Panic could rise, fueled by the uncertainty of what lies ahead and the fear of being caught or worse, falling into harm's way.

Guilt, too, may gnaw at her. Even if her home life has been difficult, she may carry the weight of leaving behind people she loves or at least feels connected to in some way. She might fear that her family will suffer in her absence—whether through worry, grief, or anger. This guilt can compound her emotional turmoil, making her question whether her decision was right or impulsive, justified or selfish. The pain of leaving could be further amplified by memories of small moments of affection, now tinged with a sense of betrayal.

Loneliness often creeps in next. Despite her decision to run, she is still a child, and the isolation of an unfamiliar world can feel unbearable. The safety net of home, however imperfect, is now out of reach. She may feel invisible—adrift in a world where no one truly knows or cares for her. This sense of abandonment deepens into profound sorrow, a hollow ache for the comfort and security she has left behind, even if those things were scarce in her previous life.

Amid this emotional tempest, she oscillates between fragile hope and overwhelming despair. At times, she convinces herself that this escape will lead to a brighter future—one where love, understanding, or freedom will finally be within reach. But these moments of hope are often punctuated by harsh realities, as the road she has chosen proves longer, lonelier, and more treacherous than she ever imagined.

In the end, she is left with a complex mix of emotions—hope tempered by fear, freedom shadowed by guilt, and a yearning for connection in constant tension with her fear of being lost and alone in a world she barely understands. Her heart becomes a battleground, torn between the need for safety and love and the daunting reality of navigating life entirely on her own.

But the figures also reveal cases that arise from far more egregious circumstances. There are many instances where children confided in their parents or older siblings but received no help, leaving them to feel trapped and ultimately prompting them to escape:

- She was being blackmailed by someone
- She was being molested by a person within her so-called comfort zone
- She made a mistake in a moment of emotional vulnerability and feared the consequences

Hide and seek is a universally beloved childhood game. Explaining its deeper meaning, Winnicott (1963) wrote, "It is a joy to be hidden and a disaster not to be found". A child simultaneously longs to be hidden and to be discovered by loved ones. This captures the tension between the desire for privacy or concealment and the profound need for acknowledgment and connection. On one hand, solitude offers safety—a private space to exist without judgment or intrusion, a brief escape from external pressures. Yet the second half of Winnicott's insight, "a disaster not to be found," underscores the emotional toll of prolonged invisibility. What begins as a desire to hide can quickly become isolation, evoking feelings of abandonment, loneliness, and despair. Even in secrecy, there is always an unspoken hope of being seen, understood, and drawn back into connection.

In the context of missing girls, this duality is striking. Some may run away seeking escape or a hidden refuge from the challenges of their world. But if they remain "unfound," not only physically but in terms of their pain and struggles, it becomes disastrous, leading to deeper societal issues such as exploitation, trafficking, or the complete erasure of their voice. The joy of being hidden transforms into a disaster when the need for connection, help, and safety goes unmet.

Symbolically, running away may reflect a child's inner self and unspoken desires: to be hidden, yet desperately wishing to be found. Some children feel invisible, as though no one cares enough to search for them. They may grow up believing they are neither noticed nor valued by the very people who matter most. Phillips (2009) notes, "Out of sight, out of mind," a phrase that tragically mirrors the reality for many traumatized children. Across the globe, studies consistently identify childhood experiences such as abuse, neglect, home instability, and poor parent–child relationships as central factors in adolescent runaway cases (Ferguson, 2009; Peled & Cohavi, 2009; Raval, Raval, & Raj, 2010).

Patrick Tomlinson suggests that understanding a child's personal history can offer crucial insight. Has running away been a recurring pattern in her life? Did significant adults in her world also flee or live transient lives? If she ran away before, what were the consequences? Was she punished, relocated, or further traumatized? Sometimes, running away may be a way of testing loved ones—seeking proof that someone cares enough to search. It may also represent an attempt to escape fears or situations rooted not only in the present but in past trauma that feels painfully alive. Tomlinson asks: Could a child's urge to flee lessen if someone were willing to sit with her pain, hold it, and help her work through it? Or would confronting her pain only intensify her need to escape? Exploring the symbolic dimensions of running away can be a deeply revealing approach.

Beyond these psychological dynamics, resource disparities introduce additional factors influencing runaway behaviour. In resource-poor countries, conditions like poverty and customary practices often play decisive roles. For example, in parts of Sub-Saharan Africa and Asia, families may arrange early marriages for daughters due to cultural beliefs. Fathers may feel obligated to secure their daughters' future economic stability or to "protect" them from sexual experiences perceived as harmful to their marriage prospects (Boyden, Pankhurst, & Tafere, 2012; Molla, 2018). Contemporary research increasingly frames runaway youth as victims, and running away itself as a social issue linked to systemic failures in family functioning and parent–child relationships (Bradley, 1997; Hyde, 2005; Miller, 1990).

For many girls, running away is not a calculated plan but an emotional eruption. She flees in pain, shame, fear, or desperation, boarding the nearest bus, train, or other available transport, with no fixed destination in mind. She carries a heavy emotional burden, leaving behind a familiar world that has failed to support her. Often, she chooses to run because she feels there is no one who will understand her turmoil or advocate for her rights. This gap highlights a systemic failure: schools lack accessible counseling services staffed by trained, empathetic individuals. Introducing such preventive measures could give adolescent girls a safe outlet before they view disappearing as their only option—a decision that feels simple in theory but proves devastating.

Research by Jone G. Lurgain and Carola Eyber in Northern Ethiopia reinforces this complexity. Two major themes emerged from interviews with young participants: first, that the decision to run was often driven by intense emotions, and second, that these escapes were carried out secretly and alone. Yet despite their solitude in fleeing, many runaway girls eventually received some form of temporary support from relatives or neighbours. A thirteen-year-old girl decided to leave her comfort zone. One of her friends at school had received a mobile phone as a gift and eagerly shared her excitement, proudly showing off her new Android device. During recess, the two girls would often slip away to a quiet corner of the school, disappearing into the digital world together. This ritual, filled with laughter and fascination, went on for months.

For the girl, this was a completely new experience. At home, her father—a daily wage labourer—owned only a basic keypad phone, the family's sole connection to the outside world. That outdated device symbolized her family's modest means. On her birthday, she asked her parents for an Android phone like her friend's. But their limited budget could not accommodate such a demand. She interpreted their refusal not as financial constraint but as a measure of their love for her—a test she had, in her mind, failed.

Determined to prove her worth and find the life she imagined, she decided to leave home. Her vision of the world beyond her small town had been shaped by the glowing screen of her friend's phone: a flamboyant world, with exuberant opportunities and buoyant humanitarianism around. She packed her few belongings, zipped her hopes tightly into her bag, and broke open her piggy bank. She had saved only ₹120. Clutching her meager treasure, she boarded a train to Nagpur—the only "big city" she had ever heard of in her thirteen years.

But the train ride was nothing like the joyful journeys she once took with her parents. She felt exposed, as though every pair of eyes was silently questioning her presence. The crowded general compartment was suffocating, and she clutched her bag as if it were her last link to safety. Memories of past trips flashed in her mind: sitting by the window, watching lush green fields pass like pages of a flipbook, giggling with family while sharing home-packed meals. Now, that sense of warmth was replaced by fear.

When the train reached Nagpur, she stepped off the platform with a fleeting sense of relief—only to be swallowed by panic moments later. The bustling crowd dispersed, and she was left paralyzed, unsure how to navigate this new world. With no guide, no Google Maps, and no plan, she realized that her imagined freedom was, in reality, a terrifying trap.

She bought a small snack from a platform vendor, leaving her with just ₹10. Sitting on a bench, she watched trains come and go, counting the shoes of hurried strangers and feeling smaller by the minute. Summoning her courage, she decided to leave the station, but as she approached the exit, the stares of strangers seemed to pierce her with an unspoken question: Where are you going? Overwhelmed, she ran back at breakneck speed to the platform where she had first arrived. The bench was still empty, a small mercy in her spiraling fear.

Heart pounding, she finally decided to call her father. At a public phone booth, she dialed his number with trembling fingers. He answered on the second ring, his voice calm, almost as if he had been waiting for her call. She choked out a single word—"Papa"—before tears overwhelmed her. Her father spoke gently, consoling her as she sobbed into the receiver. When she finally managed to share her location, relief washed over her. She was rescued that day, scarred only by guilt and remorse, but spared from the irreversible harm that so often befalls vulnerable children who disappear into the unknown.

Her story is not unique. Countless young people become ensnared in the artificial allure of digital worlds, seeking online solutions to their real-life struggles. Social media and digital culture offer unprecedented opportunities for connection, creativity, and expression. Yet, for impressionable minds, these platforms also breed comparison, insecurity, and unrealistic expectations. Excessive screen time and exposure to curated realities often exacerbate anxiety, depression, and feelings of inadequacy. Cyberbullying and privacy violations further erode young people's sense of safety and self-worth.

The rise of digital addiction has also created echo chambers, reinforcing biases and stereotypes as young people gravitate toward like-minded communities online. While these platforms promise connection, they often deepen isolation, leaving vulnerable adolescents trapped between their inner pain and a glittering but deceptive virtual world.

Many young girls find solace in forming friendships on social media because these platforms offer an escape from the restrictions and expectations of their offline lives. The anonymity and distance inherent in online spaces allow them to express themselves more freely, seeking validation and connection from people who appear to understand or appreciate them. In a world where they may feel overlooked, misunderstood, or stifled by family, friends, and societal norms, these virtual spaces become a refuge where they can construct identities that reflect their aspirations, free from the scrutiny they face in real life.

Yet, the nature of online relationships can create a false sense of intimacy and trust. Friendships formed online can quickly become intense, as girls share their innermost thoughts, dreams, and insecurities with people they've never met in person. The desire to belong is a powerful force, and social media can amplify this by fostering a culture of instant approval through likes, comments, and shares. For many, the constant pressure to meet the expectations of their online peers leads to a distorted sense of reality, where virtual acceptance becomes more important than real-world relationships.

These dynamics can become even more complex and overwhelming when group interactions are involved. Online groups often cultivate environments where conformity is rewarded, and dissent is met with ridicule or exclusion. The fear of being ostracized or abandoned can pressure young girls into compromising their values, making impulsive decisions, or engaging in risky behaviours. This peer pressure manifests in various ways, from sharing deeply personal information to agreeing to meet strangers in person—choices that can leave them vulnerable to harm.

In extreme cases, the need for acceptance can drive girls to run away, lured by the promise of a better life with someone who they believe understands them. Social media relationships often feel more exciting or emotionally charged, leading them to idealize these connections and believe that escaping their current situation is the only way to find happiness. However, this escape often exposes them to significant dangers, including exploitation, trafficking, or abusive relationships. Predators on social media are skilled at identifying vulnerable girls and exploiting their emotional needs, making them believe they are entering a safe and caring environment when, in reality, they are being manipulated.

Ultimately, the combination of emotional vulnerability, peer pressure, and the seductive allure of social media connections can push young girls to take decisions that put their safety and well-being at risk. What begins as an innocent search for friendship and belonging can quickly spiral into a dangerous situation, with long-lasting consequences.

In her desperate journey into the unknown, the missing girl encounters people and places poised to exploit her vulnerability. She is dragged into the abyss of darkness and crime, where her attempt to escape familiar discomfort becomes a prison of unimaginable suffering. The atrocities inflicted upon her strip away her individuality, drowning her spirit in the black holes of society. Shame, disgust, and humiliation weigh heavily on her, leaving her unable to summon the courage to step back into the world she once knew. She waits—hoping for a family member's embrace, for the police to rescue her—but even when rescue comes, full rehabilitation remains elusive.

"She thought the night would shelter her from all she couldn't bear,
But little did she know, the light she left was waiting there.
In fleeing from her troubles, she left her dreams behind,
Not knowing that the answers lay in what she dared not find".

If fortune favours her, she may return home, but she is no longer welcomed with warmth. Instead, she is branded as impure—a transgressor who dared to step beyond the lines society drew for her. She becomes an unfortunate cautionary tale whispered in her community, her story distorted and sensationalized, retold with layers of judgment and shame. In the eyes of society, she is no longer just a victim of circumstances; she is condemned as a criminal.

In a world still bound by narrow, patriarchal mindsets, a woman's expression is a rebellion. To question injustice is a crime. To say "no" to wrongdoing is a crime. To seek freedom is a crime. This young girl, once filled with dreams of reaching the moon, returns with her hope eclipsed. Her pursuit of comfort leaves her with scars that deepen her discomfort, and her light, once vibrant, is forever dimmed.

The moonlight

An adolescent boy and girl come together in a union fueled by love, defying every barrier of caste, creed, religion, and region. Unable to bend beneath the weight of societal expectations, they choose to follow their hearts and run away. In a quiet act of devotion, they exchange garlands before the God they worship, take vows of lifelong partnership, and embrace one another as husband and wife. They reject the oppressive customs of dowry and bride price, unaware of the legal implications of their choices, driven only by the urgency of love. For them, breaking free from the strings that bind them feels like the only way forward.

For many minor girls, the decision to run away with someone is born from a complex web of emotional, social, cultural, and psychological forces. At its core is often a deep sense of entrapment within the family home—a space that should feel safe but instead becomes suffocating. Rigid expectations, relentless scrutiny, and strict control over their behaviour create an atmosphere where girls feel voiceless and powerless. This confinement fuels a yearning for independence, for a life that reflects their dreams and aspirations rather than those imposed upon them.

The looming threat of forced or arranged marriage often intensifies this desperation. In many traditional contexts, families may value honour, reputation, or financial gain over a girl's emotional well-being, pushing her toward unions that erase her autonomy. Faced with a future that feels both predetermined and unbearable, running away can seem like the only path toward freedom. The boy she chooses becomes more than a romantic interest; he represents hope, validation, and a chance to reclaim her identity.

Adolescence itself adds another layer of vulnerability to these decisions. This stage of life is marked by emotional turbulence and a hunger for belonging, making young girls especially drawn to relationships that provide attention and affection—especially when they feel unseen or neglected at home. Romanticized portrayals of love in media and culture further reinforce the belief that such acts of defiance are courageous and liberating, overshadowing the dangers and consequences that await.

The allure of urban anonymity plays a powerful role in shaping her choices. Large cities and slum settlements offer a deceptive sense of freedom, promising escape from the constant scrutiny of her small community. The idea of starting over in a place where no one knows her can be intoxicating, especially when coupled with the hope of building a new life alongside her partner. Though these environments carry their own challenges, they are often seen as preferable to the suffocating restrictions she leaves behind.

Peer influence and social dynamics add further weight to her decision. Seeing other girls break free—whether successfully or not—can normalize the act of running away, making it seem like a courageous and viable option. This blend of societal pressure, lack of supportive structures, and limited avenues for self-expression drives her to seek liberation in the only way she knows how. The boy she chooses becomes more than a romantic partner; he embodies the possibility of choice, autonomy, and a life she can shape for herself.

Riya, a young girl raised in a deeply conservative household, has lived under rules that govern nearly every detail of her existence—what she wears, whom she speaks to, even what she should dream of becoming. Though her parents love her, their love manifests as strict protection, discipline, and rigid guidance along a path they believe to be best. Yet this constant control suffocates Riya, leaving her feeling misunderstood and disconnected from her own family.

Her world is heavy with unspoken expectations. Her mother's warnings to refrain from boys, her comments about dressing "to protect her dignity," and the constant reminders of societal judgment teach Riya to shrink herself. Over time, she hides her dreams, her frustrations, and even her true self, fearful that her thoughts and desires will be rejected—or worse, shamed.

Then, Riya meets Arjun, a boy from her school who listens without judgment, laughs at her jokes, and genuinely cares about her opinions and dreams. For the first time, she feels seen—not as a daughter bound by rules or a girl weighed down by expectations, but as an individual with her own worth. Arjun's acceptance of her fills a space in her heart she hadn't even realized was empty. With him, she feels valued not for who others think she should be, but for who she really is—a feeling so rare at home that it becomes intoxicating.

As their friendship deepens, Riya begins to see Arjun not only as a source of comfort but also as an escape route. The thought of being with him fills her with both excitement and fear—a chance to live freely without the constraints she faces at home. In his company, she feels a courage she's never known, the courage to imagine a world where she isn't constantly judged, corrected, or silenced—a world where she can simply exist as herself. Slowly, the idea of running away with Arjun becomes more than a fantasy; it feels like her only chance to break free.

On an emotional level, Riya feels a mix of hope, desperation, and inner conflict. She knows the decision to leave home isn't just risky, it's a life-altering step. Yet, the loneliness she feels at home, the silence that fills her when her thoughts are dismissed, and the pressure to live up to ideals that aren't her own weigh heavily on her. Each stolen moment with Arjun widens the gap between the acceptance she longs for and the reality of her life at home.

The night she decides to leave, Riya is overwhelmed by a mix of sorrow and courage. She's terrified of what lies ahead but even more afraid of losing the sense of self-discovery Arjun has awakened in her. It's a heartbreaking choice, but one that feels inevitable. In her mind, it is not a reckless act of rebellion, but a desperate cry for freedom—a plea for a life where she can finally feel alive, seen, and respected.

These decisions are shaped by complex dynamics, often driven by a yearning for personal freedom and a desire to escape societal restrictions. The choice of a young couple to elope often emerges from a convergence of social pressure, emotional intensity, and a lack of understanding about the wider world. Their journey is not merely an act of defiance but a desperate attempt to break free—both from oppressive traditions and the constraints imposed by their social and economic circumstances. Marriage is traditionally regarded as a legally and culturally sanctioned union between a man and a woman, intended to establish a family. In contrast, runaway marriages are viewed as a deviation from societal norms, attracting widespread stigma and disapproval. Couples who elope frequently face severe social exclusion and are often boycotted by parents, relatives, neighbours, and friends. This ostracism places them at a significant disadvantage, depriving them of access to stable housing, healthcare, basic household necessities, and education for their children—factors that hinder their full participation in society. As Lawson (1995) notes, issues such as family breakdown, gender inequality, inadequate housing, fragile community connections, and systemic prejudice against the less privileged further reinforce this cycle of social exclusion, compounding the challenges faced by these couples. In most of these cases, even when a couple makes their relationship known, it remains socially indiscernible. They live in constant fear, always on the run and hiding from others. Runaway couples are largely left to navigate life on their own terms, yet they face intense stigmatization for their choices. Both they and their children are often branded as immoral and treated differently for the rest of their lives. Within this context of social exclusion, they are largely shut out from social gatherings, family visits, and community networks. What was once considered "home," a place of joy and reverence, becomes instead a memory of confinement and pain, as recounted by many such couples (Social Exclusion and the Runaway Couples: A Study of Their Hardships – Tanveer Ahmad, Wasima Hamid, and Mohammad Swalein).

When a runaway couple relocates to a larger town in search of work—while simultaneously avoiding their families—the socio-psychological toll can be profound and multifaceted. Their emotional struggles and social challenges can be understood through several dimensions.

Often, these couples elope to escape familial and societal constraints, only to face further alienation in an unfamiliar urban environment. Cut off from their former support networks, they are thrust into isolation. This alienation is even more severe if their union challenges cultural norms, such as caste, religion, or age differences. For example, a young couple from a rural village who marries against family wishes due to caste disparity may encounter difficulties finding employment in the city, where employers often demand family background details.

This scrutiny alienates them not only from their new surroundings but also from the traditions they left behind. This experience often leads to anomie—a sense of disconnection from established social norms without successfully integrating into new ones. With no clear framework to guide them, runaway couples may feel adrift, overwhelmed by stress, and uncertain of where they belong.

The constant fear of being found by family members or even legal authorities contributes to chronic anxiety and fear. The couple lives in an uncertain state, worried that any moment could lead to confrontation or punishment. This fear can lead to hypervigilance, mistrust of others, and an inability to feel safe, all of which take a heavy toll on their mental health.

In one such case, a 17-year-old girl and her 18-year-old partner eloped to escape the restrictions of their families. While living in a small town, they constantly moved from place to place and switched jobs to avoid recognition. The relentless stress eventually led the girl to develop frequent anxiety attacks, while her partner turned to alcohol as a coping mechanism.

Guilt compounds this emotional burden, particularly for those raised in collectivist cultures where family honour and duty hold immense weight. Many runaway couples are haunted by the feeling that they have betrayed their parents, tarnished their family's reputation, or abandoned younger siblings who may still rely on them. This guilt erodes their emotional well-being, leaving them trapped between a longing for freedom and a profound sense of shame.

There is often a continuous struggle for identity, shaped by the tension between role conflict and self-concept. In urban settings, individuals' roles can shift dramatically, creating friction as couples attempt to adapt. Back in their hometowns, their roles may have been clearly defined by cultural and gender norms. However, survival in an unfamiliar city—securing jobs, managing finances, and navigating daily challenges—can force them into unfamiliar responsibilities, sparking internal and relational conflict.

For instance, a boy raised with traditional ideas of masculinity might feel emasculated if his partner secures employment first or earns more, leading to feelings of inadequacy and frustration. Meanwhile, the girl—socialized to expect protection and provision—may find herself overwhelmed by responsibilities she was never prepared for. These shifting roles can cause deep identity struggles, as both partners wrestle with self-doubt, low self-esteem, and the dissonance between old socialization and new realities.

In the face of these challenges, couples often develop coping mechanisms. Positive strategies may include cultivating resilience, seeking support networks, or redefining relationship dynamics. For example, a couple who successfully avoids family detection might begin attending support groups or working with NGOs that provide legal and psychological assistance, helping them navigate city life and build some semblance of stability, even if emotional scars remain. However, negative coping mechanisms are equally common. Substance abuse, social withdrawal, and aggression can easily surface when stress becomes overwhelming, further destabilizing their fragile sense of security and belonging.

Runaway couples often face severe economic marginalization, lacking the social capital, educational qualifications, or family support needed to secure stable employment. With limited opportunities, they are frequently pushed into the informal economy, working long hours for meager pay in precarious jobs such as factory labour, construction work, or domestic service. This financial instability compounds their emotional struggles.

Consider a young couple with no higher education who elopes to a large city, seeking freedom but finding hardship. The boy becomes a rickshaw driver, while his partner works as a maid. Their combined income barely covers rent and basic meals, leaving them physically drained and emotionally exhausted. The strain of poverty and constant uncertainty often manifests in frequent arguments, eroding their once-romantic bond.

Even in larger towns, escaping stigma proves difficult. If their background becomes known—especially if their marriage crosses caste or religious boundaries—they may face social exclusion and discrimination. Local communities can be unforgiving, and institutions often fail to offer protection or support. The couple must remain vigilant, particularly if their marriage challenges legal age requirements or if families file missing-person cases. In such circumstances, every interaction with authorities or local organizations carries the risk of exposure, deepening their sense of fear and helplessness.

The long-term psychological effects of depression and isolation on runaway couples are profound. Over time, the cumulative weight of alienation, fear, role conflict, and poverty often accelerates the onset of depression. Without family support or strong social networks, couples become increasingly isolated, their relationship strained under the constant burden of survival. After years of living in hiding and enduring relentless economic hardship, many women feel trapped in relationships where returning home is not an option, while men—exhausted by emotional and financial pressures—may grow distant. This emotional disconnect deepens loneliness and despair for both partners.

For these couples, life is not merely a physical escape but an emotional odyssey through fear, guilt, identity struggles, and profound psychological stress. Social alienation, stigma, and poverty intertwine, creating a cycle that is difficult to break without proper intervention. Research highlights that the loss of familial and kin support severely worsens their financial insecurity, restricting their ability to counter future crises. Denied refuge by their families, many are forced to live in cramped rented rooms. Their challenges intensify with the birth of children, as they must navigate schooling, food, and healthcare alone, without extended family support.

Socio-psychological theories shed light on these conditions. Émile Durkheim's concept of anomie, or normlessness, explains how the breakdown of traditional social structures leads to chronic instability. In Indian slums, where many runaway couples eventually settle, the lack of reliable institutions—such as education, healthcare, and legal protections—exacerbates feelings of disconnection and despair. Similarly, Robert K. Merton's strain theory posits that systemic inequality and the inability to achieve culturally approved goals create frustration, stress, and a sense of failure. In these marginalized spaces, alternative norms and survival strategies emerge, often perpetuating cycles of poverty and exclusion.

Living in slums, with overcrowding, economic deprivation, and social stigma, couples face relentless psychological stress, often manifested in anxiety, depression, and a pervasive sense of hopelessness. These harsh realities underline the urgent need for comprehensive support systems—social networks, mental health care, and legal protections—to help couples break free from cycles of alienation and instability.

This disconnection from mainstream society reinforces a collective identity centered on survival rather than social mobility or progress. These socio-psychological perspectives illustrate how a runaway couple seeking refuge in a slum environment faces a dual burden: material deprivation compounded by psychological strain. This intersection of poverty and stigma perpetuates cycles of marginalization and social disintegration.

Women, in particular, face extraordinary risks when they choose to leave their families. They are disproportionately vulnerable to violence, including being coerced into prostitution or even murdered by their own relatives in the name of "honour" (Hussain & Afzal, 2013). Chowdhary (2007) notes that such extreme measures are often taken to demonstrate a family's rejection of a woman's "misconduct" and to safeguard its reputation in the community.

Runaway couples lose not only their social status but also the protective network and support that comes with family membership. They are rarely welcomed back, even in moments of desperation, and often face a future of isolation with limited opportunities for asylum or compassion. Social norms dictate that such couples must shoulder their responsibilities alone, further intensifying their vulnerability.

The gender disparity in perceptions of elopement is striking. For a woman, leaving her family to marry without parental consent is regarded as a profound betrayal. Society often considers her "dead" to her family, lost forever, and beyond redemption. Her decision is framed as a moral failure, a selfish pursuit of personal desire at the expense of family honour, virtue, and respect. Once she leaves, she is expected never to return, and this act is regarded as a permanent rupture with her family and community.

By contrast, men are not subject to the same social penalties. A man's decision to marry without parental approval is not typically seen as deviant or irreparable. He retains the possibility of reconciliation with his family, and his actions rarely bring the same level of disgrace. This stark gender asymmetry reinforces patriarchal norms, where women bear the full weight of moral judgment while men retain the privilege of social reintegration.

"A step into the shadows feels like a dance with the unknown, yet in the quiet darkness, all her hopes remain alone. The path she seeks for freedom leads far from where it grows, For strength is found in facing what the heart already knows".

Emotionally, she may feel both a sense of freedom and fear. The thrill of stepping out of a controlled environment might initially bring excitement, but this is usually accompanied by anxiety about what lies ahead. She may begin to question her decisions, particularly as the realities of living independently, without financial stability, emotional support, or the societal safety nets—begin to weigh heavily on her. The absence of familiar surroundings can evoke a profound longing for home, even if her previous home life was far from ideal. This sense of homesickness is often magnified by the instability and unpredictability of her new circumstances, creating a heightened emotional vulnerability.

In terms of her mental and emotional health, she might experience an overwhelming sense of responsibility and pressure. As a minor, navigating adult relationships and responsibilities can feel disorienting and daunting. Fear of judgment, stigma, or even legal consequences might further compound her emotional turmoil.

For a woman in this situation, internal conflict is heightened. There is the desire for autonomy and self-expression, but it comes at the cost of security and predictability. The physical discomforts, such as poor living conditions or a lack of basic necessities, further amplify her sense of displacement. Ultimately, while she may have sought love, freedom, or escape, the harsh realities of being away from home, cut off from emotional and material support, can lead to profound feelings of regret, fear, and emotional exhaustion.

Even when a minor girl wishes to return to her parental home, the fear of rejection and judgment weighs heavily on her mind. Her longing to go back is overshadowed by trepidation—not because she doesn't miss the safety and familiarity of home, but because she knows her return would not be met with open arms. She anticipates the blame, the harsh words, and the inevitable ostracism that would await her. In the eyes of her parents and society, she has violated an unspoken code of conduct, a breach that will not be easily forgiven.

Her decision to run away is often viewed as an act of rebellion or dishonour, and this stigmatization amplifies her reluctance to return. The possibility of being shamed, scolded, and branded as "ruined" or "disobedient" looms large. She fears being seen not as a daughter in need of love and support, but as a source of disgrace—a burden her family would rather conceal than embrace. The thought of isolation within her own home, of being treated as an outsider, deepens her hesitation to seek the sanctuary she desperately craves.

This inner conflict is deeply painful. She longs for the comfort, protection, and acceptance of her family, yet she knows returning would mean facing condemnation not only from her parents but also from her extended family and community. In conservative or patriarchal settings, the societal pressure to preserve family honour makes it nearly impossible to imagine a warm welcome. The fear of humiliation and of being permanently labeled a "fallen" girl creates an emotional barrier, leaving her stranded in a painful limbo of guilt, regret, and loneliness.

In this state, she feels trapped—yearning for home yet convinced that home no longer holds a place for her. The emotional weight of this realization can be crushing, leaving her with a profound sense of hopelessness and abandonment that further deepens her isolation.

The crescendo

There have been cases where multiple girls from different villages—even different districts—went missing with the same man. In many such instances, the accused was not a resident of the area where the girl lived. Often employed as a petty worker, small contractor, or student, he came under the guise of work. This charmer, with his *sui generis* blend of cunning and charisma, prowled like a predator in search of prey. He projected himself as a man of respect, boasting of a comfortable life in a big city. A pseudo-package, neatly wrapped, yet hollow within.

Adolescent girls, already navigating phases of discomfort and discontent, found themselves drawn to the glitter of this illusion. The sudden dazzle blinded them, much like a child enchanted by the glow of a firefly in the dark night—innocently following the light, oblivious to the dangers of the path. But when the glow faded, they realized too late that they had wandered too far, with no way back. The spell shattered, leaving them stranded in an alien world they neither understood nor belonged to.

In such cases, the accused often lodged the girl in dingy rented rooms in slum areas, convincing her young bilked heart he only needed time to persuade his family. Trusting him, she adopted a false identity, weaving lies with complete conviction. An acquaintance of the accused would usually help procure accommodation and forge new documents. Introduced to neighbours as a distant relative studying in the city, the girl lived under a pseudo-identity, posing as an adult. Vulnerable and fearful, she was exploited in ways her young mind could scarcely process.

Soon, a stranger would be introduced—framed as a family friend or relative. The girl was displayed, tested, and eventually handed over. What began as trust ended in repeated assaults. Reduced to an object of trade, her body became currency. From a person of flesh and blood, with dreams and hopes, she was transformed into a commodity to be sold and resold, vanishing into the dark underworld of the flesh trade.

This is one of the most common forms of trafficking. The criminals who run it are deeply entrenched, their networks stretching from rural backwaters to sprawling cities. They maintain the grim "demand and supply" equilibrium of this trade with chilling precision.

When I was serving as SP in Rajgarh district, one such girl was rescued from Rajasthan. She had been lured with promises of a better life by a petty contractor working on a dam site. After a few bike rides with him, her young heart believed in the dream he painted. A school dropout, burdened with household chores to support her labourer parents, she felt as though she had found a path to the moon. Instead, she landed in a tenebrous corner of Rajasthan, where darkness swallowed every trace of hope.

In this case, fortune favored the investigation. The accused used his bank account, leaving a trace. Missing person cases often unfold like a jigsaw puzzle, with information arriving in scattered fragments. Success demands persistence, patience, and consistency from the police. Eventually, the girl was rescued.

Neighbours, when questioned, claimed they had never suspected anything. The *mangalsutra* around her neck and the vermilion in her hair convinced them she was a newly married bride. The sordid truth, however, was that the victim herself had been silenced by fear. Betrayed by the one she trusted most, she could not summon the courage to confide in anyone. Instead, she bore her pain quietly, resigning herself to the cruelty of fate.

I have named this particular phylum crescendo, as the emotional intensity gradually increases over time until it reaches a breaking point. The phenomenon of crescendo, in the emotional and mental state of a minor girl, represents a steady escalation of psychological strain that culminates in a critical tipping point. Initially, minor girls may face various stressors—family dynamics, peer pressure, academic expectations, or societal norms—that seem unmanageable.

However, as these pressures persist without adequate support or coping mechanisms, the emotional burden intensifies, manifesting as anxiety, frustration, or isolation. This internal conflict deepens as the girl struggles between her desire for freedom and autonomy and the weight of familial and cultural expectations. Eventually, this mounting pressure can lead to impulsive decisions—such as running away or engaging in risky behaviour—followed by a spectrum of emotions ranging from relief to regret as she navigates the consequences, including estrangement from family or vulnerability in unfamiliar environments.

Understanding this crescendo effect is vital for addressing the mental health needs of minor girls, underscoring the need for early intervention, supportive environments, and open communication to prevent emotional distress from escalating into crises.

In one case, a thirteen-year-old girl accompanied her aunt to a nearby village to work in chilli fields, travelling thirty kilometres daily by bus. The expense of this commute weighed heavily on their finances, so the field owner arranged for them to stay in a large shed near the fields. The village, known for chilli cultivation, attracted labourers from various regions.

After a week of work, the girl noticed a man from a neighbouring field watching her, his face partially hidden by the dense foliage of green leaves and red chillies. She ignored him, but a few days later, while finishing her day's work and heading back to the shed, she was suddenly grabbed from behind. A cloth was pressed over her mouth, and she was dragged into the bushes. The man—whom she had seen watching her—raped her. Her hands were tied, and her mouth was stuffed with cloth. Trembling with pain, anger, and fear, she somehow made her way back to the shed, where her aunt was busy preparing dinner. She wanted to tell her aunt what had happened but couldn't gather the courage. She resolved to leave for her village the next morning.

Yet, when the day broke, she changed her mind. She stayed. Back in the fields, she again noticed the same man watching her, but this time she no longer felt discomfort. That evening, the assault was repeated, but now she experienced no pain, fear, or anger. Over time, she began to develop an attachment to him, even anticipating their encounters.

Psychologists describe this phenomenon as one in which stereotypical ideas about sexual violence interfere with a person's ability to recognize assault while it is occurring. "Rape scripts," a term used in psychology, refer to mental frameworks shaped by cultural beliefs and stereotypes about how rape is "supposed" to happen. These scripts often distort a survivor's ability to acknowledge an assault. As psychologist Littleton notes, "The more someone's experience with rape differs from the script, the less likely they are to label it as such". Survivors may not categorize their assault as rape if it does not match preconceived notions—perhaps they trusted the assailant, the attack was not overtly violent, resistance was minimal, or the perpetrator was a woman. Rachel Thompson, in her work *Unacknowledged Rape: The Sexual Assault Survivors Who Hide Their Trauma—Even from Themselves*, explores how such scenarios prevent survivors from naming their experiences, compounding their trauma.

When the chilli-harvesting season ended, labourers began to leave for their home villages. Around this time, the young girl disappeared. Her parents reported her missing, and a case was opened. For five years, the investigation yielded nothing. When the case was revisited, police re-interviewed her aunt, who now recalled details she had previously omitted. Witnesses often forget or withhold information out of fear or shock, which is why revisiting testimonies at intervals is critical. Even with this new lead, finding the perpetrator was like "chasing a bird on foot". Eventually, the police received information from the field owner about seasonal workers hired in the area, which provided a breakthrough.

After a month of investigation, the missing girl was found. She was now married to the same man who had assaulted her, and together they had two children. Both worked as agricultural labourers. This case raised unsettling questions: How does a rapist become a life partner? How can trust be placed in a criminal? Why would someone leave behind family to be with a stranger? How does an assault transform into what appears to be a love affair?

The answers lie in the complexity of the human mind and instinctive behaviour. Instinct theory offers partial insight, suggesting that humans, like all animals, are driven by innate survival mechanisms. These instincts guide behaviour, often unconsciously, shaping responses to fear, intimacy, and safety. According to researcher Mila Belle Frothingham, instinct theory emphasizes that survival drives are at the core of all human behaviour, influencing actions such as seeking relationships, reproducing, and securing safety. Instincts are goal-directed and not products of education or experience; they are embedded capacities to act without deliberate reasoning.

In this context, the girl's attachment to her assailant may reflect survival-based coping strategies rather than conscious choice. Emotions—fear, dependency, isolation—interact with instincts, triggering behavioural responses that can blur moral boundaries and complicate notions of consent. What may appear incomprehensible from the outside often stems from a deeply primal drive to create a sense of stability, even within harmful dynamics.

A minor girl's decision to abandon the safety and familiarity of her home to run away with an outsider is rarely a simple act of rebellion. It often emerges from a complex interplay of emotional, psychological, and social factors, heightened by adolescence—a period when identity and self-worth are still fragile. In unsupportive or oppressive home environments, these vulnerabilities can push young girls to seek validation and connection elsewhere, sometimes at devastating cost.

When an outsider, often older and more persuasive, enters their life and offers attention, affection, or the illusion of freedom, it creates a powerful emotional pull. This figure may present himself as a source of understanding, offering an escape from what the girl perceives as a restrictive or hostile environment. The outsider may manipulate her emotions, exploiting her naivety by making her feel seen, desired, and special in ways that her immediate family or peers have failed to do.

The allure of autonomy can be intoxicating for a minor girl, especially when she has grown up in an environment where her desires, choices, or aspirations are dismissed or controlled. The outsider, then, becomes not only a symbol of romance or adventure but also a key to self-liberation, a way to break free from the perceived shackles of parental authority.

Social factors also play a role, as girls are often conditioned to value relationships above personal safety. Media representations, societal narratives around love, and peer influence can reinforce the idea that love is worth sacrificing everything for. In her mind, the outsider may appear to offer a version of life filled with the excitement, love, and independence she craves, convincing her that the unknown holds more promise than her present reality.

In essence, a combination of emotional manipulation, psychological need, and societal pressures can drive a young girl to abandon her familiar ties and embrace the uncertain allure of an outsider, despite the dangers that lie ahead. Several socio-psychological theories help in explaining the reasons, how a minor girl might be convinced that her future lies with an outsider, typically a slightly older individual. She may come to believe her future lies with someone outside her family when her emotional needs remain unmet or when she feels stifled by her environment. Within her family, she may experience neglect, a lack of understanding, or rigid expectations that undermine her sense of self-worth and autonomy. Such experiences can create a profound emotional void, fostering a yearning for connection, validation, or escape.

Psychologically, this dynamic is closely tied to idealization—the tendency to see someone as nearly perfect because they appear to fulfill an unmet need or desire. The girl, lacking the maturity or life experience to critically evaluate this person's intentions, fixates on the hope and freedom they seem to offer. Trust develops quickly as she unconsciously amplifies their positive qualities, viewing them as the solution to her struggles.

On a social level, this can also be understood through attachment displacement. When natural attachments within her home fail to provide emotional security or support, she may unconsciously redirect her need for connection toward someone who does. This creates a strong, often idealized bond with the outsider, who appears to offer understanding, freedom, and happiness. Her trust in this person deepens rapidly—not because of proven reliability, but because of her own unfulfilled desires and longing for escape.

A crescendo refers to the gradual buildup of feelings, experiences, or challenges in one's life that culminates in a peak moment of realization, transformation, or action. It could be the way excitement or anticipation builds as one pursue a goal, leading to a moment of achievement. It might describe the way stress or unresolved emotions escalate until they reach a tipping point, prompting a necessary change or decision. Ultimately, a crescendo reflects the dynamic nature of our emotional and psychological journeys, highlighting how each phase contributes to our growth and development. Life is a symphony, and every experience is a note; the crescendo builds as one embraces the highs and lows, culminating in a powerful melody that echoes in one's hearts.

The eclipse

Initially, in these cases, human traffickers lure victims with false promises of opportunities under the pretext of financial gain. Human trafficking supply chains have become increasingly organized and harder to monitor, making these cases nothing short of well-laid traps. Vulnerable communities are deliberately targeted to set the chain of exploitation in motion.

An analysis of trafficking cases reveals that locals are often chosen to identify and approach potential victims. Some of these individuals may run petty shops in rural areas, where villagers gather to purchase goods and exchange gossip. These shopkeepers, by offering a place for casual conversations, subtly position themselves as trusted members of the community. Others may work as door-to-door service providers or street vendors, selling daily necessities on foot, bicycles, or handcarts. Their frequent visits and long-standing relationships with rural families allow them to engage in unguarded conversations and gain access to private information.

Studies also underline the involvement of people connected to local health centres and schools, as they are in constant interaction with vulnerable groups. Broadly, these categories of individuals serve as disguised spotters, closely linked to the next tier in the trafficking network operating in nearby towns. This second layer often includes contractors, suppliers, transporters, and small business owners who regularly visit villages on motorbikes, covering large areas and staying well-acquainted with the local terrain. These town-based intermediaries are, in turn, connected with a more centralized trafficking network operating in larger cities.

While serving as SP Rajgarh, I handled a case that starkly illustrated this organized chain. A fourteen-year-old girl from a poor family was lured with the promise of a job as a domestic helper in Alwar, Rajasthan. The mediator in this case was a midwife who worked in the girl's village. Trusted by the family, she convinced the parents to send their daughter. She accompanied the girl and her father to Jhalawar, a bordering district, where they met a middle-aged couple at a bus station.

Over tea and snacks, the father—a landless agricultural labourer struggling to feed his family of six—was offered an advance of two thousand rupees and a promise of four thousand rupees monthly. Desperate and powerless, he accepted the offer almost immediately. The midwife received her payment on the spot. Before their tea was finished, the deal was sealed, and the girl left with the couple in their private car. The father and midwife returned home, and the family felt immense gratitude toward the midwife, seeing her as a saviour.

For two months, payments were made as promised. But after the third month, the money stopped coming. When the father approached the midwife, she assured him there was likely some delay due to unforeseen circumstances. Weeks turned into months, but no payment arrived. Slowly, the father realized he had been deceived.

He approached the local village headman for help. Instead of support, he was reminded that he had personally accompanied his daughter to Rajasthan and accepted advance payment, making him liable under child labour provisions of the Juvenile Justice Act. He was also convinced that, since the transaction occurred in Rajasthan, only the Rajasthan police could act. Believing this advice, the father began preparing to go to Rajasthan himself, borrowing money from neighbours and relatives.

Meanwhile, one of my SDPOs, Nisha Reddy, was conducting a community outreach programme in a nearby village. The distraught father shared his ordeal with her. She immediately recognized the situation for what it was and escalated the case, bringing it to our attention.

The investigation began immediately. We gathered every possible piece of evidence, but the delay in reporting had already cost us critical leads. CCTV footage from the bus stand had been automatically erased, and toll booth records of the suspects' vehicle were no longer available. However, we managed to trace a few cash transfers made to the father's account, which gave us a starting point. After a week of intense investigation, the traffickers were arrested in Jhunjhunu district, Rajasthan. The missing girl had already been sold further to a group operating in Gujarat, but she was located and rescued. In total, fifteen arrests were made in connection with this case, including the midwife who had betrayed the family's trust.

This case was yet another example of how traffickers operate within an intricate and well-organized network, resembling the hidden roots of a massive tree. On the surface, everything may appear calm and harmless, but beneath lies a sprawling and sinister system. Each piece of information is carefully concealed, requiring investigators to dig deep to uncover the truth. These crimes are wrapped in layers of deception, designed to swindle entire communities.

Human trafficking in India, especially from rural areas, is a deeply rooted and multifaceted crisis that preys on the most vulnerable sections of society. It thrives on poverty, social inequality, and a lack of education, luring individuals, often young girls and children, into modern forms of slavery. Traffickers use deceit, coercion, and force to trap their victims, offering false promises of employment, education, or marriage, while subjecting them to brutal exploitation.

The economic fragility of rural communities is one of the biggest drivers of trafficking. Families burdened by poverty are often eager to believe in promises of a better life. Parents, driven by desperation, may even allow strangers to take their children away, believing they are securing a brighter future for them. Tragically, this hope often turns into a cruel illusion, trapping their children in a cycle of abuse and exploitation.

The large-scale migration of rural populations to cities in search of jobs adds another layer of vulnerability. Migrants, who lack formal employment, legal safeguards, and social safety nets, are easy targets for traffickers who prey on their unfamiliarity with urban environments. Promised decent jobs, they are instead forced into bonded labour, domestic servitude, or worse.

In many rural areas, illiteracy and a lack of awareness about the dangers of trafficking make communities highly susceptible to deception. Traffickers present themselves as benevolent figures, offering education, jobs, or even marriage, without disclosing their true intentions. The rural population, often unaware of the prevalence of trafficking or the risks involved, are easily swayed by these fraudulent offers, entrusting their children to traffickers under false pretenses.

Certain cultural norms and practices in rural India, such as child marriage or the dowry system, exacerbate the risk of trafficking. Girls, viewed as financial burdens due to dowry obligations, may be trafficked under the guise of marriage. In other cases, runaway girls seeking to escape forced marriages or abusive households become easy prey for traffickers who exploit their desperation.

Another striking example unfolded when I was serving as SP Betul. A sixteen-year-old girl, a school dropout, was lured with the promise of a call centre job in Indore. A small recruitment office had been set up in a rented building near an internet café in Betul, an area popular with the district's youth. Eye-catching pamphlets guaranteed a monthly salary of two thousand rupees, with no educational qualifications required. Applicants were simply asked to attend an interview, which led to the recruitment of eight girls and three boys. Shortly after the recruitment process, the Betul office shut down. The selected candidates were given staggered dates to report at the Indore "office."

When the girl arrived in Indore, she was surprised to find that the so-called office was a rented residential flat near Vijay Nagar Square, lacking any semblance of a workplace. A middle-aged woman greeted her with a file in hand, took her form, and asked her to sit. There were no computers, no desks—nothing to indicate a legitimate call centre. The girl asked about her job profile, only to be told, with disdain, that she had been recruited as a "salesgirl." The woman smirked cruelly, assuring her she would "like the job".

A man soon emerged from another room—overweight, wearing an ill-fitting shirt and trousers, with dyed hair and gutka stains at the corners of his mouth. The woman instructed him to take the girl to the dormitory. Outside, a blue Maruti van awaited. After a ten-minute drive, they arrived at a house where several girls peered out from windows, curious about the newcomer. Gathering her courage, she stepped inside. A caretaker handed her a uniform, and her real "job" became clear: she was to work as a waitress at social events.

The girls received basic etiquette training and were regularly taken to functions to serve food. This continued for sixteen months. The girl managed to send money home, and when she visited her village, she lied to her family, telling them she worked at a reputable call centre in Indore. Her parents were proud of her and the money she sent back, unaware of the truth.

One day, the woman running the agency proposed a "business opportunity": a fake marriage. The girl was not forced, but heavily persuaded, with promises of substantial financial rewards. Under pressure to support her impoverished family, she agreed. A fake identity card was issued under the name Akanksha Jain, and all her credentials, including her age, were falsified. Her phone and

SIM card were confiscated, and she was threatened with legal consequences if she revealed anything.

The gang took her to a district in Maharashtra, posing as her relatives. She was shown to a man in his late thirties, and within two days, a marriage was arranged. The groom's family paid a large sum of money to her fake "relatives". The marriage ceremony was conducted with absolute Jain rituals, giving it an air of legitimacy.

She stayed in her new husband's house, expecting to be retrieved after a week as planned. But weeks turned into months. She made no contact with her parents, terrified of being implicated in a crime. She felt trapped in what she thought was her own decision, not realizing she was a pawn in a much larger scheme.

Months later, her father, worried about her silence, approached the police. He only had her switched-off mobile number as a lead. We registered the case and began investigating. Evidence in such cases is like a faint scent—it must be followed relentlessly before it dissipates. After extensive groundwork, DSP Shivcharan Bohit and his team managed to uncover key information, leading to the arrest of thirteen gang members. The girl was rescued, and in total, seventeen arrests were made, dismantling yet another trafficking ring.

This condition closely resembles Stockholm syndrome, in which kidnapping survivors develop sympathy for, conspire with, or even fall in love with their captors. The term originated in 1973, a year before the widely publicized Patty Hearst kidnapping, after a botched bank robbery in Stockholm, Sweden, where hostages unexpectedly bonded with their captors.

Melissa Goldberg Mintz, in her book *Has Your Child Been Traumatized?*, explains Stockholm syndrome as a victim's development of positive feelings toward their perpetrator. To cope with abuse, Dr. Hunter notes, victims often idealize their abuser and internalize blame for their suffering: "The victim takes on a mindset that is almost symbiotic with the abuser in order to please the caregiver and get in their good graces," Dr. Hunter elaborates. "They may believe that the more they bond with the abuser, the less likely they are to be abused—and this is often the case".

A key factor in the development of Stockholm syndrome is isolation combined with an emotional connection—fostered intentionally or unintentionally by the abuser. Clinical psychologist and trauma expert Carla Manly explains that "a perceived or actual unavailability of outside support is also critical to the development of Stockholm syndrome".

A 2018 study analyzing interviews with female sex workers across India identified four main criteria: a perceived threat to survival, displays of kindness from the captor, isolation from other perspectives or support systems, and dependence on the captor for physical or emotional needs.

In minor girls, Stockholm syndrome can severely distort emotional and cognitive functions, reshaping social and psychological identity in deeply harmful ways. From a social-psychological perspective, this begins with cognitive dissonance—the struggle to reconcile abuse with the attachment formed toward the abuser. To ease this psychological discomfort, the victim reframes harmful acts as care or protection, normalizing and justifying abuse as a survival strategy.

This is often reinforced by learned helplessness, where repeated exposure to trauma leads the victim to believe escape is impossible or futile. Within a social exchange framework, dependency deepens as the captor alternates between cruelty and kindness, creating trauma bonding. Under extreme stress, the girl's attachment system activates, strengthening loyalty and affection toward her abuser despite ongoing harm.

As the abuse continues, the minor girl may also undergo social isolation, where she becomes disconnected from her previous social world, her family, friends, and community. This isolation leads to a loss of her original social identity, as her sense of self is increasingly shaped by the abusive relationship. Over time, her social identity becomes enmeshed with the captor, erasing her previous roles and connections. This isolation is compounded by dissociation, a psychological defense mechanism where the girl emotionally detaches from the trauma to protect herself from the overwhelming distress. This coping strategy, while offering temporary relief, can leave her emotionally numb and disconnected from reality, making it harder to break free from the abusive relationship.

The socio-psychological impact of Stockholm Syndrome on a minor girl is long lasting, often leaving her with a fractured sense of trust, identity, and autonomy. Her ability to form healthy relationships, regain self-worth, and reintegrate into her social world can be deeply compromised, requiring significant psychological intervention to rebuild her sense of self and recover from the trauma.

Insights from a sociological perspective help us understand this concerning issue of why girls go missing more effectively. Structural strain theory explains how societal pressures, rigid gender norms, and patriarchal family systems can place young girls in situations where their options feel severely limited. In homes where communication is replaced with control and emotional needs are ignored, running away can become a coping mechanism—a way to escape an asphyxiating environment. The lack of proper support systems, such as counseling services and open family dynamics, worsens the problem.

From a psychological standpoint, Maslow's Hierarchy of Needs helps illustrate how these girls often lack the basic emotional and psychological safety required for healthy development. When their needs for belonging, self-esteem, or self-actualization are denied, they may experience intense psychological distress. This distress can lead to impulsive or desperate decisions, such as fleeing from home. Running away may also represent an attempt to regain control or autonomy when they feel stripped of agency by their circumstances.

A young girl, full of potential and dreams, may suddenly feel compelled to abandon her home and venture into the unknown. In that moment, it seems like the only viable choice—a way to escape mounting pressures at home, at school, or in personal relationships. The decision feels like freedom, a break from suffocating challenges. Yet what she believes is the right decision often unfolds into a journey filled with unforeseen difficulties, leaving her vulnerable in ways she hadn't imagined.

Instead of finding relief, she distances herself from opportunities that could lead to a brighter future—education, personal growth, and genuine support systems. What seems like a step toward freedom often becomes a step away from safety and resources that could help her thrive. For young girls in such situations, it is essential to recognize that running away is not a solution but a retreat from the very opportunities that could transform their lives.

The key lies in addressing the underlying factors—family conflict, societal pressure, and emotional distress—that push them toward such drastic measures. By confronting these challenges, we can create environments where young girls feel empowered to face difficulties rather than flee from them, ensuring they do not sacrifice their future in a misguided attempt to escape the present. Running away may feel like freedom in the moment, but it often leads them further from the opportunities that could truly set them free.

Identifying a missing girl from a socio-psychological perspective requires understanding both visible signs and deeper behavioural changes that signal disconnection from familiar environments. Here are key indicators anyone can look for:

She may appear displaced and disoriented, as if lost or out of place, struggling to adjust to unfamiliar surroundings and finding it difficult to navigate social spaces. This sense of unease reflects a deeper spatial disorientation and a detachment from the familiar social and geographical environments that once anchored her.

She may display visible signs of anxiety and fear, often reflected in her hyper-vigilance and heightened sensitivity to her surroundings. Social-psychologically, this can be seen in her tendency to look over her shoulder repeatedly or respond nervously during interactions, as if anticipating danger. Such behaviour stems from an overwhelming sense of insecurity and uncertainty, where she feels unsafe in an unfamiliar environment. Her emotional responses are deeply rooted in the trauma of separation from her own known and trusted world, leaving her unsettled and vulnerable in the face of new and unpredictable circumstances.

A noticeable transformation in appearance and mannerisms may emerge, reflected in changes of clothing, hygiene, and behaviour. These shifts often signify an attempt to remain inconspicuous or adapt to unfamiliar surroundings. On a psychological level, such changes are closely tied to role confusion, as the girls struggle to bridge the gap between their former identity and the realities of their current situation.

Missing girls may exhibit marked social withdrawal, consciously avoiding interaction with strangers or figures of authority, whether bullies or unfamiliar adults. Their demeanor might appear shy, reserved, or characterized by avoidant behaviour, often rooted in a fear of exposure or misjudgment. This withdrawal serves as a psychological coping mechanism, allowing them to retreat inwardly as a form of self-protection against perceived threats or confrontations Sudden dependence or attachment may emerge, as a missing girl clings to others or seeks constant reassurance. This behavioural shift reveals a profound yearning for security in the midst of unfamiliar and unsettling circumstances. Inconsistent narratives or vague details—such as hesitation when speaking about one's home or family—may signal an attempt at concealing identity, often employed as a protective defense mechanism. Trauma often manifests through emotional numbness, sudden outbursts, or difficulty in concentrating—clear indicators of psychological strain born out of fear and uncertainty."

Adolescence, as explained in Erik Erikson's theory of psychosocial development, is a pivotal stage of identity formation. During this period, many girls struggle with feelings of alienation and being misunderstood, which can sometimes result in impulsive choices such as running away. Building an atmosphere of trust and non-judgmental communication is therefore essential. When safe spaces are created where girls feel genuinely heard, respected, and valued, they are less likely to seek escape. Knowing they can express themselves openly, without fear of reprimand or dismissal, greatly reduces their vulnerability to such decisions.

By paying attention to these behavioural and emotional cues, ordinary people can play a vital role in identifying missing girls and ensuring they receive timely help and protection.

"The road away seems clearer when the heart is full of fear, but the dreams she leaves behind her are the ones that disappear. For freedom lies not in the running, nor in turning from the fight, but in the courage to keep standing, to find the way to light".

As ordinary community members, we can play a crucial role in preventing girls, especially minors, from going missing by understanding their psychological needs and providing support that addresses their emotional and developmental stages. Here are some practical ways to help, framed in psychological terms:

Attachment theory highlights the lifelong human need for secure emotional bonds. When girls feel neglected or unsupported at home, they often seek comfort elsewhere. In such situations, neighbours, friends, and mentors can play a vital role by offering consistency, attentiveness, and genuine support. This creates a psychological safety net that not only grounds them but also nurtures resilience and a sense of belonging. Fostering positive peer influence is vital, as peer dynamics profoundly shape adolescent behaviour and can, at times, steer them toward harmful choices. By cultivating a culture of support and encouraging friendships grounded in trust and respect, we help girls feel genuinely valued and included. Introducing them to inspiring role models provides constructive pathways for overcoming challenges, reinforcing their resilience and enhancing their self-worth.

Developing problem-solving and decision-making skills is essential, as cognitive development theories, notably Piaget's, highlight that adolescents are still refining their ability to assess complex situations and foresee consequences. Many girls may struggle to fully recognize the long-term risks associated with leaving home, which can make them vulnerable to impulsive actions. By walking them through realistic scenarios, exploring possible outcomes, and presenting safer alternatives, we can equip them with the capacity to think critically, weigh options wisely, and make choices that safeguard their well-being. Runaway behaviour is often driven by push factors, like family conflict or emotional neglect, and pull factors, such as romantic attachments or the promise of freedom. Responsible community members can identify signs of distress and help address these root causes by promoting healthier family dynamics, encouraging open communication, and supporting mediation between parents and daughters.

Raising awareness about the real risks is crucial. Many girls run away due to misconceptions about the outside world or an idealized notion of freedom. By educating them on the genuine dangers—such as trafficking, exploitation, and abuse—we can help reshape their understanding. Even simple awareness programs or sincere, open conversations can have a profound impact in guiding them toward safer choices. Fostering positive community engagement can play a vital role in preventing girls from running away. When girls feel connected to their surroundings, they are more likely to develop a sense of belonging and security. Encouraging participation in community activities, sports, and educational initiatives provides them with meaningful engagement, purpose, and safe outlets for their energy, strengthening their ties to the community. Empower adolescents through guidance and autonomy. Young girls flourish when they are both encouraged to take initiative and supported with care. By mentoring them to make thoughtful decisions within clear boundaries, we help them cultivate a sense of independence while ensuring they have a reliable safety net.

Ultimately, creating a community rooted in emotional security, positive role models, and open communication is key to prevention. We must recognize the girls who have lost their way—the ones standing alone in darkness, waiting for a hand to guide them home. It is our shared responsibility as individuals and as humanity to light their path, offering safety, hope, and the chance to reclaim their future.

"Empowering one another is the key to building a community where everyone feels safe and valued". Empowering one another is not only about individual growth but also about collective strength. When we empower those around us, whether through education, emotional support, sharing resources, or advocating for their rights, we create an environment where every person feels valued, respected, and capable of contributing to the community's well-being. This empowerment encourages individuals to step into roles where they can influence positive change, whether it's in families, workplaces, or larger societal structures.

A key aspect of empowerment is breaking down hierarchies of power and privilege. In many communities, power is unequally distributed, leading to marginalization of certain groups—often women, minorities, or those from lower socioeconomic backgrounds. Empowerment helps level this playing field, enabling everyone to have an equal stake in the community's progress. By fostering a culture where everyone is encouraged to voice their opinions and take on leadership roles, we build a foundation of mutual respect and inclusivity.

Empowered individuals, in turn, empower others. When one person feels capable and confident, they are more likely to uplift those around them, creating a powerful ripple effect. This is especially crucial when addressing safety and security. A community where individuals feel empowered to speak out against injustice, challenge harmful norms, and protect one another becomes a safer and more compassionate place. In such an environment, people are more likely to intervene in harmful situations, support victims, and collaborate on solutions that safeguard the vulnerable.

Empowerment also strengthens social cohesion by fostering belonging and shared purpose. When individuals feel valued and capable, they form a deeper connection to their community, knowing they are part of something greater than themselves. This sense of unity creates resilience—a community able to face crises together and emerge stronger.

Ultimately, empowerment builds a society where dignity is honoured, voices are heard, and every person plays a role in ensuring safety and well-being. It's a reciprocal process: by lifting others, we lift ourselves, creating a cycle of growth, respect, and collective security.

As we explore the reasons why minor girls go missing, we uncover a reality that extends far beyond individual choices. These disappearances are not simply acts of rebellion or impulsive decisions made in distress; they are symptoms of deeper societal fractures. Each case reflects the weight of unspoken expectations, pressures to conform, and the silent fear of judgment that young girls carry.

The home—ideally a sanctuary of love and safety—can, for some, become a place of confinement, misunderstanding, or emotional neglect. Socio-psychological factors such as familial discord, rigid gender roles, and emotional isolation may vary, but they all point to a collective failure to nurture and protect.

What's truly missing is not just the girl herself but the promise of a life that could have been—the dreams denied, the voice silenced, and the potential stifled by invisible chains. These girls are not mere statistics; they are symbols of a system that has failed to grant them true freedom, dignity, and hope.

If we are to address the issue of missing girls, we must not only intensify our search for those lost but also turn our gaze inward, towards the structures that constrain them. Real change begins when we acknowledge that to protect these young lives, we must reshape the world they live in. We must offer them not just safety, but a space to grow, to express, and to define themselves outside the narrow confines of societal expectations. It is not only to reflect on the missing girls but also on the broader changes needed in society to prevent these disappearances in the first place.

Our perceptions, often clouded by stereotypes and biases, can lead to neglect or misunderstanding about why girls go missing. When we judge their choices or blame them for their circumstances, we reinforce a culture that allows such tragedies to persist. Real change requires us to confront these internal biases and foster a mindset that values and protects every girl's life. This begins with educating ourselves about the complex factors behind their disappearance—familial pressures, emotional neglect, and the absence of safe spaces for expression.

By promoting empathy and understanding within our communities, we can create stronger support systems for girls. Prioritizing emotional intelligence and compassion fosters meaningful dialogue and healing, transforming our collective consciousness. Addressing the issue of missing girls demands more than surface-level solutions; it requires a deep shift in how we think and feel about them. Only then can we truly address the root causes and work toward prevention and recovery.

As we search for answers about why these young girls slip away, with wings as fragile as paper, from the familiar embrace of their homes, we must recognize that the truth does not lie in isolated acts of rebellion or confusion but in the heavy shadows of expectation and pressure they have lived under. What is lost is not only the girl herself but also her dreams, her voice, and her potential. To bring them back, we must search not only the streets but also the corridors of our minds and hearts—because that is where real change begins.

Chapter 3

ESCAPING THE MIST

"The law is reason, free from passion."

- Aristotle

A fifteen-year-old missing girl was rescued after a year. She was brought before the magistrate to record her statement. Without hesitation, she confessed with disarming sincerity that she had fallen in love with a nineteen-year-old boy from her village. Succumbing to social pressure, they had chosen to run away rather than remain and battle their families' disapproval. For weeks, they wandered through unfamiliar towns, surviving on scraps of hope, until luck finally smiled on them: they found jobs at a factory in Surat. There, away from prying eyes and rigid customs, they married quietly at a nearby temple. Within months, they welcomed a baby girl and began building a life of simple contentment, far from the caste divides and suffocating expectations of their village.

But a year later, the police stood at their doorstep, not to congratulate them but to "rescue" the missing girl. In the eyes of the law, she was not a wife or a mother—she was a minor who lacked the legal capacity to choose her path, a child who needed to be taken from her husband and returned to her parents.

Now, in the crowded courtroom, the runaway couple sits side by side, fingers brushing lightly, clinging to each other in the chaos. The girl, still more child than adult, wears a modest salwar kameez, her dupatta drawn tightly over her head as though to shield her from judgment. Her nervous gaze flits between the magistrate and the advocates, struggling to decode the heavy legal jargon that reduces her life to paperwork. Beside her, the boy sits stiffly, his posture both protective and tense, his face caught between defiance and fear—fear of losing her, fear of being branded a criminal for loving her.

For them, this moment feels surreal. A year ago, they had fled their village believing that love was all they needed, that their hearts could carve out a sanctuary beyond the reach of tradition. They had imagined freedom. But now, the law looms like a wall they cannot climb. Her age makes their marriage illegal. He is not only her partner but also an accused, facing charges of kidnapping and sexual exploitation.

And yet, there is a quiet defiance in the way they sit together, a shared conviction that their love is real, even if the world refuses to see it. Around them, lawyers spar over consent, morality, and legality. The magistrate studies the file before him, his face unreadable but heavy with the burden of the law. Police officers linger at the edges of the room, waiting for orders.

The girl sits silent, her thoughts whirling like a storm. She wants to speak, to tell them all that this was not coercion, that she left of her own will. But she knows her voice carries little weight here. To the system, she is still a child, her love a crime, her family's honour a priority over her happiness.

The boy, on the other hand, feels the pressure of his responsibility. He knows the law sees him as a criminal, but in his mind, he did what any man in love would do, protect the one he cares for. He wishes there was a way to explain to the stern faces in the room that his intentions were pure, that they were not running from the law but from a society that wouldn't accept their love.

In the midst of the courtroom's hustle, their love feels fragile, vulnerable to the scrutiny of a world that sees them as rebels. But for them, this love is their truth. They sit, holding onto that truth, hoping against hope that it will be enough.

It has been accredited that the cases that ought not to be criminalized are given a criminal colour by the strict wording and implementation of the Protection of Children from Sexual Offences (POCSO) Act, thereby increasing the number of cases as well as rendering precarious the plight of those that are caught within the folds of its application, as suggested in the report of Law Commission, (report no. 283). It further states that there is a growing concern that the Special courts are plagued with false cases, especially those arising out of teenage romantic relationships, which are filed by the family members who disapprove of such relationships or come to the forefront due to mandatory reporting requirements under the law. In the case of *Arhant Janardan Sunatkari vs. The state of Maharashtra*, 2021, the court opined, It has been observed that consensual sex between minors is a legal grey area as consent of a minor is no consent in the eyes of law.

There has been a continuous discourse on the matter. While some argue that the age of consent for consensual sexual relationships should be lowered to sixteen years, as it was before the enactment of the POCSO Act, others propose introducing "close-in-age" exemptions similar to those in the USA and Canada. Another perspective is that judicial discretion should be allowed in sentencing, without lowering the age of consent under any circumstances.

Two High Courts have recently made separate recommendations in this regard. In *State of Karnataka vs. Basavraj s/o Yellappa Madar* (2023), the Dharwad Bench of the Karnataka High Court considered a case where a girl aged 17 years and 9 months had eloped with the accused. The two later married and had two children. The accused was acquitted by the Special Judge due to insufficient evidence to establish the prosecution's case. The court observed that criminal prosecution in such matters often causes misunderstanding between the boy and the girl, potentially straining their relationship. Families—including parents, siblings, and spouses—suffer severe emotional trauma, social ostracism, and financial losses. Frequently, complaints are filed in the heat of the moment, often due to opposition to the marriage, but complainants and their families later turn hostile and do not support the prosecution's case.

Similarly, in *Veekesh Kalawat vs. State of Madhya Pradesh* (2023), the Gwalior Bench of the Madhya Pradesh High Court considered a case in which a minor girl eloped with a boy, and their relationship resulted in marriage and the birth of a child. The court suggested amending the POCSO Act to allow discretion for Special Judges in such cases. The court highlighted that the law's rigid application disproportionately affects marginalized communities, especially in rural Madhya Pradesh, where poverty and illiteracy exacerbate the consequences. The enforcement of POCSO often leads to devastating outcomes, such as sending the sole breadwinner to prison for a minimum of ten years, leaving wives and children vulnerable to social exploitation. The Act does not provide survivors with basic support, forcing many into precarious survival strategies, including prostitution or crime.

The court recommended amendments granting Special Courts (presided over by senior Sessions Judges) the discretion: (a) In cases where the prosecutrix is below the age of consent but de facto consent is apparent, to impose a sentence based on circumstances rather than mandating a minimum term, with the option to extend the sentence up to twenty years. (b) In cases where the prosecutrix is below the age of consent but the relationship has culminated in marriage (with or without children), to avoid imprisonment altogether and instead impose alternative correctional measures, such as community service. If a child's physical and mental development takes place in an environment full of warmth and encouragement, that child is likely to grow into a confident and successful adult. Conversely, a child who endures constant abuse and untold physical or emotional suffering often becomes a bruised and distressed individual. The hardships faced in childhood leave lasting marks on one's personality and traits.

As Mahatma Gandhi observed:

"If we are to reach real peace in this world, and if we are to carry on a real war against war, we shall have to begin with children; and if they will grow up in their natural innocence, we won't have to struggle; we won't have to pass fruitless idle resolutions, but we shall go from love to love and peace to peace, until at last all the corners of the world are covered with that peace and love for which consciously or unconsciously the whole world is hungering".

In the field of human rights and social justice, the State is entrusted with the responsibility of ensuring the development and protection of children. This obligation rests on both moral imperatives and constitutional commitments. As Justice P.N. Bhagwati stated in *Sheela Barse v. Union of India* (1986):

"If a child is a national asset, it is the duty of the State to look after the child with a view to ensuring the full development of children and shielding them from any form of exploitation".

By fulfilling these principles, the government lays the foundation for a just and healthy society, upholding every child's rights and nurturing their potential in a safe and secure environment. The concept of child rights reflects the belief that every child has the right to survival, health, education, and protection from harm.

The Law Commission, in its 259th Report on *Early Childhood Development and Legal Entitlement*, observed:

"This critical period up to the age of six years is a 'window of opportunity'. If the child receives favourable environmental inputs in health, nutrition, learning, and psychosocial development, the chances of the child's brain developing to its full potential are considerably enhanced. If environmental experiences are unfavourable and the child faces deprivation or abuse, the brain's development is negatively affected, and this 'window of opportunity' is often irrevocably lost".

The recognition of child rights is relatively modern, having taken formal shape only in the twentieth century. Christine Alice Corcos, in *The Child in International Law: A Pathfinder and Selected Bibliography*, notes that historically, any rights children possessed flowed from their dependency on parents, being viewed as property rather than independent rights-holders. A true rights-based approach emerged in the twentieth century, beginning with the *Geneva Declaration of the Rights of the Child* (1924), adopted by the League of Nations, which for the first time acknowledged child rights and the importance of special safeguards and care.

Subsequently, the *Universal Declaration of Human Rights* (1948), though not specific to children, recognized their entitlement to special care and equal social protection. The *Declaration of the Rights of the Child* (1959), adopted by the UN General Assembly, further articulated the principle of the "best interests of the child".

The most significant milestone in this field is the *United Nations Convention on the Rights of the Child* (1989), a legally binding treaty ratified by 196 countries, making it one of the most widely ratified international instruments. The UNCRC encompasses a wide range of civil, political, economic, social, and cultural rights.

Beyond child-specific instruments, recognition of children's rights is also found in broader human rights treaties, such as the *International Covenant on Economic, Social and Cultural Rights* (1966), the *International Covenant on Civil and Political Rights* (1966), and conventions of the International Labour Organization. The Law Commission Report (No. 283) stated that the move towards a rights-based approach to child rights was driven by a change in societal attitudes toward children. Children began to be viewed as autonomous individuals, separate from their parents, with unique rights, interests, and needs. Their inherent vulnerabilities compared to adults warranted a distinct legal framework for recognition and protection.

In the Indian context, the earliest traces of implicit or explicit recognition of child rights can be found in various labour laws passed during the colonial period. For instance, the *Factories Act, 1881* introduced provisions regulating child labour. Similarly, the *Apprentices Act, 1850* contained measures for the welfare of child workers and, for the first time, required that convicted children aged 10–18 years receive vocational training as part of their rehabilitation. The *Reformatory Schools Act, 1876* focused on the reformation and rehabilitation of young offenders.

The *Code of Criminal Procedure, 1898* also recognized the need for differentiated treatment of juvenile offenders. The landmark recommendations of the *Indian Jail Committee (1919–1920)* emphasized that child offenders should not be treated as adults. It proposed that juveniles should not be imprisoned but sent to remand homes, and that efforts should be made for their reformation. The committee also suggested the establishment of separate children's courts.

Following the committee's report, several provincial legislations were enacted, including the *Madras Children Act, 1920*; *Bengal Children Act, 1922*; and *Bombay Children Act, 1924*. These statutes laid down detailed procedures for the trial of child offenders, treating them as a distinct category separate from adult offenders. Another significant piece of legislation from the colonial era, the *Child Marriage Restraint Act, 1929*, aimed to safeguard children by prohibiting child marriage.

The post-independence era marks a progressive shift, with emphatic recognition of child rights explicitly embedded within the Constitution of India. Article 15(3) empowers the State to enact special laws for children, while Article 24 prohibits their employment in hazardous industries. The addition of Article 21-A in 2002, which guarantees the right to free and compulsory education for children aged 6 to 14 years, further reflects India's commitment to advancing child rights. The Directive Principles of State Policy reinforce this commitment, particularly Articles 39 and 45, which outline the government's duty to safeguard children's welfare and protection.

To meet constitutional obligations and international commitments, India has enacted several child-centric laws addressing diverse aspects of child welfare. These include the *Immoral Traffic (Prevention) Act, 1956; Child Labour (Prohibition and Regulation) Act, 1986; Child and Adolescent Labour (Prohibition and Regulation) Amendment Act, 2016; Protection of Children from Sexual Offences (POCSO) Act, 2012;* and *Juvenile Justice (Care and Protection of Children) Act, 2015.*

Although the terms "child" and "minor" are often used interchangeably, they carry distinct definitions across various legal frameworks, leading to inconsistencies in interpretation. The *Indian Majority Act, 1875; Hindu Minority and Guardianship Act, 1956;* and *Guardians and Wards Act, 1890* uniformly define a minor as an individual under 18 years of age.

By contrast, under the *Prohibition of Child Marriage Act, 2006,* a child is defined as a male under 21 years or a female under 18 years. The *Right of Children to Free and Compulsory Education Act, 2009* defines a child as a person between 6 and 14 years of age. Similarly, the *Juvenile Justice Act* and the *POCSO Act* consider anyone below 18 years a child, whereas the *Child and Adolescent Labour (Prohibition and Regulation) Act, 1986* defines a child as below 14 years and categorizes adolescents as those aged 14–18 years. The term "adolescent," however, is rarely defined in other legislations and is more commonly referenced in government policies and programmes.

The principle of *Doli Incapax*—the presumption that a child is incapable of committing a crime—has long been embedded in Indian criminal jurisprudence, reflected in both the *Indian Penal Code, 1860 (IPC)* and the *Bharatiya Nyaya Sanhita (BNS)*. This principle acknowledges that children, due to their developmental stage, may lack the capacity to fully understand the nature and consequences of their actions.

Under the IPC, immunity is provided based on specific age brackets, with varying degrees of protection. Children below seven years of age are granted absolute immunity, while those between seven and twelve years can only be held criminally liable if it is proven that they possess sufficient maturity to understand the implications of their conduct. This tiered approach ensures that young children are not unjustly prosecuted, while also recognising the importance of assessing a child's individual level of understanding. The Juvenile Justice (JJ) Act further builds upon this foundation by recognizing that different age brackets within childhood reflect varying levels of cognitive and emotional maturity. Accordingly, the JJ Act allows children between 16 and 18 years of age to be tried as adults under specific circumstances, particularly in cases of heinous offences, if it is determined that the child possessed the requisite maturity and intent for such serious actions.

The Bharatiya Nyaya Sanhita (BNS), intended as a modern update to the Indian Penal Code (IPC), seeks to contextualize and modernize these principles within contemporary Indian society. The BNS preserves the essence of Doli Incapax while emphasizing a more nuanced approach to juvenile justice. Its focus is on rehabilitation and reform rather than purely punitive measures. It continues to draw distinctions based on age, maturity, and the nature of the offence, reflecting India's commitment to a child-sensitive justice system that aligns with evolving global perspectives on juvenile justice.

Together, the BNS and JJ Act aim to protect the rights and developmental needs of children while balancing societal interests. They acknowledge that children are fundamentally different from adults in terms of cognition and morality and therefore require tailored approaches within the criminal justice system. This alignment underscores India's commitment to a progressive, reformative justice model that safeguards children's welfare and developmental rights even when addressing criminal liability.

The POCSO Act, 2012, passed by Parliament, was designed to provide comprehensive protection to children from sexual assault, harassment, and exploitation, including crimes involving pornography. The Act mandates the establishment of special courts to ensure the speedy and sensitive handling of such cases. It officially came into effect on November 14, 2012.

Before the POCSO Act, no specific legislation addressed child sexual abuse comprehensively. Such offences were prosecuted under provisions of the IPC, including Sections 375, 354, and 377. However, only Section 377 was gender-neutral, which left male victims of child sexual abuse without adequate protection. Other provisions often failed to address the gravity of sexual crimes against children, both in their definitions and punishments.

The POCSO Act introduced a gender-neutral framework for all individuals under 18 years of age. It requires the creation of special courts to safeguard child victims' interests and places strong emphasis on privacy, confidentiality, and child-friendly procedures throughout the judicial process. The preamble of the POCSO Act reflects constitutional principles, particularly Article 39(f) of the Constitution, a Directive Principle of State Policy mandating that the State ensure children's healthy development, freedom, and dignity while safeguarding their childhood and youth.

The need for such legislation stemmed from rising instances of child sexual abuse. In its 156th Report (1997), the Law Commission highlighted the alarming increase in child rape cases and proposed amendments to Sections 375, 354, and 509 of the IPC. However, it also acknowledged that these amendments alone would not comprehensively address child sexual abuse. The Supreme Court in Sakshi v. Union of India recognized this gap and called for comprehensive legislation. In this case, a writ petition sought to broaden the definition of "sexual intercourse" under Section 375 IPC to include all forms of penetration. The Court, noting the serious implications under Article 21 of the Constitution, requested a fresh examination by the Law Commission. The Commission's 172nd Report subsequently recommended a comprehensive overhaul of rape laws and suggested making them gender neutral.

The enactment of POCSO was a direct response to these recommendations and to alarming data on sexual abuse from the National Crime Records Bureau and the 2007 Study on Child Abuse: India, conducted by the Ministry of Women and Child Development. Previously, crimes against children were prosecuted under the same provisions as those against adults, offering inadequate protection and deterrence.

The POCSO Act filled this legislative vacuum, establishing strict provisions designed to curb child sexual abuse. This is particularly significant given India's demographic realities: according to the 2011 Census, over 400 million children under the age of 18 make up approximately 36.7% of the total population. The Act thus serves as a vital protective framework for one of the world's largest child populations.

The concept of the age of consent refers to the minimum legal age at which a person is considered capable of consenting to sexual activity or marriage. In India, this age is currently 18 years, as mandated by the POCSO Act. Prior to its enactment, the age of consent was determined under Section 375 of the IPC, which defines rape.

The evolution of the age of consent reflects changing societal and legal attitudes. Initially set at 10 years in 1860, it was raised to 12 years in 1891 following the Phulmoni case. In 1925, it was increased to 14 years, and in 1940, it was raised to 16 years, where it remained until POCSO raised it to 18 in 2012. During this time, the minimum legal age of marriage stayed at 18 years for women and 21 for men.

The "marital rape exception" within Section 375 also evolved, with the age below which marital relations constituted rape increasing from 10 years in 1860 to 15 years in 2012. The Law Commission's 84th Report, Rape and Allied Offences, recommended raising the age of consent to 18 years to align with the Child Marriage Restraint Act, 1929. However, Parliament chose to retain the age at 16. The Commission's 156th Report revisited the issue, recommending an increase to 18 years based on suggestions from the National Commission for Women. Despite these recommendations, Parliament retained the age at 16 until the 2013 amendment to Section 375 IPC, which aligned it with POCSO's 18-year threshold.

Let's delve deeper into both the legal and social aspects of the age of consent, highlighting additional nuances and considerations. The age of consent is set at different ages depending on the jurisdiction, leading to inconsistencies within a country. In the U.S., for example, some states set the age at 16 years, while others set it at 18 years. These differences can create legal ambiguities, especially in cases of cross-state relationships. In some countries, there are different ages of consent for different sexual acts. For example, certain sexual activities might have a higher age limit than others.

Laws often differentiate between "consent" and "capacity to consent". While a minor may legally be able to consent, they might lack the emotional maturity or life experience to make informed decisions about sexual relationships. Legal frameworks are increasingly recognizing this distinction and are working to address it through education and support services. Even where laws exist, enforcing age of consent laws can be challenging. Law enforcement may struggle with the nuances of consent in cases where both parties are minors or where cultural practices normalize earlier sexual activity. Victims of statutory rape may be reluctant to report offenses due to fear of legal repercussions for themselves or societal stigma, complicating enforcement efforts.

The rise of digital communication and dating apps has blurred traditional boundaries around age of consent. Laws that were once clear-cut are now challenged by the realities of online interactions, where minors may engage with adults across different jurisdictions. Some jurisdictions are adapting by including provisions related to online communication, but the rapid pace of technological change often outstrips legal responses. Various international treaties advocate for the protection of children and young people, influencing national laws around age of consent. The convention on the Rights of the Child, for instance, emphasizes the need for legal frameworks that protect minors from exploitation and abuse.

Different cultures have distinct beliefs about youth sexuality, which can influence the setting of the age of consent. In some cultures, early marriage is common, and laws reflect these practices, leading to lower ages of consent. In contrast, cultures that prioritize individual autonomy and sexual education may set higher ages. Changes in cultural attitudes, such as the growing acceptance of LGBTQIA+ rights, can also influence discussions around age of consent and the recognition of diverse relationships. Comprehensive sex education is often linked to the effectiveness of age of consent laws. Countries or regions that invest in education about consent, relationships, and sexual health typically see lower rates of teen pregnancies and sexually transmitted infections (STIs), suggesting that informed youth make safer choices. Programmes emphasizing communication, respect, and understanding of consent can help young people navigate their relationships responsibly.

Advocacy groups play a critical role in shaping conversations around the age of consent, pushing for reforms that protect minors while respecting their autonomy. These groups raise awareness about the importance of consent in relationships and the potential harm caused by sexual exploitation. Campaigns highlighting the experiences of survivors of abuse often bring public attention to inadequacies in existing laws and the urgent need for reform.

Gender plays a significant role in how age of consent laws are perceived and enforced. In many cultures, girls are primarily viewed as victims in cases of statutory rape, whereas boys may face less scrutiny, resulting in gender biases within both legal outcomes and societal attitudes. Discussions on consent must also take into account power dynamics, including those tied to age, gender, and social status. Recognizing the potential for older individuals to exploit younger individuals is crucial to creating a strong and protective legal framework.

The age of consent intersects with several social issues, including poverty, education, and health. In regions where educational opportunities are limited, young people may lack the information needed to navigate relationships safely. Communities facing systemic social inequality often experience higher rates of sexual violence, underscoring the need for a comprehensive and socially just approach to understanding and implementing age of consent laws.

The ethical debate surrounding the age of consent often revolves around balancing the protection of minors with respect for their autonomy. Laws that are overly strict risk criminalizing consensual relationships between peers, while overly lenient laws may leave minors vulnerable to exploitation. Establishing a universal standard is further complicated by cultural relativism, as practices deemed acceptable in one culture may be considered harmful in another. Global discourse reflects this tension, calling for culturally sensitive approaches to legislative frameworks.

The rise of social media has added new dimensions to this debate, raising ethical concerns about consent in digital spaces. As young people increasingly navigate relationships online, there is a pressing need for guidelines that address the complexities of digital communication, consent, and exploitation.

The age of consent remains a multifaceted issue encompassing legal, social, and ethical considerations. It is a crucial mechanism for safeguarding minors while respecting their rights and personal autonomy. As societal norms evolve and new challenges emerge, continuous dialogue and reform are essential to ensuring that age of consent laws remain effective. The dynamic interplay between legal standards and societal attitudes will continue to shape how these laws are understood and applied in a rapidly changing world.

The age of consent, defined as the age at which an individual is legally recognized as competent to consent to sexual activities, varies significantly across countries and is influenced by cultural, religious, and legal factors. Below is an overview of age of consent laws in different regions:

Europe

- **France**: The age of consent is 15 years. French law generally prohibits sexual activities with minors under this age, with additional protections in place for minors under 18 years to prevent exploitation.
- **Germany**: The age of consent is 14 years for consensual sexual activities. However, sexual relationships with minors between 14 and 16 years are prohibited if the partner is over 21 years and there is evidence of exploitation.
- **United Kingdom**: The age of consent is 16 years across England, Scotland, Wales, and Northern Ireland, with strict legal measures against adults engaging in sexual relationships with minors below this threshold.

North America

- **United States**: The age of consent varies by state, ranging from 16 to 18 years. For example, it is 18 years in California and New York, 17 years in Texas, and 16 years in Florida. Most states have "Romeo and Juliet" provisions, which decriminalize consensual relationships between minors close in age.
- **Canada**: The age of consent is 16 years, with additional protections for minors under 18 years, particularly to guard against exploitation by individuals in positions of authority, such as teachers or coaches.

Latin America

- **Mexico**: The age of consent varies by state, generally ranging between 16 and 18 years. Federal law provides further protection against exploitation of minors under 18 years by adults in positions of power.
- **Brazil**: The age of consent is 14 years, with additional safeguards against the exploitation of minors under 18 years.

Asia

- **Japan**: The national age of consent is 13 years, but local ordinances and prefectural laws often impose higher limits, typically around 18 years, to prevent exploitation.
- **India**: The age of consent is 18 years. Indian law includes strict provisions to protect minors from

sexual exploitation, supported by cultural norms and additional legal measures under child protection laws.

- **Philippines**: Recently raised from 12 to 16 years to strengthen protections for minors, with stricter penalties for offenders in positions of authority.

Africa

- **South Africa**: The age of consent is 16 years, with close-in-age exemptions that prevent the criminalization of consensual sexual relationships between peers.
- **Egypt**: There is no formal age of consent, as sexual activities outside of marriage are prohibited. Marriage, with a legal minimum age of 18 years, is the only lawful context for intimate relationships.

Australia

- **Australia**: The age of consent varies by state, generally 16 years in New South Wales and Victoria, and 17 years in South Australia and Tasmania. Laws also prohibit sexual relationships between minors and adults in positions of authority.

Middle East

- **Saudi Arabia**: There is no codified age of consent due to the strict prohibition of premarital sexual relationships. Marriage is the only legal context for sexual activity, with the minimum marriage age often determined by social and familial consent.

These examples demonstrate the diversity of age of consent laws worldwide. Some countries emphasize stricter legal protections for minors, while others reflect cultural or historical norms regarding relationships and maturity. Many jurisdictions include provisions that provide additional safeguards for minors to prevent exploitation by individuals in positions of authority, regardless of the age of consent.

The POCSO Act serves two primary purposes: first, to uphold every child's right to safety, security, and protection from sexual abuse and exploitation; and second, to define offences against children explicitly and assign proportionate penalties to serve as an effective deterrent. Under this Act, offences involving children below 12 years of age are treated as aggravated offences, attracting stricter penalties, including longer prison terms and higher fines.

Although the POCSO Act is gender-neutral, it is undeniable that girls face heightened threats within our society. The Supreme Court highlighted this vulnerability in *Nawab-ud Din v. State of Uttarakhand*, emphasizing that children are invaluable human resources, our nation's future, and the hope of tomorrow rests upon them. Yet, in our country, girls remain especially vulnerable to various forms of exploitation, including sexual assault and abuse. The court described such exploitation as a crime against humanity and society, underscoring that all children, and particularly girls, deserve comprehensive protection and greater care, whether in urban or rural settings.

As a society, we often fail to protect our children, leaving the courts with the essential duty to ensure that these vulnerable children receive the legal protection they need and deserve. When a child experiences sexual abuse, they are placed in an even more precarious position than an adult victim of similar abuse. For a child, facing social ostracism and enduring the mental trauma inflicted by society can be far more overwhelming. This heightened vulnerability underscores the need for additional protection, care, and support to help them heal and rebuild. The problem is further compounded by the prevailing societal attitudes towards such violence. As per the survey records, approximately 35% of male and 41% of female adolescents believe it is justified for a husband to beat his wife for reasons such as arguing or burning food. It is especially concerning that such a high percentage of female adolescents accept domestic violence as justified.

Child marriage has its own socio-economic dimension, which also appears in the context of romantic relationships under the POCSO Act. Many child brides come from specific socio-economic backgrounds, a trend similarly reflected in POCSO cases involving romantic relationships. Courts have highlighted the concerning inconsistency in these situations, acknowledging that many of these cases involve complex power dynamics and exploitation.

In instances of child marriage or trafficking, perpetrators often attempt to argue that the child has "consented". However, a child's consent is legally irrelevant due to the inherent power imbalances and the vulnerability of minors. Additionally, such "consent" may be gained through manipulation, coercion, or deception, leading a child to believe they are a willing participant when, in reality, they are being exploited. Emerging cases of online grooming are a prime example of how manipulation can create a false sense of consent.

It is also an unfortunate reality that, in many cases, a family member or someone close to the child is involved in pushing them into marriage, prostitution, or trafficking. NCRB (National crime records bureau), data reveals that in approximately 97% of cases reported under Sections 4 and 6 of the POCSO Act, the perpetrator was known to the victim.

Taking a child's "consent" into account in these cases risks adding subjectivity that can enable groomers, traffickers, and perpetrators to evade accountability.

An emerging aspect to consider is the Parliament's proposal to raise the minimum marriage age for girls to 21 years, under the Prevention of Child Marriage Act, aligning it with the age for boys. This bill has been referred to the Department-related Parliamentary Standing Committee on Education, Women, Child, Youth, and Sports for further examination. In this context, any move to reduce the age of consent could exacerbate existing challenges.

Another important factor is the link between the POCSO Act and child trafficking, including child prostitution. According to the NCRB data, in 2021, a total of 6,533 trafficking victims were reported, of which 2,877 were children. However, only 2,189 cases of trafficking were registered, with a significant percentage involving sexual exploitation through prostitution and some cases involving forced marriages. The POCSO Act serves as a crucial tool in combating such crimes. Therefore, in evaluating the age of consent under the POCSO Act, it is essential to strike a careful balance between protecting children and respecting their autonomy.

The contentious issue of prosecuting romantic relationships under the POCSO Act has attracted considerable judicial scrutiny. Various High Courts, faced with this complex issue, have reached differing conclusions. Some courts, constrained by the literal interpretation of the statute, have felt compelled to convict the accused in cases where a consensual sexual relationship was involved with a minor. On the other hand, several High Courts have taken a broader interpretative approach that moves beyond the strict confines of the POCSO Act. By adopting a more flexible reading of the law, these courts have argued that the intent of the POCSO Act was not to criminalize consensual relationships between adolescents but rather to protect minors from sexual exploitation. For instance, in *Ajay Kumar v. State (NCT of Delhi)*, the Delhi High Court observed that the purpose of the POCSO Act was to shield children under 18 years from exploitation, not to penalize young adults engaged in consensual relationships.

Conversely, in *Ravi Varsha v. State of Madras*, the Madras High Court took a stern stance, ruling that under the POCSO Act, a minor's consent holds no legal weight. The court emphasized that any individual below 18 years is legally considered a child, and as an appellate court, it must adhere to the law's explicit language without extending its interpretation. In this case, it was noted that the accused had taken the minor from her guardians without their consent and engaged in a penetrative sexual act. Thus, the court held that the offense fell under Section 5(i), punishable under Section 6 of the POCSO Act. Concerns are growing over the increasing number of cases in which minors are prosecuted under the POCSO Act for engaging in consensual sexual relationships. This issue has been repeatedly raised in proceedings before various High Courts and POCSO Special Courts across the country.

Despite statements from female minors asserting that these relationships were consensual, male partners are often convicted under the POCSO Act. This is based on the interpretation that the Act was not intended to exclude cases involving sexual intercourse, regardless of consent. The issue of consensual adolescent relationships within the judicial system is complex and deeply layered, particularly given the legal and moral nuances surrounding age, consent, and societal perceptions of relationships involving minors. Courts, especially at the high court level, frequently encounter cases where adolescents engage in relationships that, while consensual in a practical sense, fall outside the boundaries of legal consent due to age restrictions. This puts trial courts in a difficult position, as they are often bound to deny bail to accused individuals, reflecting the legal severity of cases involving minors, even when there is evidence of mutual consent.

High Courts, in contrast, have increasingly stepped in to assess these cases more sensitively, recognizing that rigid legal interpretations may not always serve justice. High courts, when confronted with rising numbers of bail applications and petitions to quash FIRs in such cases, have provided guidelines for trial courts to consider in their bail decisions. These guidelines incorporate a range of factors intended to capture the real-world dynamics of these relationships.

Key considerations include the ages of both the victim and the accused and whether they are close enough to suggest a lack of exploitation, as well as any familial or social connections between them. The H.C. also review the behaviour of the accused following the alleged offense, their treatment of the victim, and whether there is any indication of coercion, threat, or violence. Social factors, such as the comparative standing of the parties and any claims that the accused harassed or intimidated witnesses, are also examined. Importantly, high courts consider whether the victim's behaviour or statements suggest a degree of tacit consent, though such consent is not legally valid for minors.

This approach emphasizes a shift towards individualized, case-by case assessments rather than blanket judgments.

Recognizing the need for nuanced handling, H.C. underline that each case must be judged on its specific circumstances. This perspective seeks to balance the protection of minors with the avoidance of overly punitive measures in situations where the circumstances suggest mutual involvement rather than exploitation. Ultimately, this nuanced judicial approach aims to protect vulnerable individuals while respecting the complexities of adolescent relationships, considering both legal frameworks and the evolving social context.

The issue of mandatory reporting and medical termination of pregnancies involving minors under the POCSO Act (Protection of Children from Sexual Offenses) touches upon complex legal, ethical, and social dimensions. The Act, initially designed to protect minors from sexual exploitation, sets strict reporting requirements for cases of sexual abuse, including consensual relationships among minors, where consent itself is legally non-existent due to age.

A recent interpretation by the Madras High Court, in accordance with the Supreme Court's judgment in *X v. Principal Secretary Health and Family Welfare Department*, sheds light on an important but sensitive issue—the mandatory reporting of minors seeking medical termination of pregnancy resulting from consensual sexual relationships. The section 19 of the POCSO Act mandates that any knowledge or suspicion of sexual offenses involving minors must be reported to the authorities. However, this requirement has posed challenges when minors or their guardians are hesitant to reveal the minor's identity, especially in cases where the pregnancy results from consensual relations. The Madras High Court's stance allows medical practitioners not to disclose the minor's identity in such cases, thus prioritizing the minor's and family's privacy over strict procedural compliance. This decision attempts to balance mandatory reporting with considerations of privacy and the potential stigma faced by the minor.

Trial courts, which handle POCSO cases in the initial stages, often find themselves constrained by the rigid legal framework of the Act. Due to the severe implications of offenses under POCSO, courts typically refrain from granting bail or exercising discretion, even when the defense argues that the relationship between the minor and the accused was consensual. The rationale is to maintain a stringent stance on child protection. However, this rigidity has led to debate over the Act's one-size-fits-all approach, which does not differentiate between exploitative cases and consensual relationships among minors. Furthermore, the POCSO Act imposes mandatory minimum sentencing, leaving little room for judges to account for context or the contoured realities of individual cases, such as age proximity or the absence of coercion.

Decisions rendered by special courts in POCSO cases are closely monitored by the High Courts due to the serious consequences associated with offenses under the Act. Given this scrutiny, any decision that deviates from the strictures of the POCSO framework, such as granting bail or issuing a lesser sentence, must be well-justified and supported by the Act. High Courts have routinely set aside bail orders or modified sentences that they find inconsistent with the Act's intentions. This reinforces the stringent approach of POCSO but raises questions about whether this strict legal environment effectively addresses the welfare and rehabilitation needs of minors in all cases.

In an administrative response to the complexities of POCSO cases, the Mumbai Police in April 2022 introduced a directive that said cases under the POCSO Act involving molestation accusations require approval from an Assistant Commissioner of Police (ACP), with endorsement from the Zonal Deputy Commissioner of Police, before an FIR could be registered. This step aimed to filter cases, given the high societal sensitivity and potential misuse of molestation allegations. However, this directive was challenged in the Bombay High Court on the grounds that it could obstruct timely justice for genuine victims. After a series of modifications to the directive, the police ultimately limited the requirement to "controversial cases" and then eventually withdrew the circular entirely. The directive drew severe criticism from the National Commission for Protection of Child Rights (NCPCR) and the Maharashtra State Commission for Protection of Child Rights, who argued that it added unnecessary procedural barriers for victims seeking protection under POCSO. The controversy underscored the tensions between safeguarding procedural integrity and ensuring unimpeded access to justice for minors.

The discussions around mandatory reporting, judicial discretion, and administrative procedures reflect ongoing tensions in POCSO's implementation. While the Act is essential for protecting minors, its strict framework can sometimes be at odds with the fine-grained realities of cases involving minors in consensual relationships. Legal experts and child rights advocates argue that reforms may be needed to grant judges limited discretion in sentencing, particularly where circumstances suggest a lesser degree of harm or coercion.

Moreover, the judicial recognition of minors' privacy in cases of medical termination could potentially lead to broader legal adjustments in POCSO's implementation, where the welfare of the child is prioritized over strict procedural mandates. This area remains an evolving field of law, with future cases likely to further refine the balance between safeguarding minors' rights and the law. This situation sheds light on the complex intersection of legal protection, adolescent psychology, and the role of the justice system in dealing with consensual relationships among minors, especially under the POCSO Act.

The circular issued by the Director General of Police in Tamil Nadu on December 3, 2022, reflects a significant step towards carefully managing cases where young people in consensual relationships are implicated under the POCSO Act. The court had further directed the Director General of Police to identify cases involving consensual relationships from among the pending cases as already determined under previous orders of the court. In compliance with the Court orders, the Director General of police had identified that there were 1,274 pending cases out of which 111 cases have been identified as involving consensual relationship which are either at the stage of investigation or where the investigation has been completed and final report has been filed and the same is yet to be taken on file by the concerned special court. The High Court will exercise its jurisdiction ultimately to the benefit of the children involved by relieving them from the trauma of facing a criminal trial before the Court. In this light, it is amply clear that the situation regarding the rising cases of adolescent love that the courts are faced with needs to be carefully considered, keeping in mind all dimensions and balancing them to the best extent possible. Protecting children from any sexual abuse or exploitation, however, must remain the central and paramount consideration in this endeavour, as stated by the Law Commission Report (Report No. 283).

The POCSO Act, enacted to protect children from sexual offences, sets a clear boundary: any sexual activity involving minors (below 18 years) is criminalized, regardless of consent. This law thus faces challenges in cases where adolescents, often close in age, engage in consensual relationships. Applying strict legal consequences in these cases without distinction can have severe repercussions on the young individuals, potentially subjecting them to criminal trials and stigmatizing life experiences that may impact their future.

The prevailing judgments encouraged investigating officers to avoid incautious arrests in cases where adolescents were involved. Instead of immediate arrest, they were advised to apply Section 41A of the Criminal Procedure Code, which mandated issuing a notice to the accused to appear before the police. Now covered under 35(3) BNNS (Bhartiya Nagrik Suraksha Sanhita), this approach minimizes trauma for young people and prevents criminalizing behaviour that might otherwise be regarded as part of normal adolescent exploration.

Recognizing the need for ongoing judicial oversight, the Madras High Court constituted a special bench to monitor the implementation of the POCSO Act and the Juvenile Justice (JJ) Act. This bench is not only examining the legalities but is also sensitive to the social and psychological contexts surrounding these cases. Their role includes ensuring fair treatment for minors, avoiding unnecessary criminalization, and setting best practices in handling such cases. In line with prior directions, the cases are being treated with specific care to relieve children from the ordeal of facing unnecessary criminal trials. The special bench's mandate extends to establishing best practices in cases involving juveniles. For example, they are tasked with finding ways to protect minors from undue trauma, recognizing the difference between exploitation and consensual relationships, and setting benchmarks for handling similar cases.

This ongoing judicial scrutiny helps align legal interventions with the realities of adolescent behaviour and maturity levels. Despite the shift towards a more nuanced approach, the core purpose of the POCSO Act—to protect children from abuse and exploitation—remains intact. All decisions and interventions are designed to ensure that vulnerable minors are not exposed to abuse or exploitation under the guise of "consensual relationships". Authorities need to remain vigilant to the fact that seemingly consensual relationships might sometimes camouflage coercion or manipulation, especially when power dynamics are at play.

The case studies highlight how the justice system must balance protection with respect for adolescent autonomy. While the POCSO Act aims to prevent exploitation, its rigid implementation could lead to unjust outcomes when it fails to distinguish between abuse and consensual, close-in-age relationships. Thus, the courts' approach recognizes the importance of safeguarding children without ignoring their evolving capacity to form connections and make choices.

At the societal level, there is a need to address the cultural stigma surrounding adolescent relationships, especially in India, where societal norms often clash with young people's exploration of romantic relationships. Criminal trials can severely impact the social standing, emotional well-being, and educational or career prospects of adolescents, creating lifelong consequences for choices made during a formative phase.

The steps taken by Tamil Nadu's DGP and the special bench of the Madras High Court reflect a more enlightened approach that addresses the spirit of the law while respecting the realities of adolescence. Ultimately, this approach could serve as a model, guiding the rest of India in rethinking how laws like POCSO are implemented in cases involving consensual relationships among minors.

The Law Commission, recognizing the far-reaching impact of any revisions to the POCSO Act, carefully considered the complexities and varied issues surrounding the law. To ensure a comprehensive perspective, the Commission engaged in extensive consultations with a diverse group of stakeholders. These included the National Commission for Protection of Child Rights (NCPCR), civil society organizations, child rights advocates, legal experts, and academic professionals, all of whom provided valuable insights.

Additionally, the Commission sought guidance from the Ministry of Women and Child Development and reached out to all 25 High Courts in the country to gain a clear understanding of the cases currently pending under the Act. During these thorough consultations, a range of concerns were raised regarding the implementation of the Act as it stands. Notably, there was no clear consensus on the need to alter the statutory age of consent. However, experts unanimously agreed that the legal definition of a child under the POCSO Act should remain as it is, encompassing all individuals below the age of 18 years. This position ensures that children within the 16-to-18-year age group, where consent is absent, continue to be safeguarded under the Act's protective framework.

The POCSO Act extends its protection to children aged 16 to 18 years, applying stricter penalties and offering enhanced safeguards for all minors due to their heightened vulnerabilities. This protection acknowledges that while minors in different age brackets may vary in mental development and decision-making capabilities, the law should prioritize their well-being without overlooking these distinctions.A key area of consensus among experts was the critical need for age-appropriate sex education and health awareness, especially for adolescents. Schools should intensify their sex education programmes to equip young people with the knowledge to make informed and responsible choices. Beyond legal protections, it is essential to foster awareness among children about understanding their bodies, the risks linked to early sexual activity, and ways to prevent such risks effectively. Comprehensive sexual education has been shown to delay the onset of sexual activity among adolescents and positively influences responsible choices in contraception, partner selection, and reproductive health outcomes. While there are existing government initiatives addressing these concerns, it is clear that these programmes need to be restructured and expanded to better align with current realities and needs.

One of the most debated issues throughout the various consultation process is whether the age of consent should be lowered to 16 years. Advocates for lowering the age of consent or creating exceptions for minors aged 16 to 18 years, argued that setting a high age threshold overlooks the natural development of adolescent sexuality and fails to consider young people's evolving capacities. Not all minors are at the same level of maturity, and laws should reflect these developmental differences. Experts emphasized the need for balance between protecting young people and avoiding over-criminalization, suggesting that while all children should remain under the Act's protection, this protection should not become punitive for consensual relationships. Consequently, they recommended that the

Act's definition of "child" remain unchanged, ensuring legal protection for all minors under 18 years. It is proposed that most chapters of the POCSO Act should continue to apply to all children, with specific exceptions for Chapters 2, 3, and 4. Chapter 2 deals with sexual offenses against children, Chapter 3 addresses the exploitation of children in pornography, and Chapter 4 pertains to abetment and attempts to commit offenses. To address contemporary challenges more effectively, experts recommended that these chapters should not be applied to consensual sexual activity involving minors aged 16 to 18 years, as this would strike a balance between protecting young people and recognizing their emerging autonomy.

In India, comprehensive nationwide studies examining the impact of the POCSO Act on adolescent romantic relationships are lacking. However, limited but significant research by civil society groups, child rights organizations, and independent scholars has begun to shed light on this complex issue. For example, a study by the Enfold Proactive Health Trust, conducted across Assam, Maharashtra, and West Bengal, found that a substantial portion of POCSO cases in these states involved consensual relationships between adolescents. The study also highlighted that acquittals for accused individuals in these cases were common, suggesting that the law's application in such situations may often lead to outcomes where romantic, consensual relationships are punished rather than actual abuse.

Further studies in this field have questioned the unintended consequences of using the POCSO Act against adolescents. These studies have raised ethical and social concerns, noting that criminalizing consensual adolescent relationships can infringe on the dignity and privacy of young people, restrict their liberty, negatively affect their sexual and reproductive health, and place an unnecessary strain on the criminal justice system. Researchers argue that treating normative adolescent relationships as criminal offences, especially those involving individuals aged 16 to 18 years, fails to recognize the evolving maturity of young people and, in turn, undermines their best interests. They suggest that the current legal framework does not adequately differentiate between exploitation and genuine adolescent relationships.

One possible reform proposed by researchers is the introduction of a "close-in-age" exemption, as adopted by some other countries, which would provide more nuanced protection for adolescents engaged in consensual relationships. However, they caution that age alone is an insufficient measure of coercion or exploitation. They stress that multiple factors contribute to the dynamics of a relationship and that the law should focus on decriminalizing consensual, non-exploitative behaviour among adolescents while still providing safeguards against exploitative relationships.

Given that birth registration practices in our country remain inconsistent, implementing a close-in-age exemption could provide significant relief in cases where it's needed, reducing unnecessary litigation based on age discrepancies. Judicial discretion alone, as suggested by the Honourable High Court of Madhya Pradesh, may not provide a satisfactory resolution, as consensual relationships with minor age gaps would still risk criminal investigation and trial. Relying solely on judicial discretion to mitigate sentencing may not offer a viable solution. The impact of criminalizing adolescent romantic relationships extends beyond immediate legal consequences, affecting the mental and physical well-being of the young individuals involved, as well as placing additional strain on the justice system and related human resources. Case studies have highlighted the challenges faced by adolescents who engage in consensual relationships but find themselves entangled in the provisions of the POCSO Act. These cases also reveal significant gaps in the application of child-friendly procedures outlined in the Juvenile Justice Act and its corresponding rules, showing that these protective measures often remain unimplemented in practice.

The proposal to introduce a limited exception for consensual relationships involving minors aged 16 to 18 years, emphasizes that such an exception would not require changing the legal age of consent or the definition of a child. Supporters of this proposal argue that this would allow courts to differentiate between consensual adolescent relationships and genuine instances of exploitation. They stress that decriminalization should not be automatic in these cases but should depend on judicial review to determine whether consent was genuinely given and whether the relationship was exploitative. To implement this, amendments to both the POCSO Act and the IPC (and now BNS), are necessary to decriminalize consensual sexual acts involving adolescents over 16 years, while still safeguarding individuals under 18 years, against coercion or exploitation. This approach proposes maintaining the age of consent at 18 years, but carving out an exception for consensual, age-appropriate relationships among 16- to 18-year-olds. The aim is to recognize and decriminalize non-exploitative, consensual acts within this age group without weakening legal protections against abuse. It was also recommended that while the legal definition of a child remains unchanged, certain provisions could be added specifically for cases involving adolescents over 16 years. This would mean that for offenses like penetrative sexual assault or sexual assault involving minors aged 16 years and above, the courts could consider consent as a relevant factor, allowing for more nuanced handling of these cases. This approach would balance protection with fairness, ensuring that consensual relationships among older adolescents are not treated as criminal offenses while still offering full protection under the POCSO framework. Several organizations have raised strong objections to any attempt to lower the age of a child or the age of consent, cautioning that doing so could profoundly impact efforts to prevent child marriage and forced prostitution, particularly affecting young girls. Lowering these ages, they argue, could undermine legal protections and expose minors to risks with far-reaching social, psychological, and legal consequences.

From a social perspective, adolescents aged 16 to 18 years, are especially vulnerable to grooming, manipulation, and exploitation. Many young people at this age are still developing emotionally and lack the life experience to recognize or resist coercive behaviour. Permitting consent in what may be framed as "romantic" relationships between minors or between minors and adults could blur the lines between genuine relationships and exploitative ones, weakening social barriers against child marriage and increasing the risks of teenage pregnancies. These early pregnancies, in turn, are often detrimental not only to the young mother's health but also to that of the child. In many cases, this cycle leads to poorer health, limited educational attainment, and reduced economic opportunities, trapping families in multigenerational poverty.

Psychologically, adolescents are at a formative stage of emotional development, and exposure to adult relationships or responsibilities can have lasting negative impacts on their mental health and self-esteem. The demands of early marriage or parenthood can cause considerable emotional distress, especially as young individuals are ill-prepared to handle such responsibilities. Moreover, research has shown that young marriages and teenage pregnancies are associated with higher rates of depression, anxiety, and other mental health issues. Allowing adolescents to consent to adult relationships may inadvertently normalize exploitative dynamics, leading to emotional harm and stunted personal growth. Ultimately, the concern is that lowering the age of consent risks not only a violation of children's rights but also the erosion of their mental and physical dignity. The issue intersects with complex socio-economic factors, children entering such relationships are more likely to remain trapped in poverty, as early marriages and limited educational opportunities typically reduce lifetime earnings and perpetuate economic dependency. In effect, any child born from these relationships would also be pulled into the same cycle of hardship. On the legal front, altering the age of consent could weaken critical protections established under laws such as the POCSO Act and the Prohibition of Child Marriage Act (PCMA). Legal cases involving adolescent relationships frequently involve individuals who are married or planning to marry, often as a defense in court to mitigate charges. Accepting these claims could lead to a dangerous precedent, where the courts are compelled to legitimize relationships that violate child protection laws, effectively diminishing their enforceability. Furthermore, such shifts could pave the way for increased cases of trafficking, forced prostitution, and other forms of exploitation, as predators may exploit legal loopholes to justify their actions.

These organizations stress that the risks are too high to ignore. They argue that maintaining the current age limits is essential to safeguard minors from exploitation and ensuring their well-being, future opportunities, and maintaining their dignity. Legal protections must not be diluted, as doing so could lead to social and psychological harm, further marginalization, and a weakening of the societal commitment to protect vulnerable children. Lowering the age of consent carries both significant legal and social implications, particularly in relation to child marriage and the protection of minors. Legally, any decrease in the age of consent could weaken the framework established to prevent child marriage. Currently, PCMA does not specifically address the age of consent for minors in cases of sexual relations, leaving this critical protection to the POCSO Act. The POCSO Act unequivocally criminalizes sexual activities with minors, filling an essential gap left by the PCMA. This protective layer was strengthened in 2017 when the Supreme Court struck down Exception 2 to Section 375 of the IPC, which had previously exempted husbands from rape charges if their wives were between 15 and 18 years old. This landmark decision underscored the rights and autonomy of minors, recognizing their need for legal protection in marital contexts as well.

From a social standpoint, lowering the age of consent could inadvertently signal an acceptance of early marriages, giving families a perceived license to marry off girls at younger ages. This would undermine ongoing efforts to delay marriage and promote the well-being of young women, as early marriage is often associated with limited educational opportunities, early pregnancies, and restricted personal agency. Furthermore, the government is actively discussing increasing the minimum legal marriage age for girls to

21 years, aligning it with that of boys. Such a change would reflect a broader societal commitment to gender equality and a healthier transition to adulthood for young women. Any decrease in the age of consent would run counter to this progressive direction, potentially eroding the strides made in legal and social reforms aimed at protecting minors and ensuring their right to a more empowered future.

A disturbing development was highlighted from the State of Assam, wherein some parents arrange marriages between minors, or between a minor and an adult, by signing notarized agreements stating that the minor or the couple had fallen in love and, hence, the families had decided to marry them off. These incidents demonstrate that any reduction in the age of consent will inevitably provide an escape route to coerce minor girls into subjugation, marital rape, and other forms of abuse, including trafficking. A child lacks the physical and mental maturity to fully understand the concept of consent, along with the far-reaching consequences of such actions. Research by the Ministry of Women and Child Development underscores that children aged 15 to 18 years are particularly vulnerable to exploitation and abuse, a finding that raises serious concerns about the pressures and influences affecting this age group. Furthermore, the National Prevalence Study on Child Sexual Abuse by Kailash Satyarthi's Children's Foundation reveals a disturbing trend: victims of child sexual abuse frequently identify friends, romantic partners, and close acquaintances as primary perpetrators, even in severe cases involving penetrative acts.

Analysed sociologically, adolescents are navigating a complex social environment where relationships and peer influences play a significant role in shaping their understanding of trust, intimacy, and boundaries. During this formative stage, children may mistake coercion or manipulation for affection, especially when these actions are perpetrated by friends or romantic partners. This vulnerability is often compounded by social norms and pressures that discourage open conversations about consent, personal boundaries, and the risks of exploitation.

Legally, the vulnerability of children in this age group has led to strict protections under the law. Many jurisdictions have established an age of consent to guard against exploitation, recognizing that minors are not equipped to make fully informed decisions about intimate relationships. Legal frameworks, such as the POCSO Act in India, are designed to protect minors from abuse and hold perpetrators accountable, regardless of their relationship with the child. However, these protections also highlight a critical need for preventive measures, including education and awareness initiatives, to better equip young individuals to recognize abusive behaviour and seek help when needed.

By focusing on both the sociological context and the legal framework, it becomes clear that addressing child sexual abuse requires not only robust laws but also societal change, fostering an environment where children feel safe to disclose abuse and where respect for boundaries is instilled early on. Imposing alternative punishments in cases involving minors may risk trivializing the crime. However, allowing for judicial discretion with strict procedural safeguards could help ensure a fair and nuanced approach. Such discretion would enable courts to assess key factors such as the mental and physical capacity of the minor, their ability to comprehend the consequences, and the circumstances influencing the minor's consent, especially in cases involving elopement or consensual sexual relations.

When both parties are minors (under 18 years), the appropriate application of the Juvenile Justice Act (JJ Act) and its guidelines is essential. This ensures that the legal response is balanced and proportionate, preventing unjust outcomes and overly harsh consequences for young people who may lack full understanding or intent. In cases where one party is a minor and the other an adult, judicial discretion, carefully guided and applied, can offer a tailored response that accounts for differences in maturity and responsibility.

Additionally, a critical issue raised by many respondents and the beneficiaries is the limited access young girls have to essential sexual and reproductive health services. The current legal framework often deters minors from seeking help due to fear of police involvement and potential criminal charges. This limitation is both sociologically and legally problematic. On a societal level, depriving minors of health services worsens their vulnerability, often driving them towards unregulated and unsafe providers, which endangers their health and well-being. Legally, it challenges the very principles of protective law, as restrictions on health access violate minors' rights to adequate care and deepen social inequalities.

Within a sociological framework, the lack of access to these services reflects and perpetuates a culture of stigma around adolescent sexuality and reproductive health, where fear of legal repercussions overrides minors' right to necessary care. Such situations underscore the need for a balanced legal framework that protects minors without pushing them into fear, stigma, and restricted healthcare options.

The POCSO Act was introduced with the noble intention of protecting children from sexual abuse and exploitation. However, its application, especially concerning adolescent sexual behaviour, can be problematic. By criminalizing all forms of sexual activity involving minors, regardless of whether the activity was consensual or involved mutual curiosity, the law may inadvertently target and penalize young people engaging in age-appropriate exploration of their sexuality.

This creates a significant gap in the legal framework, as the law fails to distinguish between abuse and consensual exploration. For instance, adolescents often experience intense curiosity about their sexuality, which is part of normal emotional and psychological development. Criminalizing such behaviours, when no coercion or manipulation is involved, risks disproportionately penalizing minors for actions that do not align with the law's intended protective purpose.

Moreover, the law's broad application does not account for differences in age and maturity between those involved. A 16-year-old, for example, may be engaging in sexual activity with another peer, yet the law applies the same severity to their actions as it would in a case involving a child or adult perpetrator of abuse. This lack of differentiation can lead to disproportionate legal consequences, such as detention or a criminal record, which can follow these young individuals into adulthood, severely affecting their future prospects.

From a social frame of reference, this stance has serious consequences for young people and families. Adolescents, as they go through stages of sexual development, often look to their peers or even older individuals for guidance. In a society with limited open discussions about sexuality, this lack of communication leaves young people with limited understanding of their sexual rights, consent, and personal boundaries. This educational gap exacerbates the risk of misunderstandings, which may then be subjected to the criminal justice system rather than being addressed in a context of education, awareness, and guidance.

Furthermore, such a rigid legal framework can fuel unnecessary stigmatization. Adolescents who might otherwise be in a relationship of mutual affection or interest may be criminalized, creating an environment of shame and fear. Families of such individuals may be placed in difficult positions, where they must defend their child from legal consequences rather than offering them emotional support or counsel on how to navigate their sexual development.

Moreover, the broader societal implications include the reinforcement of a repressive environment around the topic of sexual education. When adolescents fear criminal repercussions for engaging in sexual activity, they may become less likely to seek help, guidance, or counselling when they face confusion, peer pressure, or exploitative situations. Ironically, instead of providing protection, the law may isolate vulnerable children and adolescents, making them less likely to speak up about genuine abuses they may face in other contexts.

The psychological toll on young individuals caught in this legal quagmire can be profound. Adolescents who find themselves labelled as offenders due to consensual yet criminalized sexual activity may experience feelings of shame, guilt, and confusion. These emotions can leave lasting scars on their self-esteem, potentially leading to issues in future relationships and sexual development. The criminalization of sexual exploration, without taking into account the developmental stage of the individuals involved, may prevent young people from fully understanding the concept of consent and respect in relationships.

Moreover, the social isolation that follows such legal repercussions can lead to increased mental health challenges, including anxiety and depression. It is crucial that the law takes into account not just the age but the emotional and psychological context of the individuals involved in such incidents, focusing on rehabilitation rather than punishment.

To align with its original intent of protecting children, the POCSO Act may need to reconsider its approach to cases involving consensual sexual activity among adolescents. A possible reform could be the introduction of differentiated legal standards that acknowledge the developmental stage of the individuals involved, allowing for more nuanced and restorative justice processes. For instance, educational programmes, counselling, and rehabilitation could be offered as alternatives to harsh legal penalties for minors who engage in consensual sexual activity.

Additionally, the law could be revised to place a stronger emphasis on distinguishing between abuse and consensual exploration, ensuring that only those who truly intend to harm or exploit children face criminal charges, while those who are engaging in mutual sexual exploration are provided with guidance, education, and resources to understand the complexities of relationships, boundaries, and consent.

In conclusion, while the POCSO Act's protective intentions are clear, its broad application can inadvertently cause harm to the very individuals it seeks to safeguard. A more refined, context-sensitive approach to the law, focusing on education, support, and rehabilitation rather than criminalization, would better serve the interests of both children and society at large.

Granting a blanket exemption to consensual sexual acts for individuals above the age of 16 years may appear to address immediate issues. However, in both legal and sociological contexts, such an exemption could create significant unintended consequences. Legally, establishing a broad exemption risks undermining protective statutes for minors by enabling de facto decriminalization whenever consent is asserted as a defence. Consent, in this regard, may become a shield too readily available, potentially leading to legal outcomes that are difficult to monitor or challenge effectively.

From a sociological perspective, consent is not always a straightforward or purely voluntary act, particularly for minors who may face coercion, manipulation, or other pressures. The structural power imbalances and social dynamics involved make it possible for consent to be manufactured or extracted, thus calling into question its authenticity. Without stringent checks, the system could inadvertently legitimize exploitative relationships, often to the detriment of vulnerable young individuals. Therefore, while a blanket exemption might simplify some legal processes, it also risks facilitating harmful social consequences, raising the need for a more subtle and cautious approach.

The proposal to carve out a limited exception for sexual relations with children aged 16 years and above is fraught with serious concerns and is highly susceptible to misuse. It is crucial to recognize that the concept of consent from a child is fundamentally flawed; any agreement made by a minor cannot be deemed valid or informed. Interpreting consent in this context is not only problematic but also detrimental to the protection of vulnerable populations.

All children deserve the full protection afforded by the specialized laws enacted for their safety and welfare. By diluting the age of consent, we risk endangering a significant portion of the child population, particularly young girls aged 16 to 18 years. This demographic would be stripped of crucial legal safeguards, exposing them to the threat of exploitation and abuse in various forms.

Additionally, the increasing prevalence of grooming and cybercrimes against minors highlights the urgent need for robust protective measures. Any legal reforms must carefully consider the broader implications, ensuring that they do not inadvertently facilitate further victimization of already at-risk individuals.

In light of these considerations, it is imperative that we uphold and strengthen existing protections for children, ensuring that they are shielded from exploitation and provided with the safe environment they deserve. In cases involving minors between the ages of 16 and 18 years, the introduction of legal exceptions has sparked discussions on the adequacy of current laws to protect vulnerable youth from exploitation. Various studies presented to the Commission, such as the one conducted by Enfold Proactive Health Trust and reviewed by the NCPCR, underscore significant gaps in understanding the nuanced dynamics involved in these cases. However, no single study provides a fully accurate or comprehensive portrayal, as most tend to focus on statistical outcomes rather than exploring the complex social realities these minors face.

From a sociological interpretive framework, adolescents are at a unique stage of development where they may be more susceptible to manipulation, particularly in relationships marked by an age gap. This stage of development is characterized by identity formation and a search for autonomy, which can make minors vulnerable to grooming by older individuals. Grooming involves an intentional process whereby an older individual may exploit the emotional and psychological vulnerabilities of a younger person, often leading them to believe the relationship is consensual when, in fact, it may involve coercive elements. When the age gap is wide, this concern becomes even more pronounced, raising questions about the authenticity of the minor's consent and the power dynamics at play. Legally, there is a tendency for courts to adopt a lenient approach, especially regarding age determination.

In many instances, courts may favour interpreting the victim as a major, which influences case outcomes significantly. This approach can weaken the protective legal framework intended to shield minors from exploitation, as it allows potential abusers to exploit legal loopholes, portraying these relationships as consensual, adult interactions. The absence of a deeper analysis into the conditions surrounding the minor's consent, such as social, psychological, and power dynamics, means that critical factors go unaddressed. Furthermore, the lack of legal scrutiny on these aspects can result in the court overlooking critical indicators of grooming or abuse. In these cases, courts might not fully consider the impact of coercion, psychological manipulation, or societal pressure on the minor's decision-making process, which undermines the spirit of laws designed to protect children from exploitation. By failing to examine the specific circumstances of the victim's consent and the potential influence of an age gap, the system risks legitimizing exploitative relationships. Therefore, a more significant approach is needed within the legal framework to balance the autonomy of older minors with protections that account for their developmental and social vulnerabilities. The introduction of standards to assess power imbalances, especially when significant age differences exist, and a requirement for rigorous analysis of the consent circumstances could enhance protections for minors. These changes would align legal outcomes more closely with sociological insights, ensuring that laws serve to protect children comprehensively from any form of grooming or exploitation.

One argument presented in favour of creating exceptions for cases involving individuals aged 16 to 18 years, is that the age of consent and the legal age for marriage serve distinct purposes and therefore should not be directly compared. The age of consent is intended to protect minors from exploitation, while the age of marriage upholds societal and legal frameworks around family and partnership. However, while this distinction may seem clear in theory, in practice, particularly given our social context, the two are often deeply intertwined. This connection is evident in numerous High Court cases where bail is granted or legal proceedings are quashed because the victim and the accused are married, sometimes even with children. In such cases, the existence of marriage becomes a significant factor in judicial decisions, reinforcing that age of consent and age of marriage cannot be viewed as separate issues. This conjunction between marriage and consent suggests a need for detailed consideration within the legal system, especially for young individuals in this age range. When sexual intercourse results in pregnancy, marriage often becomes the immediate social and legal solution, seen as a way to 'restore honour' or mitigate perceived damage to the victim.

However, separating the age of consent from the legal age of marriage presents a significant loophole. Defendants can manipulate this separation to argue retroactive 'consent' simply by marrying the victim after the offense, suggesting that marriage implies acceptance or agreement. Courts have increasingly recognized that, in many cases, accused individuals exploit this gap in the law. They may enter into marriages with their victims, not out of sincere intent, but rather as a calculated legal strategy to evade prosecution. By appearing to 'legitimize' the relationship, they shift the narrative away from criminal accountability. This tactic undermines the legal protections designed for minors; marriage becomes a shield for perpetrators rather than a safeguard for victims.

Often, once bail is granted or charges are dismissed, the accused will abandon the victim, leaving her with social stigma and emotional trauma, and with little legal recourse. Such misuse of the law reveals a critical flaw. By allowing 'consent' to be inferred through marriage, the legal system inadvertently enables child abusers to manipulate statutory protections, evade accountability, and perpetuate harm. This exploitation of consent in cases involving minors underscores the urgent need to close such loopholes, reinforcing the law's role in protecting vulnerable individuals, rather than providing a means for exploitation. Introducing judicial discretion in sentencing for cases involving sexual acts with individuals aged 16 to 18 years, represents a nuanced legal approach. It aims to balance two core objectives: safeguarding minors from sexual exploitation and recognizing the complexity of situations where factual consent may exist. In contrast to a blanket decriminalization, which could inadvertently overlook potential risks, limited judicial discretion allows the judiciary to assess each case's unique circumstances at the sentencing stage. This discretion would not be automatic but would instead operate within well-defined parameters set out in specific legal codes or guidelines.

These codes could specify the criteria under which discretion applies, such as the apparent existence of factual consent from the minor, free from coercion, deception, undue influence, or any other form of manipulation. Only a judicially trained mind, supported by expert assessments in psychology, sociology, or child development, would be equipped to evaluate the modulation of each case, including the context of consent and the maturity of the minor involved. In practice, the judge's discretion would involve a careful, evidence-based examination of factors such as the minor's age, mental and emotional maturity, and the relationship dynamics. The judge would also consider any indications of pressure, fraud, or authority that may compromise the minor's ability to provide genuine consent. By involving experts and setting clear criteria for exercising discretion, the judiciary could make informed determinations that respect the minor's autonomy while maintaining strong protective measures against exploitation.

The judicial discretion in such cases would not equate to leniency but would instead provide a structured framework allowing judges to consider the individual facts of each case. It would give them the latitude to render fair and context-sensitive decisions, promoting justice while upholding the legal and moral commitment to protect minors. This issue necessitates a comprehensive investigation and the careful presentation of evidence to ascertain whether a reduction in sentence is justified. Concerns surrounding broad judicial discretion, which may lead to arbitrary decisions influenced by gender stereotypes, are significant and have been acknowledged by the Supreme Court in *Aparna Bhatt and Ors. v. State of Madhya Pradesh and Anr.* In light of these concerns, the various commissions have contended that the discretionary authority of the Special Court in assessing consent should be both limited and structured to prevent potential misuse.

The determination of factual consent should not be left entirely in the hands of investigative agencies, as this creates opportunities for abuse and arbitrary applications of the law. Furthermore, to protect individuals from unnecessary harassment and to streamline protective proceedings, it is essential to enhance and fortify the existing frameworks for investigation and judicial determination. This approach will ensure that trials are conducted expeditiously, in accordance with the provisions of the POCSO Act, thereby reinforcing the socio-legal commitment to safeguarding the rights and dignity of vulnerable individuals while upholding justice. The intersection of consensual romantic relationships among adolescents and legal frameworks like the POCSO Act and the JJ Act raises complex socio-legal issues.

These cases often highlight the tensions between protecting minors from exploitation and acknowledging their autonomy in relationships. Firstly, the POCSO Act aims to safeguard children from sexual offenses, recognizing that minors are particularly vulnerable to exploitation. However, when it comes to consensual relationships between adolescents aged 16 to 18 years, the application of this law can lead to unintended consequences. Both parties in such relationships are technically victims of a system that criminalizes their mutual consent, yet societal perceptions often lead to a gendered narrative where boys are predominantly labeled as offenders and girls as victims. This dichotomy not only reinforces harmful stereotypes about gender roles but also undermines the shared responsibility and agency of both individuals in the relationship. From a socio-legal perspective, this situation poses significant challenges. The application of the JJ Act, which allows for more moderate considerations in cases involving minors, should ideally address these complexities.

This Act permits a more rehabilitative approach to juvenile offenders, taking into account their developmental stage and the circumstances surrounding their actions. However, when cases are treated as heinous offenses under the POCSO Act, there is a risk that the legal system may respond punitively, overlooking the underlying dynamics of adolescent relationships. Moreover, the prospect of prosecuting a child as an adult for heinous offences raises serious ethical questions. It challenges the principle of proportionality in justice, where the punishment should fit the crime and take into account the age and maturity of the offender. Treating adolescents as adults in these contexts can have lifelong implications for their futures, stifling their potential for rehabilitation and reintegration into society. Furthermore, societal attitudes towards teenage relationships often reflect broader cultural narratives that stigmatize adolescent sexuality. This stigma can lead to the criminalization of natural developmental behaviours, pushing young individuals into a system that may not adequately understand or address their needs. As such, there is a pressing need for legal reforms that not only clarify the application of existing laws but also foster a more compassionate understanding of adolescent relationships. The socio-legal implications of prosecuting consensual relationships among adolescents under the POCSO Act and the JJ Act are profound. There is a critical need for a legal framework that balances the protection of minors with a recognition of their agency, fostering a more equitable and just approach to adolescent relationships in the eyes of the law.

The complexities surrounding alleged consensual relationships between minors (16 years and older) and adults highlights several critical issues that need addressing. Here are some key points to consider further: The inherent power imbalance in adult-child relationships, often skewed by age, experience, and social status, makes it crucial to evaluate consent carefully. This evolving power dynamics between children and adolescents may not possess the emotional or cognitive maturity required to make informed decisions about relationships with significantly older individuals. Courts often struggle to differentiate between consensual relationships and exploitative ones. The focus should shift to understanding the nuances of consent, particularly in cases where the adult might exploit a child's feelings. It's essential to assess not just whether consent was given but also whether it was genuinely informed and free from coercion. The law commission's stance on recognizing the age difference as a relevant factor is significant. It acknowledges that exploitation can occur even in relationships where both parties may initially perceive their connection as consensual.

Courts must not only consider the technical age of consent but also the relational dynamics influenced by significant age disparities. The law should be attentive to coercive factors inherent in relationships where age differences are pronounced. For instance, the presence of financial dependence, social isolation, or emotional manipulation can profoundly affect a child's ability to consent freely. Introducing judicial discretion, particularly in cases where the age difference is minimal (less than three years), can be a valuable approach to ensure that the legal response is proportionate and sensitive to the realities of adolescent relationships. However, this discretion must be applied with caution to avoid undermining protections against exploitation. Consider advocating for legal reforms that provide clearer guidelines for courts when assessing cases involving alleged consensual relationships between minors and adults. This could include establishing specific criteria to evaluate the nature of the relationship, the degree of coercion, and the emotional maturity of the child. There is a need for broader public awareness regarding the implications of these relationships, particularly among young people. Educational programmes aimed at highlighting the risks of such relationships and the importance of recognizing manipulative behaviours could empower adolescents to make safer choices.

By addressing these complexities, the legal system can better protect vulnerable individuals while recognizing the realities of their experiences. These insights would contribute to an important dialogue about safeguarding children and ensuring that the law is responsive to the nuances of their relationships. The legal framework surrounding the POCSO Act and Section 63 of the BNS presents a complex interplay between protecting minors and navigating cases of adolescent relationships. Legally, the POCSO Act is stringent in its aim to protect children under 18 years, from sexual offenses, imposing strict liability regardless of context. Earlier, Section 375 of the IPC defined sexual acts involving minors as statutory rape, with an exception for marital relationships where the wife is over 15 years.

Yet, even within this provision, if the wife was under 18 years, the act was still classified as rape, reflecting a more appropriate alignment of laws with child protection standards. This legal position, however, gives rise to dilemmas, particularly in cases of consensual adolescent relationships. On one hand, the law's strict provisions seek to safeguard minors from coercion or exploitation. But on the other, the absence of flexibility can criminalize young couples who may willingly engage in relationships, not out of exploitation but emotional and romantic attachment. These laws, rooted in moral and protective imperatives, face challenges in distinguishing between consensual adolescent relationships and genuine instances of exploitation or abuse.

From a sociological stance, the law's rigid stance does not account for the nuances of teenage behaviour, particularly in societies where socialization around relationships is shifting rapidly. Modern adolescents, especially in urban settings, are increasingly exposed to ideas of romantic freedom and autonomy through digital media and societal changes. The law's inability to differentiate between consensual adolescent relationships and cases of abuse has the unintended effect of stigmatizing these young people, often placing families, the accused, and even the judiciary in a difficult position.

Thus, there is a need to reconsider how best to approach cases involving minors in consensual relationships. Some argue for limited judicial discretion to allow leniency in cases where a genuine romantic relationship exists, while still upholding the spirit of the law to protect children from exploitation. Balancing these competing interests is essential, as it would foster a legal framework that protects minors without criminalizing young relationships indiscriminately. The mandatory reporting requirement under the POCSO Act presents a significant sociological and legal barrier to accessing essential sexual and reproductive health services for minors. This hesitation can drive them toward unsafe alternatives, such as unregulated or clandestine abortions, which can lead to severe health complications or even death. The lack of awareness surrounding child sexual abuse poses significant challenges both to individual well-being and the justice system.

Children who are unaware of what constitutes abuse, or who lack the confidence to report it, remain vulnerable and unprotected. This has far-reaching consequences not only for their mental and physical health but also for the ability of law enforcement and child protection agencies to intervene and prevent further harm. In many cases, abuse goes unreported due to a lack of understanding or fear of social repercussions, which can leave perpetrators unpunished and create a cycle of continued victimization. The legal framework has evolved to recognize the rights of children and to provide mechanisms for reporting and addressing abuse. However, without a strong foundation of awareness, these laws alone are insufficient. Educational programmes that promote age-appropriate understanding of rights and boundaries are essential to empower children. These programmes could be incorporated into school curricula, with a focus not only on recognizing abusive behaviour but also on understanding that seeking help is a right, not a source of shame or stigma. Moreover, initiatives like the Rashtriya Kishor Swasthya Karyakram play an essential role in this awareness-building, as they promote adolescent health and well-being. Expanding such initiatives would address the need for more robust support systems for young people and would help instill a sense of legal empowerment.

If children understand both the nature of abuse and the protective legal mechanisms available, they are more likely to feel secure in reporting abuse, leading to better enforcement of laws and greater accountability for offenders. The socio-legal approach, therefore, demands not only laws and systems but also a shift in cultural attitudes that stigmatize victims rather than protect them. Creating awareness, building trust in support mechanisms, and ensuring that the justice system is accessible and child-friendly are all vital to breaking the cycle of abuse and silence. This integrated approach fosters an environment where children understand their rights and feel encouraged to exercise them, ultimately promoting a safer, more just society.

The rising backlog in POCSO cases, despite the establishment of fast-track special courts, reflects the judiciary's expanding responsibilities. It also highlights the challenges of ensuring justice in cases requiring immediate attention. As of January 2023, with 764 fast-track courts, including 411 dedicated POCSO courts across the country, these courts have made progress by clearing over 1,44,000 cases. However, high pendency remains, especially in cases under the POCSO Act, prompting serious concern from the Supreme Court. One factor contributing to this backlog is the inclusion of cases involving consensual adolescent relationships, which often fall under statutory interpretation as POCSO cases due to the age of those involved. These cases, though legally within the ambit of POCSO, differ in nature from cases involving actual abuse or exploitation, which demand urgent judicial attention.

The influx of consensual cases clogs an already strained system, causing delays in cases of severe abuse that critically need swift resolution. Judicial discretion could alleviate this strain by allowing courts to triage cases based on the nature and urgency of the allegations. When discretion is restored to the judiciary, fast-track courts can prioritize genuine cases of abuse, streamlining processes for handling more nuanced cases, such as those involving consensual adolescent relationships. This would significantly reduce the burden on the judicial system, allowing courts to expedite trials for cases that genuinely merit the protections of the POCSO Act. Consequently, the higher judiciary, too, would face fewer bail applications and petitions to quash proceedings, allowing it to focus on cases with profound societal impact. This shift could reorient the focus of POCSO courts toward protecting children from genuine harm while respecting the complexities of adolescent relationships, providing a more balanced, humane approach.

By refining how cases are handled based on their social and legal gravity, the judiciary can ensure that the intent behind the POCSO Act, to safeguard children, remains effective, emphasizing genuine justice over procedural congestion. This is a subtle perspective accentuating the complexities of adolescent development and the need for a measured legal approach when dealing with juveniles. Given that adolescents' brains are still developing well into early adulthood, their capacity for impulse control, risk assessment, and understanding long-term consequences remains limited. Socio-emotional development, tied to feelings of reward or punishment, can drive teens—especially those between 16 to 18 years—to engage in risky behaviours impulsively, often without fully grasping the consequences. The law, therefore, must strike a balance between acknowledging the evolving capacities of these young individuals and protecting them from potential harm, both from external influences and their own decisions.

Since physical maturity often precedes mental maturity, teens may appear adult-like in behaviour, but this doesn't necessarily equate to an adult level of understanding or responsibility. As the scientific evidence shows, the brain's decision-making and impulse-control areas are still developing well beyond adolescence, with maturity potentially extending into the mid-twenties. This delicate legal balance is crucial, as overly punitive measures might overlook the developmental limitations of adolescents, while a lenient approach could fail to address the risks associated with their behaviours. Ultimately, a comprehensive understanding of adolescent psychology and neuroscience should inform policies and interventions, ensuring they are age-appropriate and focused on rehabilitation rather than punishment. Introducing any element of consent for minors between the ages of 16 and 18 years, carries significant risks.

When a child is induced or pressured into a situation that they might not fully understand or later regret, they may initially appear to consent, but they lack the maturity and legal capacity to make informed decisions about such serious matters. If the legal system treats this initial "consent" as valid, it can lead to dismissing genuine cases where the child later realizes the exploitative nature of the situation. A limited exception or reduction in the age of consent could further complicate prosecutions, as the accused might claim that any subsequent sexual contact was voluntary, even if the child objected.

This situation could discourage children from coming forward and make it harder to protect them from repeated exploitation. Given the vulnerability and developmental stage of 16- to 18-year-olds, it's critical to preserve their high level of legal protection to prevent these apertures. Protecting this age group without any ambiguity around consent is essential, as minors in this range are still maturing emotionally and cognitively. Thus, maintaining strict laws around the age of consent ensures that any exploitation is recognized and acted upon, avoiding any misinterpretations that could otherwise harm the child. Aligning with the caution courts must exercise when dealing with cases involving adolescent relationships. Indeed, adolescence is a complex phase where impulsive decisions driven by emotions like love often blur the lines between innocence and perceived criminality. The courts, therefore, face the challenging task of distinguishing consensual relationships from exploitative ones while respecting both the autonomy and vulnerability of young individuals.

The factors such as age ambiguity, coherence in the victim's statements, and absence of inducement or threat are essential in establishing the nature of the relationship. This reinforces the importance of not only judicial prudence but also a sensitive approach that considers the potential impact of trauma or external pressures on victims. Cases involving adolescent love especially call for judicial discernment. The courts' guidance to view each case individually, with a particular focus on the consensual aspect, underscores the need for a balanced, fact-sensitive approach. This is crucial to prevent a one-size-fits-all treatment that might otherwise lead to injustice, either by wrongfully penalizing consensual acts or by failing to protect against genuine abuse. When we consider the experience of minor girls who run away from home, we can see how the tension between law and society directly impacts their lives. These girls often leave home due to a variety of factors, abusive family environments, oppressive social norms, the desire for freedom, or even the lure of romantic relationships. In many cases, their decisions are shaped by immediate pressures they feel, such as fear of punishment, violence, or a lack of autonomy, and not necessarily a clear understanding of the legal consequences of their actions.

From a sociological understanding, when these girls run away, they are stepping outside the comfort and norms of their family and community, seeking to escape oppressive conditions that may feel unbearable to them. They may be leaving a life where their social worth is tied to expectations of obedience, submission, or restricted freedom, essentially, an environment where their rights are not respected or even recognized. This personal decision, though motivated by the desire to escape, clashes with society's laws, which are structured to protect minors, prevent elopements, and ensure their safety within prescribed social and familial boundaries. As a result, these girls, who initially see their escape as an act of seeking freedom or self-expression, often end up in legal conflict. Once they are found, they are categorized as "children against the law", meaning that they have violated legal expectations set by society. The law, in this case, does not necessarily recognize the girl's reasons for leaving as valid or sympathetic, but rather views her actions as transgressions that need to be corrected. This is where the dichotomy becomes evident.

On one hand, the law is meant to protect minors, ensuring their safety, preventing exploitation, and promoting their welfare. But in the case of runaways, the law doesn't always consider the underlying socio psychological factors that led them to make this decision. The girl's actions are treated as violations of the law, running away, which may even be perceived as illegal or immoral in some societies, but the societal factors that made her feel compelled to flee are largely ignored. The girl is thus treated as a legal "offender," even though her decision may have been driven by a desire to escape abusive, oppressive, or harmful conditions. The law, in this context, creates a paradox: it is meant to protect, yet it does not always account for the subjective, personal, and socio-cultural realities that drive young girls to run away. When these girls are found, they may be punished or forced into rehabilitation, often without addressing the root causes of their decision to escape. Family violence, social pressures, or emotional distress are rarely addressed directly by the legal system, which instead focuses on enforcing societal norms, even when these norms are disconnected from the lived realities of these girls.

Moreover, these girls may end up in situations where they are further vulnerable to exploitation or harm—such as trafficking, forced labour, or abusive relationships—because they lack adequate legal protection. The system's failure to understand and respond to the psychological, emotional, and cultural reasons behind their flight leads to a punitive rather than restorative approach. In such cases, the law in its rigid form not only fails to protect these girls but may inadvertently place them at greater risk.

The key sociological issue here is how the law interacts with societal norms and lived experience. For these minors, the law rarely offers a compassionate or nuanced response. Instead, it often casts them as rule-breakers, ignoring the broader socio-cultural context that pushed them to seek agency or freedom. This creates a cycle where the law enforces conformity without addressing root causes, leaving these girls vulnerable—caught between oppressive forces that drove them to flee and a legal system that punishes them for doing so.

Thus, the contradiction lies in the law's dual role as both protector and enforcer, often out of step with the emotional and social realities these girls face. While society may fail to grasp the complexity of their choices, the law's rigidity deepens their alienation, compounding their vulnerability and limiting opportunities for recovery and reintegration.

A minor girl, barely old enough to understand the depth of her emotions, finds herself thrust into a world of confusion, heartbreak, and regret. When she left with him, she was driven by the thrill of love, the innocence of shared smiles, and dreams whispered in quiet corners of her village. To her, he was an escape from a life of restrictions—a hope for a future defined by choice rather than convention. Together, they imagined a life beyond the boundaries of her home and her parents' control.

But now, as she stands before the magistrate, watching him led away in shackles, a crushing weight settles over her. The world she imagined collapses under a reality she never foresaw. Her love, once a source of strength, now feels like a crime in the eyes of those around her. She is too young to fully understand the legalities but old enough to feel the shame and guilt thrust upon her.

Her heart breaks as she sees him—her partner in what she thought was love—now cast as a criminal. Questions swirl in her mind: *Did I do this to him? Am I to blame?* She feels abandoned in a world that condemns her without understanding, a world that sees her as foolish or rebellious. Every whispered judgment and disapproving glance deepens her isolation.

Guilt gnaws at her, but anger and confusion simmer beneath. Why can't they understand? She feels betrayed, not by him but by the adults who reduced her dreams and choices to misbehaviour to be corrected with punishment. The warmth of their imagined life has been replaced by the coldness of judgment, and she feels trapped between love and the cage of her reality.

In quiet moments, she cries for him, for the loss of their shared future. Yet the love she felt lingers, tangled with pain and regret. She wishes she could turn back time—not to erase her love, but to spare him the suffering it has caused.

The law is not always justice, and justice is not always the law".

–Author unknown

The concept of law and society is built on the relationship between formal rules and the way people live both within and beyond those rules. Society is shaped by evolving traditions, beliefs, values, and behaviours that are often fluid, subjective, and rooted in cultural practices, norms, and power structures. In contrast, law is a system of formalized rules enforced through institutions such as courts, police, and legislatures.

At the heart of the tension between law and society lies a conflict between legal mandates and societal norms. Laws are designed to impose order, justice, and equality, yet societal values do not always align with these frameworks. Cultural practices—such as gender norms or traditional family structures—can clash with laws promoting equality or individual freedoms. This creates a disconnect between legal ideals and people's lived experiences.

For example, while many societies have laws demanding gender equality, deep-rooted cultural expectations may continue to dictate roles for men and women. In such cases, the law represents an ideal of equality, while society lags behind in shifting mindsets and behaviour.

Despite this tension, law plays an essential role in regulating society. Without it, there would be no universally accepted mechanism to resolve disputes, protect rights, or maintain peace. Laws provide a framework for justice and fairness, safeguarding vulnerable groups and ensuring progress is inclusive.

However, as society evolves, law must adapt. This gap is most visible when laws struggle to keep pace with rapid social changes—such as technological advances or new social movements. Legal systems often lag, allowing societal norms to shift in ways that challenge or bypass existing frameworks. For example, digital platforms have revolutionized communication and commerce, yet laws continue to struggle with regulating online behaviour or protecting privacy effectively.

Law, therefore, becomes both a stabilising force and a source of friction. While it protects individuals from harm and exploitation, it can also reflect outdated norms, creating a gap between intent and application. Ideally, laws should evolve alongside society, balancing the preservation of order with the protection of freedoms and rights.

In a complex and diverse country like India, law is not merely a set of rules but a transformative instrument that challenges entrenched hierarchies and reshapes collective psychology. It actively redefines values, attitudes, and norms. Constitutional guarantees of equality, for example, are not just legal promises; they destabilize oppressive social structures and encourage people to view themselves and others through a lens of dignity.

Legal reforms often normalize protections for marginalized groups, gradually shifting societal perceptions. Laws like the Scheduled Castes and Tribes (Prevention of Atrocities) Act or those for women's safety not only provide protection but also signal that these groups deserve respect and inclusion. Over time, these legal standards filter into social consciousness, replacing stereotypes with empathy.

Laws initiate behavioural change not by coercion but by making progressive actions "the new normal". The Right to Education Act, for example, does more than guarantee schooling; it signals that education is a societal value, reshaping how families and communities view opportunity and childhood.

In deeply traditional societies, laws bridge the gap between custom and modernity. Legislation addressing domestic violence or child marriage, for instance, pushes communities to re-examine relationships and expectations, encouraging a progressive outlook that respects cultural identity while rejecting harmful practices.

The legal system also shapes collective memory, redefining what society honours and protects. Policies like reservations for historically marginalized communities acknowledge systemic injustices and chart a path toward healing, embedding fairness and equity into cultural identity.

Finally, laws like the Right to Information Act and anti-corruption measures strengthen trust in institutions by promoting transparency and accountability. When people see justice upheld, trust in governance deepens, reshaping the social contract and fostering a citizenry that believes in law as a tool for justice and societal transformation.

A society evolves when individuals feel empowered to assert their rights. Landmark judicial decisions, like the decriminalization of homosexuality or the recognition of privacy rights, empower individuals to live without fear of discrimination or persecution. This empowerment is transformative because it encourages people to challenge limiting beliefs about themselves and others, fostering a more liberated, inclusive society where personal dignity becomes a shared value. In essence, law in a society as multi-layered as India is not simply about enforcement; it is about gradually guiding society to recognize its most inclusive, just, and humane self. Legal frameworks evolve into social frameworks that prompt people to question, learn, and, ultimately, grow. By subtly reshaping mindsets and relationships, the law becomes an enduring tool for societal transformation, paving the way for unity amid diversity, respect amid difference, and progress that honours everyone's right to belong. The mist in the sky can be cleared only through the sagacious contrivance of law. Otherwise, it will dampen the paper wings with which these girls aspire to fly in the sky!

Chapter 4

THE SKY'S PROMISE

"Don't make me feel guilty or punish me, going missing might be how I cope when I can't ask for help."
- **Missing People**, Registered charity in England and Wales (1020419) and in Scotland (SC047419)

She went out in search of something she earnestly wanted. In this inordinate ordeal, she lost everything she had, everything she was. A missing case was registered with the police to find her. And then, they found her. All the physical characteristics mentioned in the case regarding her age, height, weight, identification marks on the body, colour of her hair, skin, and the list can go on. Everything matched perfectly. The photograph given by the family was of the same girl who was found. Each physical attribute mentioned in the case diary was the same, but the person who went missing and the person found were not the same. A young girl with a dream in her eyes and conviction in her heart went missing. But what was found was a young girl with fear in her eyes and an inconsolable heart. A girl went missing, and a victim was found. The case eventually stands closed with the police.

Do we really need to underline this homologous gap between what is lost and what is found? Can we ever, recouple the fallen leaf with the tree it belonged to? Is this grave concern shadowed by our callous conscience? These questions are often found oscillating between essentialism and the existing functional imperatives.

There are undoubtedly myriad factors that engender this missing menace, as mentioned in the previous chapters. During my stint as Superintendent of Police in Betul district, I organized a one-day workshop for all the girls who had gone missing and were rescued by the police over a period of two years. The sole attempt was to interact with these girls—just to know their version of the story in an informal setting. A private marriage lawn was selected for this purpose. Counters of various departments were also placed to apprise these young lives of ongoing government schemes and programmes. To our surprise, almost eighty percent of the girls turned up, some accompanied by their husbands and children.

All supervisory officers of police at the sub-divisional level in the district, along with a few officers working at the police station level, were invited to participate in this interactive workshop. The idea was to learn their perspective on things and try to understand any post-rescue trauma they were experiencing. The girls spoke about the discomfort they faced in court, the threatening encounters from the family of the accused—which they and their family members had to confront—the change in attitude of their family and friends towards them, and the confusion and anxiety they felt when thinking about their future. We didn't have solutions to many, or I may confess, the majority of these problems. But at least the police was present to listen and comprehend their plight.

In all the districts I have served so far, two-wheeler parties of women police were formed in each police station. Apart from their regular police duties, they maintained a register of female victims of all cases residing in their jurisdiction. Regular visits were made to the victims' residences to inquire about their well-being. However, these interactions often took place within the victims' own ecosystems, which meant that we frequently received guarded responses, tutored replies, and shadowed opinions. This workshop, however, provided them with the opportunity to breathe freely and speak fearlessly. Nevertheless, it was the police who benefitted the most. Interacting with victims always deepens our comprehension of crime and sharpens our interpretation of crime patterns. The workshop also helped the girls discover a sense of conviviality with one another. The guilt, pain, and anger burning inside them seemed to diffuse, to some extent, with the assurance that they were not alone—that many others had endured similar turbulence in their lives. Many exchanged contact details, formed new friendships, and found solace in this shared experience.

Often, for the purpose of rehabilitation, every victim is subsumed under one category. We fail to account for the nuances involved. The only common thread running through all of them is that they are victims under the purview of Section 363 IPC, now Section 137 BNS. The empirical variations shaping each victim's journey—from provenance to fate—are invariably overlooked. That one day spent was an eye-opening experience for me. A one-size-fits-all approach has proved ineffectual in the process of rehabilitation. When the stories are different, how can the endings be the same? How can wounds of varying severity be treated with the same medicine? When each victim has a unique story of victimization, how can a single, standardized rehabilitation programme suffice? Rehabilitation efforts must deal with the specifics of each case.

A victim should not be studied solely on the basis of the crime inflicted upon her. Rather, this partial analysis needs to be complemented with an understanding of the prevailing simultaneous socio-psychological equations. Every individual is a product of complex codes and the organizational structures to which they belong. Through the process of socialization, individuals adapt to and internalize the norms, values, customs, and behaviours of their shared social group (Lutfey & Mortimer, 2006; Parsons, 1951). The degree to which children learn how to participate in and be accepted by society has important consequences for their development and future lives.

In her research article *Socialization in Childhood and Adolescence*, Lara Perez-Felkner enumerates that the social codes children and adolescents learn are specific not only to nation-states and regions of the globe but also to historical periods and social groups within larger societies. The socio-historical context is a critical dimension of the socialization of children and adolescents, both in terms of their status within society (as compared to adults) and their social roles. It is also vital to consider that individuals in the same society do not necessarily share a sense of belonging to the dominant culture within that group. While studies of socialization theory often emphasize the influence of broader society, individuals frequently experience simultaneous socialization pressures from the dominant culture as well as from marginalized subcultures. Notably, research has documented the socializing influence of adolescent peer cultures and of parent cultures in reproducing social class and other social divisions (S. Hall & Jefferson, 1976; Willis, 1977).

In recent times, a new sociology of childhood has emerged. This scholarship aims to elevate the status of childhood and promote in-depth research on the subject. New childhood scholars argue that children are agentic beings and should be framed as such in research (King, 2007; Pufall & Unsworth, 2004). More specifically, this literature breaks away from a focus on how children are socialized into future adults, focusing instead on childhood as a topic worthy of serious study, not merely a stage on the path to adulthood (James, Jenks, & Prout, 2005; Mathews, 2007). This shift in how children are theorized in research characterizes childhood as a socially constructed category that is understood differently over time (Handel et al., 2007).

Adolescence was first identified by G. Stanley Hall (1904), who characterized young people in this stage as experiencing emotional, behavioural, and psychological upheaval as they transit biologically from childhood to adulthood (Perez-Felkner, Lara). At present, adolescence as a phenomenon emerged following industrialization and the elongation of compulsory schooling, which clustered young people together in urban areas. With growing independence from their families, young people were increasingly free to engage in political revolutions, crime, deviance, and to loosen their sexual mores (Kett, 1977).

However, globalization has influenced social changes in the life course across nations, making adolescence a stage of life increasingly experienced by young people (Larson & Wilson, 2004; Shanahan, 2000). It is certain, however, that "normal" adolescence and the transition to adulthood vary across time, subgroups, and cultures (Schoon, McCulloch, Joshi, Wiggins, & Bynner, 2001; Shanahan, 2000). Social and economic conditions can alter normative patterns in young people's transitions from childhood to adulthood. Societal challenges such as poverty and violence can constrain youth's ability to develop independence and meet traditional age markers, disrupting the possibility of occupying traditional adult roles (Cole, 2011). Similarly, the introduction of global capitalism can shift traditional norms for youth and foster rejection of traditional lifestyles in favour of new ones (Liechty, 2003).

Economic and societal changes can disrupt normative pathways to adulthood (Cole, 2005). For example, departure from the family home and other such markers of adulthood can be shaped not only by age norms but also by economic shifts (Billari & Liefbroer, 2007; Settersten, 1998). Indeed, norms and pressures around the timing of leaving the family home have been found to be culturally and historically specific (Holdsworth, 2000). For this and other reasons, it is especially important to use careful and rigorous methods to understand the development of young people and how various forces in their lives socially influence their growth. These factors impose intense reverberations on the way a victim reacts to a particular crime inflicted on her. The consequential ramifications differ for every victim.

Presently, the policies and programmes are drafted only cater to a broader group or category. I believe that these generalized assumptions should also accommodate for factualism in its approach. Although, individualistic desideratum cannot be accounted for but the approach in policy and programme designing should be all-encompassing and more inclusive to yield tangible results. In reference to the victims in the existing context, relief should be in conjunction with the grief. Following categories can broadly be identified for relatively better understanding of the victims.

Conscience-stricken

An adolescent girl in pursuit of her own ideas about life and self, finds herself lost in the mundane world. A once-confident soul is rescinded by the realism. Her confidence is confronted by the complications of the real world and she is compelled to return home. Sometimes, the guilt is so overwhelming that she waits for a family member or the police to take her back. When she left home, she was phlegmatic about herself and optimistic about her avocation. She falls flat on her face from the apotheosis of her imagination.

During this ordeal, she is cheated by her known acquaintances, she is disappointed by the turn of events, deeply afflicted by her circumstances and anguished by the decisions she made. The state of her mind is extremely frangible. She experiences low self-esteem, depression and hopelessness.

In such cases, attempts should be made to address self-esteem deficits. An adolescent mind with low self-esteem evaluates itself as unworthy and incompetent, which has a profound influence on her thoughts, emotions, and responses to stressful life events. During adolescence, there is an increased focus on the self and the internal world of thoughts and feelings (Harter, 1990; Rosenberg, 1986). Adolescents become increasingly self-aware and better able to evaluate themselves, making self-esteem more salient during this stage of life.

Therefore, when self-esteem is low, it is likely to be a persistent issue and may become a central focus of the adolescent's life. Such a consuming problem can cause significant emotional distress (James C. Overholser, Dalia M. Adams, Kim L. Lenhart, David C. Brinkman). Low self-esteem appears to become a more prominent feature of depression as a child matures. This becomes even more relevant during adolescence because many other changes coincide with this phase of life, including new interests, greater responsibilities, and frequent stress from peers, school, and family (Larson & Ham, 1993). Adolescence is often a period of considerable self-criticism and turmoil in terms of self-concept (Rosenberg, 1985).

Low self-esteem in children can significantly influence their decisions to run away from home, even after being rescued. Children with low self-esteem often feel inadequate, unworthy, or unloved, which can create a profound sense of isolation.

Children who struggle with low self-esteem may perceive their home environment as a source of criticism or neglect. They may feel that they do not belong or are not valued by their families, leading them to consider running away as an escape from the emotional pain they experience at home.

These children might believe that they will find acceptance or validation outside their homes. They may be drawn to peers or groups that offer a sense of belonging, even if these relationships are unhealthy or risky.

Low self-esteem can impair a child's ability to make thoughtful decisions. They may act impulsively, feeling that quarantine is a viable solution to their problems without considering the potential dangers or consequences of their actions.

When children feel powerless in their circumstances, setting apart may appear to be one of the few options they have to regain control over their lives. This need for agency can overshadow the potential risks associated with leaving home.

Children with low self-esteem are often more vulnerable to manipulation and exploitation. They in search of acceptance, only find themselves in dangerous situations or become victims of exploitation, such as human trafficking.

They may lack the coping strategies necessary to deal with challenges or conflicts at home. Instead of seeking help or communicating their feelings, they may resort to suicidal ideation as a misguided solution.

As recapitulated, low self-esteem can create a cycle of negative emotions and thoughts that push children to consider running away from home. Addressing self-esteem issues early on is crucial to helping children develop resilience and healthier coping mechanisms. Low self-esteem may indirectly increase the risk of suicidal ideation by increasing the adolescent's hopelessness and pessimism about the future. Hopelessness involves the perception that current problems are likely to continue with little expectation of any positive change. The victim may feel unable to bring about positive changes in her life and is likely to have negative expectations for the life ahead. Over the years many counselling techniques have been developed to provide evidence-based outpatient therapy to the adolescent victims. The wide range of counselling approaches prominently used to address the unique needs of teens are

Cognitive Behavioural Therapy (CBT): This approach focuses on identifying and changing negative thought patterns and behaviours. It helps teens who struggle with anxiety, depression and other mood disorders. It is a short term, goal-oriented approach that yields quick results. The counsellor needs to take account of the background of the victim and nuances of the crime setting. Clifford Geertz (1973) famously explains that simple behaviours can have complex meanings that can only be understood if the researcher also understands the culture in which that behaviour occurs.

Dialectical Behavioural Therapy (DBT): This combines elements of CBT with mindfulness practices. It is effective in dealing with teens who struggle with intense emotions, self-harm or suicidal thoughts. Every action and the reaction of the victim to every action needs to be studied by the counsellor. Arriving at the same platform with the victim is a prerequisite to this therapy.

Trauma-focussed Cognitive Behavioural Therapy (TF-CBT): This evidence-based approach helps teens process traumatic experiences in a safe and supportive environment. It promotes coping skills and fosters a sense of empowerment and control. TF-CBT provides a constructive outlet for emotions, helping to release pain and reduce emotional distress.

Following any one or a mix of these approaches can help replace a victim's negative thoughts with more positive and constructive ideas. The counsellor's expertise is essential to ensure positive results; without it, the process risks being reduced to an official formality—mere paper-shuffling of a case diary. The task is akin to replanting a derooted plant in its original soil. It is both tough and delicate. The soil must first be carefully loosened and nourished so the plant can take root again—strongly enough that it never becomes derooted. Undoubtedly, the victim's family has a climacteric role in this process. Parents must be counselled to understand the emotional instability and turmoil their child is experiencing. They must also learn to appreciate her vision for life, her aspirations, and her ambitions, and these must be accommodated within the family structure. The plant cannot simply be placed back into the same soil; the soil must first be prepared, as this is the essential first step for lasting healing.

Early socialization is thought to occur primarily within the family (Grusec, 2011). Psychologists have long emphasized the parent–child relationship, with particular focus on mother–child dyads (Gardner, Ward, Burton, & Wilson, 2003; Spinard, 2007). Research from psychology, anthropology, and other disciplines has documented how families prepare children for the social world around them. Briggs' ethnographic study (1970) detailed how Inuit families train their children to regulate emotional behaviour into more socially acceptable forms—specifically, prohibiting displays of anger. Recent studies similarly confirm that families are a key context for emotional socialization, both across and within cultures (Friedlmeier, Corapci, & Cole, 2011).

Research also shows that families strongly influence children's orientation toward education. Adolescents whose parents engage them in conversations about school tend to hold higher educational aspirations and perform better academically (Juang & Silbereisen, 2002). Likewise, parents' high expectations are associated with greater academic achievement (Pong, Hao, & Gardner, 2005). Although the effects of parental involvement on adolescents' performance may wane during high school (Muller, 1998), family background and parents' expectations remain critical in shaping adolescents' educational and career ambitions, as well as their later accomplishments (Hauser, Tsai, & Sewell, 1983).

In majority of the missing children cases, however, it is observed that parents are often preoccupied with securing the family's basic needs, leaving little time to converse meaningfully with their children. Financial strain may also limit parents' ability to understand or nurture their children's aspirations. This gap is particularly stark for girls, who often have fewer opportunities to be heard or understood. When an outsider finally lends an ear to these unspoken desires, they may be perceived as a rare saviour—a dynamic that can easily spiral into manipulation or exploitation.

The decision of a child, particularly a girl, to move out or run away from her family is often influenced by various aspects of socialization within the family environment. This phenomenon can be examined through the lens of certain social psychological theories, in order to consolidate the rehabilitation efforts and understand what a child expects. Each of these frameworks provides insights into how family dynamics shape a child's behaviour and choices.

Social Learning Theory, proposed by Albert Bandura, posits that individuals learn behaviours, attitudes, and values through observation and imitation of others, especially significant role models in their lives, such as parents and siblings. In a family context, a child may observe behaviours related to conflict resolution, emotional expression, or coping mechanisms. If a child witnesses frequent conflict, neglect, or abuse, she may learn that leaving the home is a viable option for escaping negative situations. For instance, a girl who sees her mother tolerating abuse or unhappiness without taking action may internalize the belief that her own suffering is inevitable. Conversely, if she observes a sibling or peer successfully leaving a troubling situation and thriving independently, this may serve as a powerful model, prompting her to consider running away as a means of asserting her autonomy and seeking a better life.

Another framework is set forth by the Role Theory, which focuses on the expectations and behaviours associated with social roles, can also shed light on a child's decision to leave home. In many families, traditional gender roles dictate specific behaviours and responsibilities for girls, often centered around nurturing, obedience, and subservience. When a girl feels constrained by these roles, she may experience a sense of entrapment. For example, if her family expects her to prioritize domestic responsibilities over personal ambitions or education, she may feel that her identity is limited. The pressure to conform to these roles can lead to resentment and a desire for escape. In this context, running away becomes a form of rebellion against the restrictive expectations imposed by her family and society.

Another perspective is offered by the Theory of Planned Behaviour, developed by Icek Ajzen, which suggests that an individual's intention to engage in a behaviour is shaped by attitudes, subjective norms, and perceived behavioural control. For a girl considering escape, her attitudes toward running away may stem from her family dynamics and the broader social context. If she views leaving home as a necessary response to abuse or lack of autonomy, her intention to act may strengthen. Subjective norms—her perception of how peers or community members view running away—can further influence her choice. If she believes her peers support escaping difficult family circumstances, she may feel validated. Perceived behavioural control, or her belief in her ability to manage life independently, also plays a role. A girl with financial resources or social support may feel more confident and see running away as a realistic option.

The socialization process within a family plays a crucial role in shaping a child's attitudes and behaviours, influencing choices such as running away from home. By examining this issue through the lenses of these socio - psychological frameworks, we can better understand the complex interplay of environmental factors, social roles, and personal agency that contribute to such significant life choices. This underscores the importance of nurturing healthy family dynamics and providing children with the emotional and psychological support they need to thrive within their familial contexts, once they are rescued.

While I was serving as a trainee IPS officer (Asst. SP) in district Indore, Madhya Pradesh, the daughter of a petty grocery shop owner went missing. Her mother stitched clothes for a living. The couple had four daughters, and both husband and wife worked from home. The grocery shop was just a large window of their house opening toward the road, and the mother worked on a hand-held sewing machine inside. Despite the parents being present at home all the time, the family rarely interacted in a way that could build a harmonious relationship. Conversations were mostly restricted to mundane exchanges.

The girl who went missing wanted to pursue a career as a badminton player. She tried to express her dreams on various occasions at home, but her aspirations were dismissed with conventional reasoning. After several failed attempts to be heard, she decided to leave. She was already training at a local badminton academy in Indore, the best her family could afford. A male friend suggested that to pursue badminton professionally, she needed admission to a renowned national-level academy. He assured her, he had the contacts to make it happen. She trusted his false claims.

She left home with all her parents' savings to join this man on her journey to achieve her dream. He was in his late twenties, married, and a father of two. Together, they boarded a train and reached Hyderabad, where she attempted trials at a reputed academy. She was rejected in the initial tests. Soon, all the savings of her parents were spent on food, accommodation, and travel. Her confidence crumbled along with her dreams.

Shattered, she stayed at the Hyderabad railway station, unable to summon the courage to return home. The man left for Indore using a ticket purchased with her money. Three days later, the police rescued her from the station. When she saw us, she broke into tears, relieved to be saved from what had become a long and traumatic ordeal. She returned home, clinging to the hope of starting afresh.

The girl came back with the police to Indore, to her family. The economics of the family was such that it compelled the parents to relentlessly blame the girl. They blamed her for the disrespect she effectuated to the family, the lost savings which was their only reinforcement. Many counselling sessions were conducted. But in this particular case, the counsellors failed to establish an empathic alliance with the victim. They could not even succeed in achieving affinity towards the concern of the parents. The situation retrogressed to the initial status. Unable to sail through the troubled waters, the girl committed suicide. A thirteen-year-old, who had all the probability in the world to accomplish what she desired to become. But the existing mechanism we had could not convince her. We could not make her parents understand that her life was far more valuable than their savings of fifty thousand rupees. Everyone failed her.

We rescued her and inveigled her to stay in the same set of situations from which she ran. How can we expect her to survive in a situation that has worsened? Indeed, it is criminal to leave the victim on their own for the survivorship. The differentials existing in every case are often not counted upon during rehabilitation. The prevailing schemes carved out to recuperate the victim need to factor in these stark differentials that exist in every case.

Emotional deficits are likely to have generalized and lasting impact on an adolescent's social and emotional adjustment, potentially increasing tendencies for depression and hopelessness. Furthermore, low self-esteem can inhibit participation in activities that could otherwise help to enhance a person's self-esteem. This may become self-perpetuating whereby social withdrawal further reduces the person's confidence level. Improving the person's ability and willingness to engage in different social activities may serve an important role in the treatment of low self-esteem (Brennan, 1985). Programmes designed to identify self-esteem deficits early could make positive changes that would reduce the risk of adolescent's becoming depressed or suicidal. For many victims, their definition of self is fragile and limited to a few general areas of their life. For example, social functioning may play an important role in the self-esteem of some adolescents, whereas athletic or academic skills may be important for others. The self-esteem in males is often based on the accomplishment of specific goals whereas females emphasize social relationships and personal qualities (Overholser, 1993). Improvement in one or more areas related to self-esteem can have a profound impact on the person's emotional well-being.

Rehabilitation programmes need to be restructured and redesigned to enhance self-esteem by working on the particular strengths and interests of each individual.

Regular counselling sessions need to be conducted for the parents of the affected children. It is an arduous exercise to change the mindset of the parents as their perspectives and the attitude towards life are conveniently predetermined. Effort can be made to help them in accommodating the ambitions and aspirations of their child. Once the parents become permissive, it easier to persuade other members of the family, which may include grandparents and siblings. The aim is to make the family asset to the child and not to become impediment in realization of her dreams.

Dyed in the wool

A young life, in her quest for the unknown, gets trapped in the dark tunnels of society. Her body and mind are forced to submit to the monstrosities inflicted upon her. Regular doses of drugs administered to her make her appear older than her years. Her mind is conditioned to accept the terms of the business she has been thrust into. Her brutal present is hardened into what she comes to see as her ultimate fate. She is made to believe that she is anchored irrevocably to her final destination.

This becomes all the more challenging as the victim's vision is completely blinded by the darkness of society's deepest den. One sees only what one has been inured to see. One of my colleagues in a neighbouring district rescued three sisters, aged between nine and twelve. Under the pretext of a minor family quarrel, they had left their home in the early hours and made their way to the highway.

There, they were lured and abducted by a truck driver. All three were sold in a red-light area in a district of Rajasthan.

After a prolonged and painstaking six-month effort, the girls were rescued. It was a task of immense pride for the police, given that the evidence available was fragile and scattered. The parents were filled with gratitude and admiration for the officers involved. This trailblazing case even became part of the curriculum in police training academies. From the police perspective, the case can be considered closed—what was missing was found and safely returned.

Out of curiosity about the case, I called my colleague. I wanted to acquaint myself with the nuances of the investigation carried out by the team. To my surprise, the SP was still grappling with emerging issues months after the rescue operation. All three girls were readmitted mid-academic session, following an assiduous effort by the police, to the local school in their village. Yet, after two months, they dropped out again.

Instead of shielding the girls from prying eyes and curbing the dubious attitudes of the school staff and their peers, the school administration sided with the police through a cautiously admonishing stance. They claimed, with near clairvoyance, that they had already predicted this outcome. Consequently, the police faced accusations of failing to believe in the school's "prophecy". The unfolding events had rendered the police the sole guardians of these three young girls.

Research has shown that during adolescence, young people often begin affiliating with larger peer groups or crowds associated with particular identities. These affiliations typically wane as adolescents develop a stronger sense of self independent of the crowd (Brown, Eicher &

Petrie, 1986). Young people actively engaged in school and its activities tend to show more positive adjustment than those focused primarily on peer acceptance (Barber, Eccles & Stone, 2001; Feldman & Matjasko, 2005). Schools serve as a primary site of socialization for children and adolescents, where relationships outside the home gain increasing importance (Eccles & Roeser, 2011; Schneider, 2010).

Although schooling structures can perpetuate existing social class hierarchies (Bourdieu, 2000; Willis, 1977), they also function as mechanisms for upward mobility. School social contexts critically shape socialization toward education and career, directly influencing students' outcomes (Hallinan, 2006; Stanton-Salazar & Spina, 2000). Relationships formed through school provide access to resources and support, fostering the achievement of academic and career goals. The quality of these relationships has proven to be a significant factor in youth academic achievement (Bryk & Schneider, 2002; Crosnoe, Johnson & Elder, 2004). Within schools, students and staff exchange social capital—norms, expectations, and sanctions—to enhance educational outcomes (Coleman, 1988). Access to these resources, however, is complicated by racial, ethnic, and class differences, which may limit underrepresented families' ability to build ties with teachers and highly educated families (Carter, 2003; Lareau & Horvat, 1999; Ream, 2005).

To understand how the present education system contributes to the increased incidence of missing girls or school dropout rates, particularly in the Indian and rural context, it is essential to examine the deeper structural, social, and theoretical underpinnings that exacerbate these phenomena. Theories from sociology, education, and feminist studies offer critical insights into how systemic failures intersect with societal norms, leading to the vulnerabilities faced by young girls.

Pierre Bourdieu's theory of cultural capital offers an important framework for understanding how schools, as institutions, often reinforce existing social inequalities rather than serve as mechanisms for mobility. In rural India, the education system does not function as a neutral space; instead, it perpetuates patriarchal and caste-based hierarchies. Schools often prioritize curricula that implicitly reinforce traditional gender roles, perpetuating the idea that girls' primary roles are domestic, rather than intellectual or professional. This institutional bias can alienate girls who, recognizing the incongruence between their education and the limited roles society allows them, may feel education is irrelevant to their future prospects, leading to disengagement and eventual dropout.

The hidden curriculum—the unspoken norms and values conveyed within educational settings—often supports the reproduction of these inequalities. Girls in rural areas are not merely passive recipients of this education; they are actively negotiating the social expectations placed upon them. When education fails to challenge these expectations and instead upholds them, it increases the pressure on girls to conform to familial and societal roles, such as early marriage or domestic labour. In some cases, girls may run away as an act of resistance against these limitations, seeking autonomy in a world that offers them few legitimate options.

Paulo Freire's theory of critical pedagogy emphasizes the role of education in liberating oppressed populations through a dialogic process that fosters critical consciousness. However, in the rural Indian context, the education system often falls short of this emancipatory potential. Schools rarely encourage girls to question their social circumstances or to engage critically with the gender norms that shape their lives. Instead, they are often taught to accept their roles within the domestic sphere, reinforcing their subordination.

This lack of critical engagement leads to a kind of "banking education," where information is deposited into students without fostering any meaningful understanding or transformation. Girls may internalize the message that education is not a path to independence but merely a phase before marriage, leading to high dropout rates. Furthermore, the lack of critical consciousness-building opportunities makes it difficult for girls to envision alternative futures for themselves, leaving them vulnerable to elopement, exploitation, or even trafficking when they seek escape from oppressive home environments.

Kimberlé Crenshaw's theory of intersectionality is particularly useful in analyzing the challenges faced by rural girls. In addition to gender, factors like caste, class, and geography intersect to create unique forms of marginalization. For example, Dalit girls in rural areas face both gender-based discrimination and caste-based exclusion, which severely limits their access to quality education and social mobility. The educational system, as it exists, does not address these compounded vulnerabilities, instead perpetuating exclusion through segregated schools, caste-biased curricula, and teacher prejudices.

The intersection of economic hardship and educational marginalization plays a crucial role in high dropout rates. Families in poverty often view education as a luxury they cannot afford, especially for daughters, who are expected to contribute to household labour or marry early. Theories of social reproduction, such as those proposed by Bourdieu and Jean Anyon, emphasize how schools often reflect the economic disparities of society, with fewer resources allocated to rural and marginalized communities. This under-resourcing further entrenches the cycle of poverty and illiteracy, further disillusioning girls who see little benefit in continuing their education.

Feminist geographers such as Doreen Massey argue that space and mobility are inherently gendered, particularly in rural contexts where the movement of women and girls is heavily restricted by social norms. In the Indian rural context, schools may be located at considerable distances from girls' homes, and the routes to school are often unsafe due to risks of sexual harassment, assault, and even abduction. The lack of physical safety acts as a powerful deterrent to school attendance, particularly once girls reach puberty.

The feminist theory of "patriarchal bargaining," coined by Deniz Kandiyoti, suggests that women and girls make strategic choices within the constraints of patriarchy to maximize their autonomy and safety. For young girls in rural areas, running away or eloping may be seen as the only viable option to escape an environment that denies them education, safety, and autonomy. This is not merely an act of rebellion but a calculated response to oppressive social structures that restrict their agency and confine them to roles of domestic servitude.

From a structuralist perspective, Immanuel Wallerstein's world-systems theory provides insights into how global economic inequalities manifest locally, particularly in rural India. Economic pressures on rural families, exacerbated by agrarian crises, unemployment, and lack of government support, mean that educating daughters is often seen as an economic burden rather than an investment. The opportunity cost of sending a girl to school, when she could be contributing to household labour, becomes too high for many families.

Additionally, the neoliberal policies of privatization and cuts in public funding for education have disproportionately affected rural areas. Underfunded government schools lack basic infrastructure, qualified teachers, and gender-sensitive facilities such as safe sanitation, making them inhospitable environments for girls. This underfunding aligns with Nancy Fraser's concept of "participatory parity," which argues that justice requires equal participation for all members of society. In this case, the structural denial of adequate educational resources to rural girls represents a fundamental injustice, leading to their disengagement from formal education.

Efforts to prevent girls from dropping out or running away are hampered by multiple systemic failures. The lack of a gender-responsive education system, combined with deeply rooted cultural norms, creates an environment where girls are socialized to believe that their role is secondary to men's, both within the family and society. Moreover, there is an absence of comprehensive, community-based approaches that engage with families, address gendered violence, and provide economic incentives to keep girls in school. Inadequacies in legal and social frameworks also play a role. While policies such as the Right to Education Act exist, their implementation is weak, particularly in rural areas where girls are most vulnerable. The failure to provide vocational and life-skills education leaves girls without practical skills or confidence to navigate the challenges of adulthood, making marriage or running away seem like the only viable options. To address these issues, a radical transformation is needed—one that involves restructuring the curriculum, providing comprehensive safety and support mechanisms, and challenging the social norms that confine girls to subservient roles.

Over time, when victims accept and adapt to the darkness as the ultimate truth of their lives, any light that comes their way appears unbearable. In this case, the parents found it arduous to protect their daughters in their surroundings from the humiliating label of being "available". The parents were daily wage earners and could not guard their children at all times from every gaze and comment in the village. The girls had developed an inclination toward a comfortable life away from the hardships of rural living. The parents approached the police again with their concerns. After a lengthy process of deliberations with another department, the girls were admitted to a tribal hostel. Within a month, one of the girls escaped from the hostel with a boy she knew from a neighbouring village. She was rescued and readmitted to the hostel.

During the process of transition, change must not only be accepted but actively implemented. The unpredictability of emotions makes change management challenging. Willingness to change must be established before the change itself occurs. This can be achieved through regular counselling sessions led by experts well-versed in the socio-psychological dynamics at the local level. Regional counsellors should be identified and trained in national institutes to ensure they are culturally and socially acceptable to those they counsel.

The acceptability of the counsellor is a prerequisite for effective change. Without a strong rapport between counsellor and victim, sessions risk being perceived as routine official formalities. At present, counselling directives are often treated like sermons to be heard rather than acted upon. This is similar to attempts to teach foreign languages in remote areas, where unfamiliar examples fail to resonate—just as "A" can stand for both "apple" and "aam" (mango). References must be relatable to the local context. Effective counselling should combine scientific techniques with regional expressions and cultural relevance.

Proper documentation is essential to monitor a child's progress. Without it, rehabilitation becomes generic, and improvements remain unmapped. Scientific counselling in the local dialect by a local counsellor yields the best results, particularly in sensitive cases. The number of counsellors and the quality of rehabilitation sessions must be carefully managed. Every life is valuable, and victims cannot be left to survive on their own.

Juvenile and impressionable minds effortlessly absorb whatever comes their way. Once these young minds are "painted" with a certain perspective, it becomes difficult to remove, though attempts can be made to fade it and eventually repaint it positively. A persistent approach is required to address the issues present in the victim's surroundings.

These special cases certainly require specialized expertise to execute the change. More distinctive training programmes for the teaching staff should be designed to handle such delinquent students who are readmitted after dropping out from the same school. Special counsellors with appropriate psychological proficiency may be appointed at the schools as well. The school staff and the school mates should understand the special situation the child is confronting, rather than deflating him or her. The parents along with other family members needs to be oriented towards the exceptional needs the turn of events have created.

This experience recounted by my colleague reminded me of an exploration undertaken by my mother with the Banchhada community in Ratlam district, Madhya Pradesh. The Banchhada are a tribe in central India traditionally associated with prostitution, which has been passed down through generations, with young girls groomed for the profession. At that time, my father was posted as the district administrator of Ratlam—this was nearly thirty-five years ago.

My mother published an intriguing article in the leading Hindi magazine *Dharmyug*, bringing the issue to public attention. Substantial efforts were made to improve the community's circumstances. Special hostels were established for children who wished to study; intra-community marriages were encouraged; new houses and colonies were constructed; community spaces were created for regular counselling and vocational training; and agricultural land was distributed. This multifaceted, pragmatic approach became a flagship programme during my father's tenure.

However, with the end of his term, the momentum dissipated. The colony, which had been relocated far from the highway after months of effort, returned and resettled near the highway in just a few days. Men in the community, who had depended on the income of female members, found it difficult to cultivate land and support their families. Middlemen, who had facilitated the community's traditional business while shielding them from legal repercussions, actively opposed these development initiatives. The status quo heavily benefited both the men and the middlemen.

Nevertheless, some positive outcomes were achieved. A few children admitted to the hostels completed their education and secured respectable jobs. Others who wished to live dignified lives found opportunities to do so. Yet, even today, the tribe largely remains in the same geographic location and continues with the profession for which it was historically notorious.

In my family, I am the third generation to enter the civil services and all three of us belong to the same cadre. I have witnessed officer-centric initiatives aimed at addressing problems in specific districts. Often, the spark that triggers change, dies down when the successors fail to demonstrate the same level of vigour to sustain progress. Change does occur, but it tends to be short-lived and restricted to the peripheral level.

Enduring change requires sustained effort over a considerable period to reach the core and become permanent. Change must be systemic, organic, and deeply rooted. Simply associating an initiative with the name of a particular officer does not ensure its continuation. Without institutionalization, the efforts and resources invested in new initiatives are often squandered.

Civil servants join the service to effect meaningful change in the system. Individual efforts should not perish after a single tenure. Successive officers' limited interventions should be institutionalized so that initiatives do not fade during the transition phase. These initiatives can be incorporated into government policies and programs, ensuring continuity. Regular evaluation and adaptation are essential to strengthen the administrative framework and enhance the delivery of services.

Many existing schemes and programmes are designed primarily to cater to 'women of the street'. Generally, a rehabilitation centre implements structured policy programmes consisting of a preparation stage, a planting and control awareness stage, a channeling and directing stage, a monitoring stage and an evaluation stage. These programmes are expected to change the concept of self and create normative life and prevent them to return to their former job.

However, our focus here is on adolescent girls. They do not merely need to be resettled in another profession; they need to be pulled out of that sinister environment and reintegrated into their own families and homes. The challenge in these cases lies in both the limited scope and capacity of existing schemes and the complex issues surrounding the girls themselves.

An all-inclusive, integrated effort involving all relevant departments is required to arrange the repatriation of victims, ensure their acceptance by families, and support their gradual reintegration into community life. They need to be appreciated and adequately rewarded for every small step toward change. Nonetheless, rescue is only the beginning of a long struggle to restore the victim's life after exposure to oppressive conditions.

Many changes are abandoned due to resistance, confusion, and lack of regular communication. A need-based approach should be implemented for such cases. Convincing the victim of the need to change is crucial to initiating progress. Training and experience can help mental health professionals recognize subtle acts of defiance, address them, and strengthen collaboration with the victim (Austin & Johnson, 2017).

According to Miller (1999), victim resistance may take different forms, in the discussed context:

Arguing - The victim contests the accuracy of what is said by the therapist, questions their expertise and authority and acts with hostility.

Interrupting - The victim repeatedly interrupts the therapists by talking over them or cutting them off.

Denying - The victim is unwilling to recognize the problems, accept responsibility or take advice, like blaming others for their own problems, making excuses for their behaviour, being unwilling to change.

Ignoring - The victim ignores the therapist by not paying attention, not answering, giving no audible reply or changing the conversation's direction.

It is important to remember that the therapeutic relationship is ultimately the priority. Observing and navigating resistance may require changing approaches and interventions (Austin & Johnson, 2017). In cases where the victim keeps resisting and the therapist gets irritated or annoyed, one lands in a situation where two people are fighting one another and the therapeutic relationship breaks down. The victim needs to be encouraged to explore and explain her feelings and the counsellor needs to recognize and understand them. Change will come only when it is sustained and reinforced.

In the blue funk

A rape victim can be rescued from the nocuous durance of the criminal, but it is far more difficult to rescue her from the pain and agony imprinted on her mind for life. In the majority of the rape cases, it is not the stranger danger equation as the studies have shown. On the contrary, most culprits are familiar to the victim. Familiarity with the offender complicates the equivalence between the crime and justice.

In district Betul, two tribal girls aged between five and eight years were enticed with a chocolate by a man they knew from their village. He took them on his bike, on which they had taken many joy rides on through the narrow lane passing in front of their house. They were expecting the man to stop the bike at the grocer's shop, from where they usually purchased chocolates. But the man didn't stop there. They passed the grocer's shop, crossed the narrow lane in front of their house, but the bike didn't stop.

Eventually, the man brought them deep into a dense forest. No one was in sight. Birds flew high in murmuration. As the girls got absorbed in watching the flock swooping and swirling, the man pounced. Their screams for help only echoed back from the tall trees. The little birds were trapped. Snatched feathers hung suspended in the helpless air of the forest.

He abandoned the girls there to find their way in the dark woods and fled to the neighbouring district of Amrawati, where he worked as a daily wage labour.

Back home, the villagers started searching for them. Someone suggested looking for them in the forest. A few men with torches in their hands headed towards the forest. The girls were found. The shocked villagers wrapped them in a stole and rushed to the hospital with the two girls drenched in blood. They were admitted to the hospital and the police was informed. A case was registered and the accused was arrested from Amrawati district. After twelve days, the girls were discharged from the hospital. However, they were unable to talk about the incident. In fact, they were not even able to comprehend anything about the incident. We were sitting in their porch with the girls. They were telling us about their school, friends, and family. The investigating officer was recording their statements. With a pause, I attempted to ask about the incident. They brushed aside the question and continued playing with their handmade plushies. I hesitantly offered them a packet of biscuits. The elder one opened the packet and shared a biscuit with her younger sister. With the biscuits in hand, they were looking at us with questioning eyes. We had a few questions to ask but they had many.

Even after several months, the memory of the incident continues to trouble the young girl like a dark shadow. Every night, the 12-year-old holds on tightly to her mother for comfort before she can sleep. She was betrayed by a 40-year-old auto driver from her neighbourhood, who tricked her into going with him and then harmed her in a deserted house. Although the man has been arrested and remains in jail, the fear still lingers in her life. Members of the Child Welfare Committee and the police have counseled her many times and encouraged her to return to school, but rebuilding her sense of safety and trust is a slow and ongoing process.

In many cases involving young survivors, investigating officers often rely on responses from caregivers or guardians rather than from the child directly. Inquiry methods need to be carefully tailored to the child's level of comprehension. It is essential to provide the victim with a safe environment in which the therapist is empathetic and non-judgmental. In such a space, the child experiences acceptance, openness, and unconditional positive regard. These ideas are powerfully articulated by Carl Rogers: "People are just as wonderful as sunsets if you let them be. When I look at the sunset, I don't find myself saying, soften the orange a bit on the right-hand corner. I don't try to control a sunset. I watch with awe as it unfolds".

Trauma often forces children to drop out of school. Some may even run away from home, entering marriages with men they barely know, only to live lives burdened with secrecy, guilt, and shame.

According to Prakriti Ambasht's research paper, "most of the wrongs committed by males are termed as mistakes and innumerable chances are given to them to overcome such behaviour. But it only acts as a motivating factor for them to continue committing wrongful acts because they know that they will not be punished and people will take it in a mild manner. On the other hand, people tend to be way stricter with slightest of the mistakes committed by the females in the society. In such a scenario, the limits as well as domain of the rights of individuals get diminished and in no time, people believe that their rights extend to the body and property of others as well because there is no authority to prevent them from doing so".

According to the website Help Guide, the legal system has failed to identify the trauma a woman goes through after being a victim of rape. Their article, 'Recovering from Rape and Sexual Trauma' quotes:

"The impact of sexual violence goes far beyond physical injuries. The trauma of being raped or sexually assaulted can be shattering, leaving you feeling scared, ashamed, and alone or plagued by nightmares, flashbacks and other unpleasant memories. The world doesn't feel like a safe place anymore. You no longer trust others. You don't even trust yourself. You may question your judgement, your self-worth, and even your sanity. You blame yourself for what happened or believe that you are dirty or damaged goods. Relationships feel dangerous, intimacy impossible. And on top of that, like many rape survivors, you may struggle with PTSD, anxiety and depression".

As a matter of fact, there is no institutional mechanism to provide psychological counselling for rape survivors in India. According to R. K. Vij, senior IPS officer, in his article "Healing the Minds of Rape Survivors," says that most Indian laws—such as the IPC, POCSO Act, Protection of Women from Domestic Violence Act, and the Sexual Harassment of Women at Workplace Act—have provisions only for awarding monetary compensation to victims of criminal offences. Even after the 2012 Nirbhaya gang rape, the IPC was amended to mandate that all hospitals, public or private, whether run by the Union government, state government, local bodies, or any other authority, must provide first aid or medical treatment free of cost to rape and acid attack victims. However, these provisions still fall short of offering counselling support, which at times becomes even more crucial than awarding monetary compensation or providing medical treatment to the survivor.

The One Stop Centre (also known as Sakhi Centre) scheme, launched in April 2015, does provide for psychosocial counselling services on a "call-on" basis, but these services are meant only for cases requiring "emergency response and rescue". These centres are already struggling with inadequate infrastructure. Moreover, they are incapacitated by dilettantish staff who cannot effectively cater to the range of violent sexual assault cases where counselling is required.

Victim compensation is a relatively new idea in the Indian justice system, as pointed out by Ambasht. She further notes that this concept emerged with the development of victimology, where the victim was recognized as the primary sufferer of the offence committed against them. Although victim compensation was included in the Code of Criminal Procedure, 1898, it became more victim-centric after independence. Nevertheless, it was necessary to realize the idea of justice enshrined in the Preamble of the Constitution.

For victims, this was recognized as part of Article 21 in the case of *Rudal Shah vs. State of Bihar*. The Supreme Court in this case observed: "Article 21, which guarantees the right to life and liberty, will be denuded of its significant content if the power of this Court were limited to passing orders of relief from illegal detention. One of the telling ways in which the violation of that right can reasonably be prevented and due compliance with the mandate of Article 21 secured is to mulct its violators in the payment of monetary compensation".

Further, in *Rattan Singh vs. State of Punjab*, Justice Krishna Iyer noted: "It is a weakness of our jurisprudence that the victims of the crime, and the distress of the dependents of the prisoner, do not attract the attention of the law. Indeed, victim reparation is still the vanishing point of our criminal law. This is a deficiency in the system which must be rectified by the Legislature. We can only draw attention in this matter".

In May 2018, the Supreme Court directed all states and union territories to implement the Compensation Scheme for Women Victims/Survivors of Sexual Assault/Other Crimes, 2018 (a sub-scheme within the existing Victim Compensation Scheme), without omitting or diluting any of its provisions.

This sub-scheme was prepared by a committee constituted by NALSA in pursuance of the Court's order in *Nipun Saxena vs. Union of India* (2012). It enables the victim as well as her dependents to claim compensation from the government for the loss suffered. Section 4 of the scheme lays down the eligibility criteria to claim compensation. Importantly, the section does not bar the victim from claiming compensation under other schemes. A victim may seek benefits from multiple schemes, though the final amount awarded under this scheme will be determined only after accounting for compensation already provided elsewhere. One of the factors to be considered while awarding compensation under this scheme includes "expenditure incurred or likely to be incurred on the medical treatment for physical and/or mental health, including counselling of the victim". However, even this novel scheme speaks only of compensation and does not establish a clear mechanism for providing counselling to rape survivors.

In 1994, for the first time, the Supreme Court—while hearing a petition on behalf of the Delhi Domestic Working Women's Forum in a case where six tribal domestic workers were sexually assaulted by Army personnel while travelling on a train—directed the National Commission for Women "to evolve such [compensation] scheme as to wipe out the tears of such unfortunate victims". In its judgment, the Court cited *The Oxford Handbook of Criminology*, which not only traced the historical development of compensation in London but also highlighted "a major shift in penological thinking, reflecting the growing importance attached to restitution and reparation over more narrowly retributive aims of conventional punishment." Despite this, the procedural law was amended only in December 2009, when Section 357-A was added to the Code of Criminal Procedure to formally incorporate the Victim Compensation Scheme.

The 1993 *UN Declaration on the Elimination of Violence Against Women* also emphasized the creation of support structures to promote safety and to provide physical and psychological rehabilitation for women. In this context, existing schemes in India need to be revised to better address the needs of survivors. Globally, many compensation models provide not only for the victim but also for immediate family members and even witnesses. These schemes often mandate a minimum number of counselling hours, which may be increased depending on the victim's needs. In most cases, payments for counselling are made directly to the service provider, with rates determined by the counsellor's qualifications, experience, and professional accreditation.

The rebel soul

These young lives grow restless under the familiar air that surrounds them. They believe life is meant to soar freely in the open sky. This desire drives them to move away from their place of origin. Yet, these wandering souls must be anchored firmly to their roots; otherwise, they are easily swept away by the winds. These winds often blow against the norms and values of the family they belong to. The more tightly the string of the kite is pulled, the farther it strains to fly. As science reminds us, upthrust and anchor act in opposite directions. At times, the pressure of the wind becomes so strong that it forces the kite to break free. Once the thread is severed, securing the kite again becomes a grueling task. The tension between the anchor's pull and the wind's push creates a new paradigm—one that cocoons and reshapes an individual's state of mind.

Theories of socialization have alternately framed children as being passive recipients of socializing messages or active agents engaged in the process of adapting to society (Corsaro, 2011). The passive socialization theories depict a malleable child who can be moulded to fit society.

In Bronfenbrenner's ecological model (1977), individuals develop through the process of accommodation to their environmental contexts, specifically concentric rings of influence, from family to neighbourhoods and schools to cultural forces in society. Pierre Bourdieu (1984) similarly presents individual socialization as a process by which individuals are influenced by class- specific cultural milieu in which he or she is being reared: the tastes and ways of speaking and acting that represent their habitus. In Bourdieu's model, these class-specific preferences and behaviours signify social class to others and in turn serve as a mechanism for reinforcing rigidly stratified social status categories in certain societies, a phenomenon known as social reproduction (Bourdieu, 2000; Chin & Phillips, 2004). Taking this perspective further, Michael Foucault (1979) depicted socialization as a disciplining process originating from a seemingly invisible power structure transmitting norm-enforcing pressures which appear to permeate society and restrict an individual's agency. He further acknowledges that individuals are not mere objects shaped by society but rather can enact their own subjectivities (Foucault, Martin, Gutman & Hutton, 1988).

A child's understanding of self is often full of contradictions. Young teens may see themselves as outgoing but also withdrawn, happy yet often moody, both smart and completely clueless (Harter, 2012). Studies have underlined that these contradictions, along with the teen's growing recognition that their personality and behaviour seem to change depending on who they are with or where they are, can lead the young teen to feel like a fraud. With their parents they may seem angrier and sullen, with their friends they are more outgoing and goofier, and at work they are quiet and cautious. "Which one is really me?" may be the refrain of the young teenager (Human Behaviour and the Social Environment by Susan Tyler). Harter (2012) found that adolescents emphasize traits such as being friendly and considerate more than do children, highlighting their increasing concern about how others may see them. Harter also found that older teens add values and moral standards to their self-descriptions. As self-concept differentiates, so too does self-esteem. In addition to the academic, social, appearance, and physical/athletic dimensions of self-esteem in middle and late childhood, teens also add perceptions of their competency in romantic relationships, on the job, and in close friendships (Harter, 2006). Self-esteem often drops when children transit from one school setting to another, such as shifting from elementary to middle school or junior high to high school (Ryan, Shim & Makara, 2013). These drops are usually temporary, unless there are additional stressors such as parental conflict or other family disruptions (De Wit, Karioja, Rye, & Shain, 2011). Self-esteem rises from mid to late adolescence for most teenagers, especially if they feel competent in their peer relationships, their appearance, and athletic abilities (Birkeland, Melkivik, Holsen, & Wold, 2012).

Erikson believed that the primary psychosocial task of adolescence was establishing an identity. Teens struggle with the question "Who am I?" This includes questions regarding their appearance, vocational choices and career aspirations, education, relationships, sexuality, political and social views, personality, and interests. Erikson saw this as a period of confusion and experimentation regarding identity and one's life path. During adolescence we experience psychological moratorium, where teens put on hold commitment to an identity while exploring the options. The culmination of this exploration is a more coherent view of oneself. Those who are unsuccessful at resolving this stage may either withdraw further into social isolation or become lost in the crowd. However, more recent research suggests that few leave this age period with identity achievement, and that most identity formation occurs during young adulthood (Cote, 2006).

Children usually learn and form opinions from what they observe and experience around them. If there is disintegration in the family, continuous fights between the parents which have become the norm of each day, lack of love and affection among the family members, or broken families, it will affect a child's growth and development mentally, physically, and emotionally. Moreover, if the child counts low on intellectual faculties, the incessant pressure to perform makes the child all the more aggressive and pugnacious. Initially, to cope with this strenuous situation, children tend to develop their own pressure system which defends them and shields them from the pressing situation. Structural breaks in the family lead to tension, quarrels, and disruption of a peaceful family, which has a traumatic impact on the child. The existing fissures widen with every passing day. The curiosity to know about the unknown is another prominent reason that induces these stripling minds towards taking unbeaten tracks. The lack of education regarding existing biological differences, biological processes, and consequences of any illegal or unlawful act can put them in extremis. At times, the underprivileged and the impecunious status of the family impels the child to indulge in deplorable acts. During my stint as SP of Betul district, a twelve-year-old girl was found to provide venereal gratification to an octogenarian man in lieu of just twenty rupees. She was unable to ask for this money from her parents, who were already struggling to cope with the demands of her seven siblings. It is sad, it is shocking, yet it is shamefully true.

The kite, with its flamboyant colours, vivid graphics, and upthrust vigour, fails to acknowledge the fact that it is made of frangible material which cannot stand the precariousness of the wind. The strings certainly need to be in the right hands to secure it from taking uncertain paths. Any deviant behaviour in the child should be checked at an early stage. The nascent stage leaves some scope for reparation.

An eleven-year-old girl went missing from Jabalpur railway station platform in 2022. A year after she went missing, I joined as SP Railways in 2023. The father of the girl came to meet me in my office. He was physically challenged. His neighbour was also accompanying him for support — supporting him corporeally by driving his tricycle through the slender lanes with unbridled traffic leading to my office, located in the dense area of Kanch Ghar, and supporting him mentally so that he could gather himself and express his grief in words. With a lot of difficulty and some support from his neighbour and my stick man, he occupied the chair. He was a middle-aged man, who taught children in a local madarsa. He had lost one of his legs in a road accident around five years ago. After having a glass of water, his eyes were able to hold back the tears. He started recounting the incident in a bereaved voice.

His daughter was studying in sixth standard in an English-medium convent school in Jabalpur. Her two siblings also attended the same school. As compared to her elder sister and younger brother, she was not putting in the requisite amount of effort to improve her performance in school. As a result of this negligence on her part, she was often scolded by her father at home. The neighbour accompanying the father interrupted in between; he added that she was also beaten at times and was locked in a room by her father for her poor academic results. Many a time she had taken shelter at the neighbour's place.

The father continued with a blameable undertone: "It was the day of Chehlum (signifying the fortieth day of the pious month of Moharrum in Muslims). All three children accompanied me to attend the procession. Devotional offerings were being made to the devotees participating in the procession. Children were running in different groups, observing the religious activities being performed. As the main procession was about to reach the finishing point, a group of devotees separated from the leading group and moved towards the railway station. During the period of Moharrum, groups associated with different religious places meander into divergent areas to spread their religious preachings and collect any contributions made by the devotees. This group boarded the train going to Ajmer in Rajasthan. My daughter followed this group and probably boarded the train. She was last captured in the camera at the platform. Posters were pasted at all the probable railway stations. Her photograph was published in a pamphlet and distributed all over, in different railway stations coming on the route. No information was received about her from anywhere".

The father concluded with great expectation in his eyes. He added, "I just wanted her to get a good life, which is possible only through education. I worked day and night just to provide my children better educational opportunities which I couldn't get as a child". His throat was choking in despair as he relived the whole year while he narrated his struggle to find her. The pool of tears he was managing to hold in his eyes reflected the light of my office. He was explaining his efforts to me, trying to convince me to help him. In spite of all his disability, this person went to enquire at all possible stations and checked all predictable places throughout the year. No sight of her presence was found.

I have observed an absorbing trend in police; whenever a new officer joins the office, the victims of the pending cases or the people associated with the victim come and meet the officer with an expectation that some efficacious efforts will be made to solve the unsolved. Somehow, I always feel this expectation baggage to be quite substantial. I usually start with assuaging this burden whenever I join a new assignment. We tried to connect all the missing links in this case. Fresh evidence, based on the family and friends' statements, was retaken and evidence was collected. After a month's exercise we located the girl in a shelter home in Mumbai.

This was a unique case, as the girl never wanted to go back to her home in Jabalpur. All the information given by her at the shelter home was false. She said that she belonged to Amravati district in Maharashtra. She was travelling with her parents to Mumbai to attend a marriage in the family. Due to enormous rush at the Mumbai railway station, she was separated from her family, she endorsed. Police teams from Mumbai went to the fake address given by her for the enquiry. Regular correspondence was being done on the basis of this false story narrated by the girl. The shelter home staff also communicated regularly with the Amravati police, but the girl could not be traced. It was a futile exercise in smoke and mirrors.

Life in a shelter home for her was like a free bird in a cage. Away from the pressure to perform in school, she was happy to play with the children at the shelter home.

There was no one around to scold her for not studying. The present confinement was better than the dark, dingy room where she was often locked up for not meeting the expectations of the school and her parents.

This girl was completely averse to the concept of studying in school—so much so that she was ready to leave her home and stay away from her family. What was supposed to be an opportunity in her father's opinion was a burden to her. When she was rescued and questioned about her decision to run away and stay away, she gave a very clear reply about her idea of life. She said she had decided that she would stay at the shelter home until she attained the age of maturity. She added, "As an adult I will go back to my parents and family, get married to the person of my parents' choice, and settle down".

Her idea of liberation was moving from one confinement to another. She was a free soul. She hated interventions. She wanted to live life on her own terms. In this particular case, the parents had to be counselled to understand that each child is unique. What is considered good for children by the parents may not necessarily be taken the same way by a child. Finally, the parents agreed to her terms for life, and she came back home.

While childhood is largely known as a period of developing physical, emotional, and behavioural competencies, the central task of adolescence has been characterized as having a more conscious focus. Erikson suggests that adolescents are tasked with developing some central perspective and direction—some working unity—out of the effective remnants of childhood and the hope of anticipated adulthood. Erikson refers to this process as an identity crisis, from which an individual must detect some meaningful resemblance between what one comes to see in oneself and what one's sharpened awareness tells one, and the way others judge and expect one to be.

In her research findings, Susan Tyler mentions that children in middle and late childhood are increasingly granted greater freedom regarding moment-to-moment decision-making. This continues in adolescence, as teens demand greater control in decisions that affect their daily lives. This can increase conflict between parents and their teenagers. For many adolescents, this conflict centers on chores, homework, curfew, dating, and personal appearance. These are all things many teens believe they should manage, whereas parents previously had considerable control over them. Teens report more conflict with their mothers, as many mothers believe they should still have some control over these areas, yet teens often report their mothers to be more encouraging and supportive (Costigan, Cauce, & Etchison, 2007). As teens grow older, more compromise is reached between parents and teenagers (Smetana, 2011). Parents are more controlling of daughters, especially early-maturing girls, than they are of sons (Caspi, Lynam, Moffitt, & Silva, 1993). In addition, culture and ethnicity also play a role in how restrictive parents are with the daily lives of their children (Chen, Vansteenkiste, Beyers, Soensens, & Van Petegen, 2013).

Many research studies conducted to decipher the process of identity development among marginalized youth concluded, as Perez-Felkner sums it: while adolescents are tasked with developing a sense of self within the context of society as a whole, they may be simultaneously integrating particular dimensions of their identity with their internalized sense of society's expectations for them. Adolescents who identify with a marginalized group—like racial, ethnic, and sexual minority youths, for example—may particularly experience this phenomenon. With respect to racial–ethnic minorities, W.E.B. Du Bois (1903) maintained that African Americans experience a double consciousness in which they view themselves simultaneously through their own eyes and those of white society. Phinney and colleagues extended Erikson's identity development framework to include ethnic identity development, under which an ethnic identity crisis might emerge should ethnic minority youth develop strong and stable affiliations with their ethnic group but not with the dominant culture, or vice versa (J. Phinney, 1992; J.S. Phinney, Cantu & Kurtz, 1997).

Parents often fail to understand that their vision for life may not be the same as that of their child. Some parents want to live their unfulfilled dreams through their children. This sense of ownership in parents suffocates the children. Young minds are intensely sensitive to the events happening around them and are immensely impressionable about the repercussions of these events. Under the facile supposition of human universals, parents tend to brush aside existing individualistic determinants.

Having supportive, less conflict-ridden relationships with parents also benefits teenagers. Research on attachment in adolescence finds that teens who are still securely attached to their parents have fewer emotional problems (Rawatlal, Kliewer & Pillay, 2015), are less likely to engage in drug abuse and other criminal behaviours (Meeus, Branje & Overbeek, 2004), and have more positive peer relationships (Shomaker & Furman, 2009).

Maybe this unknotted kite feels free when it gets stuck on a tall tree or an electric pole wire—so high, so much so that no one is able to get hold of it. For others, it is stuck, but for the kite it is a free state—independent, on its own, away from any knots. The challenge here is to bridge the gap between these two vehement coordinates. The mental utopian framework that subsists at each end needs to be reoriented with existential reality. Reality can be comprehensible only through communication. The existing framework of rehabilitation agencies needs to take account of this prerequisite. The provisions for the development, treatment, correction, and reintegration of children need to embrace this integrant.

The entire rescue–restoration process, the custodial and the judicial procedures immediately post-rescue are usually not victim friendly and make the survivor believe that her journey of victimization is a never-ending rigmarole. There exists a fundamental feature which is ingrained in the basic structure of Indian society: the position of women in society. Furthermore, the status of a young girl is always the dependent one; she needs to confirm that she is accepted by the people around her. In other words, she fears being abandoned by her own family members. This is a pivotal reason why many crimes are scuffled to death within the four walls of the house and go unreported. Why do victims give tutored replies in the court of law, in favour of the criminal? The question of survival takes over the demand for justice. Even after getting compensation, she has to live within her existing framework of cognate consanguinity and the same social ties that will constantly judge her. The society, including some family members, will keep abrading her wounds so much so that she remembers and lives with it for life.

The rehabilitative process should be reconstructive in a manner to establish a plan for treatment and rehabilitation of the child according to her needs and situation. To be effective, counselling techniques must be attuned to the distinctive needs and developmental stage of the child. The goal needs to be supportive to deal with complicated feelings and situations. Freud was also concerned with the impact of early experiences and unconscious drives on behaviour. Freud quoted: "The conscious mind may be compared to a fountain playing in the sun and falling back into the great subterranean pool of subconscious from which it rises". The approach needs to be age-appropriate, engaging, and relevant to their individual experiences. There are some phenomenal differences between counselling for teens and adults as identified by the Idaho Youth Ranch Therapy and Counselling Centre:

Teen counselling approaches must take into account the unique developmental needs of adolescents. Teens are in a stage of rapid growth and change, both physically and emotionally. Counsellors must be aware of these changes and be able to adapt their approach to meet the needs of the teen.

Counselling must be engaging and interactive to hold their attention and keep them involved in the process. Teen counselling approaches often incorporate activities and exercises designed to be fun and engaging, such as games or art projects.

Teens are often hesitant to seek counselling due to concerns about confidentiality. Counsellors who work with teens must be able to assure them that their sessions will be confidential and that their privacy will be respected.

While teens may resist involving their parents in the counselling process, parental involvement can be essential to their success. Counsellors must be skilled in engaging parents and helping them support their teens in the counselling process.

Counselling for teens must take a holistic approach, addressing not just their mental health challenges but also their physical health, social relationships, and other factors that may be impacting their well-being. This approach can help teens develop a sense of balance and empowerment.

Certain early signs can also be identified in the victim, such as persistent feelings of sadness, anxiety or hopelessness; changes in sleep or eating habits; loss of interest in activities they used to enjoy; difficulty in concentrating or making decisions; withdrawal from friends and family; increased aggression or acting out; self-harm or suicidal thoughts.

This phase requires collaboration between the fields of medicine, psychology, social work, and law. The process should begin with an analysis of the child's physical and mental pathology. One needs to identify the way in which the symptoms and syndromes materialize by assessing both primary and secondary causes. This can be achieved through interviews, observation, and record-keeping of the victim. Efforts should be drawn up through collaboration between psychiatrists, psychologists, and social workers working closely with the child and her family. The child's rehabilitation should be conducted on parallel lines with that of the family.

After the process of rehabilitation, the next step is reintegration of the child into her normal life. This process should begin with an assessment of risks involved or the existing push and pull factors within the child's family, community, and school. Action plans should subsequently be created to address these factors. In the event that they cannot be adequately addressed, the team should concentrate on life-skill development for the child so that she is able to seek timely assistance when needed.

Actions involving the child's family in the reintegration process require the family's effectual cooperation, as well as assistance by the legal expert as per the existing provisions of child protection legislation. It is important to note that the family's agreement to assist must be combined with the critical support of the counsellor. The assessment of the existing factors as well as implementation of the plan for reintegration must be carefully followed to be truly effective. If the child's social environment cannot be sufficiently altered to allow safe reintegration, the child would have to be removed from the community and the school and relocated to a shelter or other care centre, a manoeuvre that would not be possible without the assistance of the legal expert. Legal expertise is also necessary in cases in which the child's identity must be concealed in order to keep her experience of abuse confidential.

Social-psychological theories of re-victimization provide insights into why certain individuals, particularly children, experience repeated victimization after an initial trauma. Understanding these theories helps explain why children who go missing, run away from home, or escape from shelter homes may remain vulnerable to further harm or exploitation, and how their rehabilitation can be approached more effectively.

Martin Seligman's Learned Helplessness theory posits that individuals exposed to repeated, uncontrollable negative experiences develop a sense of powerlessness. For children who have been neglected, abused, or exploited, this can manifest as the belief that they have no control over their lives. Consequently, they may become passive or resigned, making them more susceptible to re-victimization. Runaway children, for instance, may tolerate or be drawn into new exploitative situations because they feel incapable of escape.

Rehabilitation efforts should focus on empowering these children, helping them regain a sense of control and agency. Programmes should build self-worth, teach coping strategies, and develop decision-making skills to break the cycle of helplessness. Trauma-informed care, which acknowledges the long-term psychological impact of prior trauma, is crucial for fostering resilience and independence.

Cycle of Violence Theory suggests that exposure to violence or abuse at a young age increases the risk of becoming either victims or perpetrators of violence later in life. Children who run away to escape abusive environments may, without proper support, encounter similarly violent or exploitative situations, such as human trafficking or gang involvement, perpetuating the cycle. Breaking this cycle requires providing a safe, nurturing environment where children can experience trust and stability. Counselling and support networks should help children process trauma and understand healthy relationships.

John Bowlby's Attachment Theory explains how early relationships with caregivers shape an individual's sense of security and future relationships. Neglected or abused children often develop insecure attachments, which can lead them to seek unhealthy or exploitative relationships. Rehabilitation should focus on rebuilding secure attachment patterns through consistent and supportive relationships with caregivers or social workers. Teaching children to identify and form healthy relationships is key to reducing the risk of re-victimization.

Recognizing and addressing trauma bonding is essential in rehabilitation. Trauma bonding refers to the emotional attachment that can develop between a victim and their abuser. For example, a trafficked child may develop loyalty to their trafficker due to intermittent kindness, making it difficult to break free from exploitation. Recognizing and addressing trauma bonding is essential in rehabilitation. Counsellors and social workers must offer targeted support to help children dissociate emotionally from abusers, and facilitate gradual reintegration into healthy environments.

Victim Precipitation Theory suggests that some individuals, often unconsciously, behave in ways that increase their risk of re-victimization. Runaway children may engage in risky behaviours or associate with dangerous individuals, shaped by prior experiences of abuse or neglect. Rehabilitation should teach children to recognize and avoid high-risk situations through life skills training, therapy, and awareness programmes. Equipping them with emotional intelligence and resilience strategies reduces the likelihood of future re-victimization. These social-psychological theories illustrate the complex ways trauma can perpetuate cycles of abuse, neglect, and exploitation. Effective rehabilitation requires a holistic approach that addresses both psychological needs and societal factors contributing to vulnerability. Applying these theories allows professionals in child welfare, law enforcement, and social services to design interventions that break the cycle of re-victimization, giving children the tools to rebuild their lives and prevent future harm. Those who need to be involved at this stage include school staff, community social workers, hospital staff and police officers. Indicators for the evaluation of such risk factors are typically developed through an organization's experience in providing services to the victims. These tools or standards should be tested against specific target groups, such as child victims or vulnerable children, who utilize the organization's services. Systems at the community level must be established to provide a foundation for better communication and cooperation between the multidisciplinary team and the child's family and community as well as to facilitate referral of cases. Mental health and criminal justice staff can potentially re-victimize trauma survivors by being insensitive to their needs, engaging in victim blaming, or casting doubt on victimization evidence. During the ongoing court cases, a victim is required to give evidence, relive their experience and potentially be cross-examined in courts. All these legal procedures can stimulate stress and anxiety, which in turn can induce psychological symptoms, panic attacks and further PTSD symptoms. The justice system moves at its own pace. The procedures which are required to be followed can be slow, drawn out and ongoing.

Miller's research highlights that PTSD is higher among those who have to endure criminal proceedings in the justice system compared to crime victims in general. Flashbacks and nightmares, interpersonal distancing, cognitive function impairment, anger, grief, fear, anxiety, all are present, leaving a sufferer struggling. Victims of abuse require services, support and assistance from mental health and criminal justice personnel in the immediate aftermath of their victimization. The compassion and respect with which these professionals handle victims may play a key role in their process of recovery.

The scientific techniques and rehabilitation approaches need to be integrated with socio-psychological premises of the victim. Understanding the reasons behind every case was suitably mentioned in the lines from *Missing in Care* (2021, p. 31) say - 'The young people who were consulted want carers, social workers and the police to avoid making assumptions about them and why they might have gone missing. These professionals should try to understand their reasons, acknowledging that every child is different and will be facing different challenges.'

Few studies have suggested that restorative justice can be effective in reducing the harmful effects of violent victimization. In a systematic review conducted by Nascimento et al. (2023), a broader range of psychological impacts of restorative justice, including emotional restoration, were examined. Their findings indicated that restorative justice is promising with regard to its psychological impact on victims, as it helps reduce not only post-traumatic stress syndrome but also anxiety, distress, and fear.

Aligned with the scholarly discourse on cognitive behaviour therapy, which seeks to amend maladaptive cognitions stemming from a traumatic incident through cognitive restructuring (Bourdon et al., 2019), existing research on recovery from violent victimization suggests that making meaning of the traumatic experience is a crucial step towards recovery. Those who are able to reframe their traumatic memories into something meaningful in their present day are more likely to recover. Similarly, other research has shown that account-making—defined as "people's story-like constructions of events that include explanations, descriptions, predictions about relevant future events, and affective reactions"—is linked to successful coping and better mental health among victims of sexual assault (Orbuch et al., 1994) and survivors of child sexual abuse (Easton, 2013). Thus, making sense of the harm caused can assist victims of violence in "escaping the dungeon" (Draucker & Petrovic, 1996) of the enduring impact of violence, enabling them to live with the experience while regaining control over their bodies and the narratives of their lives.

The shattered assumptions theory, proposed by Janoff-Bulman (1992), posits that individuals generally view themselves as intrinsically valuable. The self of victims may become severely impaired because violence has both physical and ontological consequences, including a threat to one's existence and a loss of personal autonomy (Pemberton, 2019). Recovery therefore requires restoring the damaged self by reclaiming one's sense of identity, which helps victims regain faith in themselves and the ability to manage traumatic experiences (Benight & Bandura, 2004). Research demonstrates that recovery from violent victimization necessitates a reconstruction of self-identity.

For victims of violence, transforming self-confidence may be essential to revive the "buried self" resulting from violent victimization (Godbey & Hutchinson, 1996) and to construct "a new residence" for the recovered self (Draucker, 1992). During this transformative process, victims may undergo a cognitive shift (Allen & Woznaik, 2010), beginning to reassert self-worth (Song & Shih, 2010) and assume responsibility for their lives once again (Reynolds & Shepherd, 2011). Taken together, by reclaiming their self-identity, victims of violent crime may start to experience a renewed sense of control over their future (Hou et al., 2013).

Restorative justice can facilitate the development of the core recovery factors outlined above because it prioritizes dialogue rather than mere settlement (Hansen & Umbreit, 2018). First, restorative justice can help victims create meaning from violent victimization through validation. In the restorative justice process, victims are given the opportunity to ask the justice-involved person the "why me" question and receive an explanation of why the offence occurred and why they were targeted as a victim (Kirkwood, 2021).

Direct engagement with the perpetrator acts as a catalyst for trauma processing (Angel et al., 2014) and helps victims comprehend their lack of culpability in the traumatic event (Strang et al., 2006). These elements represent shared components of restorative justice and cognitive behavioural therapy, the latter of which has demonstrated efficacy in mitigating PTSD symptoms in victims of violence (Billette et al., 2008).

In addition, restorative justice encourages justice-involved persons to actively take responsibility for their actions and fosters genuine remorse (Braithwaite & Roche, 2011). Acknowledging victims' experiences and recognizing that violent victimization is not their fault may help victims validate their experiences and make sense of the harm inflicted upon them. The connection between validation of victimization and meaning-making was highlighted by Elliot et al. (2014). Drawing on procedural justice, Elliot examined the impact of interactions between victims and police on trauma reduction. They found that validation of victims' experiences by police alleviated the adverse psychological effects of victimization by providing a sense of closure, empowerment, and safety.

Restorative justice is a theory that seeks to address crime and wrongdoing through reconciliation between the victim, offender, and the community, rather than through punitive measures alone. Its social-psychological impact is significant because it fundamentally reshapes the way individuals and society understand and respond to conflict.

At its core, restorative justice emphasizes healing, dialogue, and the restoration of relationships over punishment and retribution.

Traditional justice systems often marginalize victims, reducing them to witnesses in their own cases. Restorative justice, by contrast, actively involves them in the process, giving them a voice and an opportunity to express their pain, needs, and desires for resolution. This can empower victims to regain a sense of control, dignity, and closure.

Instead of focusing solely on punishment, restorative justice encourages offenders to take responsibility for their actions. This can lead to genuine remorse and the desire to make amends, which can be psychologically transformative for offenders. The process can foster empathy by confronting offenders with the real human impact of their actions, potentially reducing recidivism.

Restorative justice also aims to repair the harm caused to the community and rebuild trust between its members. This collective healing can reduce feelings of alienation and prevent future conflicts by fostering a sense of shared responsibility and collective well-being.

By promoting understanding and dialogue, restorative justice can help reduce negative emotions like fear, anger, and revenge, which are often perpetuated by traditional punitive systems. This approach helps individuals move towards forgiveness and emotional healing, which can be particularly beneficial in cases involving deep personal or communal conflict.

Various scholars have explored restorative justice from different angles, each offering insights into its applicability and effectiveness. Howard Zehr, often referred to as the "grandfather of restorative justice," emphasizes that the system moves beyond just the legal aspects of crime to address its broader social implications. He argues that restorative justice allows communities to become more resilient by addressing the underlying causes of crime and fostering reconciliation. John Braithwaite, an Australian criminologist, highlights the concept of "reintegrative shaming" in restorative justice. According to Braithwaite, shaming the behaviour (not the person) in a supportive environment can help offenders reintegrate into society without the stigma that often accompanies traditional punitive approaches. Paul McCold and Ted Wachtel stress the importance of restorative practices in schools and communities, demonstrates how these methods can prevent conflicts and address issues such as bullying and juvenile delinquency. They argue that restorative justice fosters a culture of dialogue and accountability that can reduce the need for more severe interventions later. Nils Christie, a Norwegian criminologist, introduced the idea that conflicts are "property" belonging to those directly involved, not the state. He critiques the traditional justice system for "stealing" conflicts from victims and offenders. Restorative justice, in his view, returns the ownership of these conflicts to the individuals and communities involved, giving them the power to resolve matters in a more personal and meaningful way.

In India, restorative justice has gained attention as an alternative to the overburdened and often adversarial criminal justice system. Its application has been discussed in various contexts, from juvenile justice to community-level disputes. Scholars argue that India's rich cultural traditions, such as the Panchayat system, inherently align with restorative justice principles, fostering reconciliation and community involvement. Restorative justice resonates with India's long-standing traditions of community-based conflict resolution, where elders mediate and focus on reconciliation rather than retribution. This system has been practiced in various forms, particularly in rural areas, long before the modern legal system was introduced. With a judicial system burdened by millions of pending cases, restorative justice offers a practical solution to resolve less severe disputes without lengthy legal proceedings, helping expedite justice and reduce stress on formal courts. Restorative practices are recognized as especially beneficial in the context of juvenile justice, emphasizing rehabilitation and reintegration over punishment, which aligns with India's goals for juvenile offenders. The Juvenile Justice (Care and Protection of Children) Act of 2015 provides space for restorative justice, aiming to reform and reintegrate rather than punish young offenders.

Where communal, caste, and ethnic conflicts have historically caused deep wounds, restorative justice can serve as a tool for healing societal divisions. By fostering dialogue between conflicting parties, it can address underlying grievances that fuel communal tensions.

In a society where crimes against women are a serious concern, restorative justice may offer a complementary approach, allowing victims to voice their suffering directly to offenders in a controlled, supportive environment, potentially fostering personal healing and raising societal awareness of gender-based violence. However, caution is necessary to ensure that it is not used to diminish the severity of crimes such as sexual assault or domestic violence.

While restorative justice holds promise, several scholars caution against its uncritical adoption. Power imbalances may prevent genuine dialogue and fairness, as marginalized groups may feel pressured to accept inadequate compensation or apologies. Some critics worry that restorative justice could be misused to trivialize serious offences, especially crimes against women, by prioritizing reconciliation over justice. While the concept aligns with India's traditional systems, its implementation within a modern legal framework remains a challenge. Policymakers need to develop clear guidelines to ensure that restorative justice complements, rather than undermines, formal legal processes.

In conclusion, restorative justice offers profound social-psychological benefits by fostering accountability, healing, and community resilience. Scholars largely agree on its potential, but in the Indian context, careful consideration is required to ensure it is applied equitably and effectively. When integrated with India's cultural values and legal structures, restorative justice can play a significant role in transforming how society addresses crime and conflict.

The process of rehabilitation involves multifarious agencies, each having its own dextered procedure to accomplish the task. But at the end of this chapter, we can arrive at a consensus that rehabilitation is not a task but a process, which needs to be perpetuated invariably and counted upon regularly to channelize the change. Any victim should not be viewed as a single seamless monolith. Each case is deeply embedded in the spasmodic, perplexing socio-psychological context. Prevailing rehabilitation system is oblivious to the non-victimization of the victim. The present vacuous objective of counselling simply serves as an insouciant shrug-off of the basic objective of the whole process of rehabilitation. The rehabilitation of victims, especially those who have experienced severe trauma such as missing girls or survivors of human trafficking, necessitates a multifaceted approach that engages various agencies, each playing a crucial role in the victim's recovery journey. A comprehensive rehabilitation strategy involves not only addressing the immediate physical and emotional needs of the victim but also facilitating their reintegration into society. The effectiveness of this process can be significantly enhanced through coordinated efforts among legal, medical, psychological, social, and community agencies.

Legal Agencies are fundamental in ensuring that justice is served and the rights of the victim are upheld. Their primary responsibility is to prosecute offenders and provide protective measures to safeguard victims from further harm. However, the role of legal agencies can be augmented by adopting a victim-centered approach that prioritizes the needs and well-being of the survivor. This includes establishing specialized units within law enforcement that focus on the unique circumstances surrounding cases of violence against women and children, ensuring that investigations are conducted sensitively and efficiently. Legal advocates can assist victims in navigating the judicial system, empowering them to reclaim agency over their lives.

Medical and Psychological Agencies play a pivotal role in addressing the physical and psychological scars left by trauma. Immediate medical intervention is critical for treating injuries, but long-term care is equally essential for fostering holistic recovery. Psychologists and mental health professionals must implement trauma-informed care that recognizes the profound effects of trauma on the psyche. Therapeutic modalities such as Cognitive Behavioural Therapy (CBT) and Eye Movement Desensitization and Reprocessing (EMDR) can facilitate emotional healing and help victims develop coping strategies. Collaboration between medical and psychological practitioners enables integrated care, treating physical and mental health simultaneously.

Social workers and rehabilitation programmes are instrumental in creating supportive environments that facilitate the victim's reintegration into society. This includes providing essential services such as safe housing, vocational training, and educational opportunities that enable victims to regain independence. Social agencies must enhance their outreach efforts by proactively engaging with victims and tailoring support services to their specific needs. By fostering strong connections with community resources, social workers can ensure that victims have access to comprehensive support systems that address their physical, emotional, and economic needs.

Community-based organizations and non-governmental organizations (NGOs) are crucial in advocating for the rights of victims and providing practical support services. Their roles can be amplified by fostering partnerships with government agencies to ensure a more streamlined approach to victim rehabilitation. These organizations often provide essential services such as legal assistance, counseling, and safe havens, but they must also focus on preventive measures, such as community education and awareness campaigns. By challenging societal norms that perpetuate stigma and discrimination against victims, NGOs can help create a more supportive environment that fosters healing and reintegration.

The role of family and community cannot be overstated in the rehabilitation process. Victims often require a stable and nurturing environment to heal and reintegrate successfully. Interventions aimed at restoring family connections, where safe and appropriate, can significantly impact the victim's recovery. This includes educating family members about trauma and its effects, thereby equipping them to provide informed support.

Furthermore, community sensitization programmes can play a vital role in fostering empathy and understanding toward victims, ultimately reducing stigma and facilitating social acceptance.

From a psychological perspective, rehabilitation encompasses more than mere recovery; it is a transformative journey toward reclaiming identity and agency. Trauma-informed care emphasizes the importance of understanding the intricate dynamics of trauma and its lasting impact on behaviour and emotional health. Ensuring that all agencies involved are trained in trauma-informed practices is essential for creating a safe environment where victims can begin to heal.

Social theories, such as Goffman's concept of stigma management, illuminate the challenges victims face in societal reintegration. Victims of violence and exploitation often contend with societal prejudice, which can impede their healing process. Therefore, community education initiatives that challenge harmful stereotypes and promote empathy can foster an environment conducive to rehabilitation.

Additionally, Maslow's Hierarchy of Needs provides a useful framework for understanding the sequential nature of recovery. Victims must first have their basic needs for safety, shelter, and security met before they can pursue higher-order psychological needs such as self-esteem and self-actualization. Rehabilitation programmes should prioritize establishing a sense of safety and stability, enabling victims to focus on personal growth and development.

Rehabilitation of victims is not just about healing past wounds; it is about empowering them to reclaim their futures with strength, hope, and resilience.

"Everyone is different, so don't treat us all the same. We do things for different reasons; you need to know and … talk to me, get to know me, don't judge me, understand why I might go missing, and help me manage those feelings and situations before it gets out of hand. Young people go missing for a reason; try to understand that. When we go, don't be angry or make us feel bad".
— Referencing quotes from young people, Missing in Care (p.17)

In concluding this chapter on the rehabilitation of minor victims, it is crucial to recognize the multi-faceted nature of the process, which involves various theories and agencies working in concert to support the healing and reintegration of these vulnerable individuals. The application of psychological, sociological, and legal theories underscores the importance of a holistic approach that addresses the emotional, social, and legal dimensions of a victim's experience.

Different agencies, including social services, law enforcement, educational institutions, and mental health organizations, play pivotal roles in the rehabilitation journey. Each agency contributes its unique expertise—whether through counselling, educational support, or legal advocacy—to create a comprehensive support network tailored to the specific needs of the victim. Collaboration among these entities is essential, as it ensures a continuum of care that fosters resilience and empowers victims to reclaim their lives.

However, while existing frameworks provide valuable support, it is evident that a more concatenated approach is needed to enhance the effectiveness of rehabilitation efforts. Moving forward, it is imperative to prioritize the development of interdisciplinary models that foster collaboration among various stakeholders. This includes promoting communication and coordination between agencies, investing in training programmes for professionals working with victims, and actively involving victims and their families in the rehabilitation process.

By embracing a more holistic and collaborative approach, we can better address the complex needs of minor victims, ultimately leading to more effectual rehabilitation outcomes. It is our collective responsibility to ensure that every victim receives the support necessary to heal and thrive, transforming their trauma into a narrative of strength and resilience.

Rehabilitation of minor girls is a journey of healing hearts—where broken dreams are gently mended, lost innocence is tenderly reclaimed, and every soul is given the chance to rise from the shadows, discovering the strength to hope and believe in life once again!

Chapter 5

WHISPERS OF A NEW DAWN

"There are no facts, only interpretations."
- Friedrich Nietzsche,
Beyond Good and Evil (1886)

There is no objective reality or absolute truth. All knowledge and understanding of the world is sieved through our subjective perspectives and biases. What we acknowledge as facts are actually interpretations moulded by our views, values, and prejudices. The objective reality is what we see in the mirror of our subjective experiences. Truth and fear are often difficult to acknowledge. Truth is daunting to accept, and fear requires courage to be revealed. As human beings, we are inherently apprehensive of the truth, for it often threatens the fragile illusions we construct around ourselves. The truth, when unveiled, forces us to confront uncomfortable realities, shaking the very foundation of our beliefs and exposing our deepest insecurities. The fear is not merely about the truth itself but what it demands from us—the potential for profound change, the risk of loss, and the dismantling of the safe, predictable environments we cling to. Revealing the truth feels perilous because it has the power to unsettle relationships, tarnish reputations, or strip away the false sense of security we find in ignorance. In much the same way, we fear our internal struggles because they bring us face-to-face with our vulnerabilities and the unpredictable, uncontrollable nature of existence.

However, when we shy away from the truth or conceal it, we plunge ourselves deeper into a cycle of consternation and denial. By avoiding these realities, we become ensnared in a web of self-deception, which alienates us from authentic growth and distorts our interactions with others. To shield ourselves from the truth is to foreclose the possibility of resolution and genuine understanding; it is to choose stagnation over transformation.

The virtuous path, though fraught with difficulty, lies in embracing both the truth and our fears with courage and vulnerability. To reveal the truth, regardless of how unsettling it may be, is to walk the road of integrity and self-liberation. It is painful, yes, but it ultimately clears the way for clarity, reconciliation, and meaningful progress. Likewise, confronting our fears empowers us, stripping them of their hold over us. In accepting and embracing the truth, along with the fears that accompany it, we free ourselves from the chains of pretence and self-delusion. In doing so, we open the door to personal evolution, deeper connections with others, and a life lived with genuine purpose and authenticity.

Between this predicament of fear and truth, human beings must always be kept at the heart of every endeavor, whether in politics, governance, or administration. Too often, systems and institutions are built on abstract principles, where the complexities and vulnerabilities of individuals are overshadowed by impersonal frameworks. When fear dictates these structures, it leads to oppression, manipulation, and the suppression of voices. Conversely, when truth is the guiding principle, it paves the way for transparency, accountability, and the empowerment of individuals. Yet neither fear nor truth should be isolated from the essential fact that at the core of every policy, decision, or strategy are human lives—complex, fragile, and deeply interconnected.

In administration, this congruent principle holds. Rules, regulations, and processes are necessary, but they must never lose sight of the individuals they are meant to serve. An administration that is rigid and indifferent to the human experience fails in its most basic function—that is, to enhance the well-being of its people. When decisions are made without regard to the human element, they become sterile, bureaucratic impositions that lack empathy and effectiveness. However, when truth informs these decisions, and when the fears and hopes of individuals are genuinely understood, governance can become more responsive, humane, and equitable.

Despite human beings being positioned at the core of governmental programmes and administrative policies, the failure to fully derive benefit from these initiatives stems from deep structural, sociological, and psychological factors. One prominent issue is the misalignment between policy formulation and the actual lived experiences of individuals. From a sociological perspective, this can be understood as a disjunction between the "system" (institutional structures and regulations) and the "lifeworld" (the everyday experiences of individuals). Policies are often designed in a top-down manner, driven by macro-level considerations and bureaucratic rationality, which often fails to account for the complexities of diverse social realities. This results in an inadequate response to the specific needs of marginalized groups, exacerbating existing inequalities.

Psychologically, individuals may experience alienation or disengagement from these programmes due to a lack of trust in the institutions that administer them. When people perceive government systems as impersonal, inaccessible, or corrupt, it leads to a form of "learned helplessness," a psychological state where individuals feel powerless to change their circumstances, even when help is theoretically available. The perceived inefficacy of governmental interventions, combined with structural inefficiencies such as corruption and administrative bottlenecks, creates a cycle of disillusionment and non-engagement.

Additionally, many government programmes operate under a technocratic, undifferentiated model, ignoring the sociocultural context in which they are implemented. This disregard for social stratification, cultural norms, and local knowledge creates barriers to participation. For instance, marginalized populations, ethnic minorities, and economically disadvantaged groups often face intersectional challenges that these programmes do not adequately address. From a sociological standpoint, this reflects a failure to incorporate a holistic, intersectional framework in policy design, where multiple dimensions of disadvantage are recognized and addressed.

Furthermore, governments and administrations frequently prioritize populism over long-term structural change. The pressure to cater to the will of the general public or political constituents often leads to a focus on superficial, symbolic policies rather than substantive, systemic reforms. In this context, the concept of "political expediency" dominates, where decisions are made based on short-term gain or public approval rather than sustainable, evidence-based solutions. This reflects a psychological tendency toward "loss aversion," where political actors are more concerned with avoiding public discontent than pursuing difficult but necessary reforms.

To address these challenges, it is essential to adopt a human-centric approach that integrates sociological insight and psychological empathy. Policies must move beyond bureaucratic rationality and engage with the lived realities of individuals through participatory governance models. This requires genuine dialogical engagement between policymakers and citizens, fostering an environment of trust, accountability, and inclusion. In sociological terms, this shift would involve bridging the gap between the "system" and the "lifeworld" through bottom-up policy processes, ensuring that programmes are responsive to the needs of diverse social groups.

In this light of truth, away from the shadows of fear, we can assess the gravity of the issue of missing girls. We can realize the emotional agony of parents whose minor daughter is missing—it goes beyond words. Each morning, they awaken to a brutal reality: their child is gone, and they do not know where. The start of each day means yet another journey into uncertainty, another walk through fear and longing that can feel like it tears their hearts open anew. These parents pour all their hopes and energy into the search for their daughter, visiting the police station repeatedly, inquiring and pleading, only to be met with silence or, sometimes, vague assurances that feel as hollow as their hearts. With each visit, they grow more desperate, more exhausted, yet they find no peace, no relief.

The police station, which once seemed a place of protection, now becomes a place of despair. They sit in the waiting area, watching officers busy with routine tasks, realizing that for these officers, their missing daughter is just one case among many. They try to catch the officer's eye, to gain a sympathetic ear, but are often brushed off, told to wait, or offered only a few words that give them no answers, no hope. They see each officer as a potential lifeline, and when those lifelines fail, it feels like another crack in their already broken world.

At home, the ache continues. They go through their neighbourhood, their friends, their relatives, asking, searching, holding up a photograph, hoping someone might have seen her or heard something. Every time someone avoids their gaze or hesitates before answering, it sparks a new dread in them. They feel ashamed and vulnerable, putting themselves at the mercy of others, but they keep asking, hoping against hope that one of these conversations might lead to her. Yet each unanswered question feels like another wall built up between them and the daughter they so desperately long to hold again.

Their relatives and friends, well-meaning at first, sometimes grow tired of the questions, the sadness, the constant reminder of a tragedy they don't know how to comfort. Some even suggest that it's time to move on, to come to terms with the fact that she might not return. But for the parents, these words are impossible to hear. How can they move on when they don't know if she's cold, hungry, or in pain? The uncertainty grips them with guilt. They feel as if they are somehow failing her by not doing enough, by not pushing harder, by not finding the answers. They blame themselves, they blame the system, and sometimes, they even turn against each other, struggling to hold on to their own sense of sanity amidst an unspeakable grief.

Each passing week wears down their bodies and minds. The sparkle in their eyes long gone. They cannot rest, cannot laugh, cannot relish anything because a part of them is gone, and nothing makes sense without her. Every small object, every familiar scent, every sound in the house reminds them of her absence. Her room becomes a sanctuary they both cherish and dread, as it remains a symbol of everything they've lost and everything they still hope to regain.

It's not just despair; it's a living nightmare that these parents endure. The pain is endless because, unlike grief, it has no closure, no finality. They cannot cry out their sorrow and begin to heal because, for them, every tear brings a sense of betrayal, as though, by mourning, they are letting go of the chance that she might still come back. In this emotional purgatory, they live for a return that may never come, and yet, they cannot afford to stop hoping. For them, that hope is all that remains. It's all that keeps them going. But it is also what chains them to a suffering that is as endless as it is profound.

When parents approach the police, they are not simply reporting a case, they are sharing a part of their pain, a depth of vulnerability that we need to understand. They look into the eyes of the officers with an unspoken plea, not only for action but for empathy, for understanding, and for the assurance that someone cares as much about finding their daughter as they do. This simple, silent exchange places a weight on the officers that sometimes extends beyond their professional responsibilities.

For the police, this means much more than following leads or conducting searches. Each case becomes personal, as they absorb the parents' fears and silent prayers. They carry the knowledge that, for some families, this hope in the police is the only hope they have left. This adds an emotional weight to their work, a weight that cannot be measured in hours logged or cases closed, but only in the hearts touched, the lives reunited, and, in some cases, the painful reality of sharing a family's grief.

The responsibility then transforms, blending duty with compassion, as the police take on a role that is part protector, part investigator, and part emotional lifeline. They understand that every visit, every phone call, every bit of news, good or bad, ripples through the lives of these parents, who are clinging to a last thread of resilience. And while they bear this burden willingly, the emotional toll on both sides is fervent, binding the police to the parents in an unspoken pact of hope, one that reaffirms the human core at the heart of every investigation.

In midst of all this, a call comes from the police station that chilled the parents to their core. The call said the police had found an unidentified body that could be their missing daughter. What the parents go through in that moment needs to be understood in its true light by every human. The parents, the missing girl and the police who shoulder this pain, all deserve to be understood by each member of the society.

Every agonizing second spent traveling to the hospital felt like a lifetime, with fear clutching their hearts in a relentless grip. Their legs were shaking and they could barely support their weight as the parents took each step towards what could be the end of all hope. The call from the police shattered the fragile peace of their lives, reverberating like a thunderclap in the stillness of their home. Panic gripped their hearts, a cold, unyielding hand that made it hard to breathe. As they rushed to the hospital, time stretched and warped; every second felt like an eternity, filled with visions of their daughter's smiling face, the sound of her laughter echoing in their minds. The burden of fear was too much to bear.

When they arrived, the sterile smell of antiseptic mingled with their anxiety, creating an almost suffocating atmosphere. Every step toward the examination room felt monumental, each footfall a battle against their overwhelming dread. How could they face the unimaginable? How could they possibly gather the courage to confirm what they feared most? The walls seemed to close in around them, amplifying their trepidation, making their hearts pound like a relentless drum.

Inside the room, the air was thick with tension. The police officer's expression was grave, and in his eyes glinted sympathy as he prepared to uncover the face of the unidentified body. In that agonizing moment, a kaleidoscope of emotions surged through them—fear, dread, despair, and a deep, aching love for their daughter that felt almost unbearable.

As the officer gently pulled back the sheet, time stood still. They held their breath, eyes fixed on the figure before them, hearts racing with the desperate hope that it wouldn't be her. A million thoughts rushed through their minds—memories of her childhood, her dreams, her smile—every moment replaying like a film on loop.

Then came the moment of truth. As the sheet fell away, they finally saw the face of the deceased. Relief washed over them in an overwhelming wave, a torrent of emotions crashing together: thankfulness mingled with sorrow for the life lost, and gratitude that their daughter was still alive. It felt like narrowly escaping a nightmare—the kind that leaves scars on the heart.

Tears filled their eyes, not just tears of relief but also for the mother who would never see her child again, a deep empathy blooming within their own grief. In that moment, they were both free and imprisoned—heartened by hope for their daughter's safety, yet mourning for a stranger whose life had ended too soon. The bittersweet mix of emotions lingered long after they left the hospital, a reminder of life's fragility and the relentless grip of uncertainty shadowing their days. Whispering silent prayers, they wished for her safe return, reaffirming their commitment to search for her, however long it might take. Their hearts were bruised but not broken; the relief of identification had fortified their resolve, igniting determination to pursue every lead and exhaust every possibility. They were still parents, still searching, still loving her with every ounce of their being.

Yet, as they closed the door of their house behind them, they were acutely aware that the world outside continued, indifferent to their suffering. Each ticking clock seemed to mock their anguish, each mundane sound a reminder of unresolved grief. But amidst the turmoil, they clung to belief—that someday, their daughter would walk through that door and they would embrace her tightly, erasing the shadows of fear.

To view this missing girl, or others like her, as merely a statistic is to overlook the profound personal and social loss her absence represents. Statistics can quantify the problem but cannot convey the human experience behind each number—the dreams, the relationships, and the life that girl once lived. Each missing child is an individual with her own story: a family who loves her, friends who feel her absence, and a community that wonders what might have been done to protect her. Her story is rich with detail, reflecting her aspirations, her talents, her fears, and her potential.

Every girl who goes missing leaves a hole in the lives of those who know and love her, creating a ripple effect of sorrow and concern that no statistic can fully capture. Parents live with the ache of loss, waiting for news, clinging to hope, and experiencing a daily anguish that data points can't convey. Friends and neighbours are left with the lingering impact of her absence, feeling less secure and wondering if their own daughters and sisters might also be at risk. When society views missing girls as mere statistics, there's a risk of becoming desensitized, of letting these cases blend into the background. Numbers can create distance, allowing us to perceive these girls as part of a distant problem rather than as irreplaceable individuals who should still be here, fulfilling their dreams. This perspective hinders empathy and action, reducing a profoundly human issue to something abstract.

Recognizing that each missing girl is much, much more than a mere statistic is essential to building a society that truly values and protects its members. It pushes us to think beyond policies and procedures, inspiring deeper, more committed efforts toward prevention, protection, and justice. It reminds us that each girl is part of a family, an irreplaceable presence, whose dignity and safety deserve unwavering respect and proactive safeguarding. This shift in perception can drive real change, making it clear that our responsibility is not only to bring every missing girl home but to create a world where she is safe, valued, and never forgotten.

Preventing cases of missing girls is a multifaceted responsibility that extends far beyond the realm of law enforcement; it requires a cohesive and collaborative effort from families, schools, communities, and various social institutions. Families serve as the first line of defence, and their role is crucial in fostering an environment of trust and open communication. By encouraging dialogue, parents and guardians empower young girls to voice their concerns, fears, and experiences without the apprehension of judgment or punishment. It is vital for families to remain vigilant, recognizing signs of distress such as withdrawal, secrecy, or changes in social circles that may indicate potential problems or outside influences. Furthermore, equipping girls with self-advocacy skills enables them to resist coercion and navigate difficult situations more effectively, fostering resilience against manipulative behaviour.

Schools play an equally significant role in this preventative framework. They can implement educational programmes that teach students about personal rights, self-protection, and the importance of mental health. Accessible counselling services within schools provide a confidential space for students to discuss their feelings and experiences with trained professionals. Peer support groups can also be established to create a sense of belonging and solidarity among students, where they can share challenges and support one another in times of distress.

Community involvement is essential to building a proactive environment where girls feel safe and supported. Neighbourhood watch initiatives and local awareness campaigns can promote vigilance and encourage community members to look out for one another. Creating safe spaces where girls can turn in times of crisis, along with promoting helplines and resources, offers immediate support for those who feel threatened or distressed. Additionally, community leaders and organizations can host workshops that educate families on recognizing early signs of distress or exploitation, equipping them with the knowledge to act swiftly when needed.

The involvement of mental health professionals is equally critical in preventing cases of missing girls. Access to mental health services can address underlying issues, such as trauma or anxiety, that may drive a girl to consider leaving home. By making counselling accessible and reducing the stigma surrounding mental health, families can better support their daughters in navigating difficult emotions and circumstances.

Media campaigns and community workshops also play a pivotal role in raising awareness about the issue of missing girls. These initiatives can educate the public on signs of distress, human trafficking, and the importance of mental well-being. By spreading knowledge and dispelling myths, communities can empower individuals to take action and support one another.

Ultimately, creating a safer society for young girls requires the collective efforts of families, schools, communities, law enforcement, and mental health professionals. Each stakeholder must understand their unique role in prevention, fostering an environment where girls feel safe, supported, and empowered to seek help when needed. Through collaboration and proactive engagement, we can work towards significantly reducing the instances of girls going missing and build a more secure future for them.

For police officers, cases of missing girls are raw, conflicting, and layered with a depth of helplessness that outsiders rarely see. Behind the uniform and professional stoicism lies a heavy personal burden. Each case isn't just a file; it's the story of a child who could be scared, hurt, or trafficked. The officer feels an intense sense of responsibility, knowing that time is crucial and that every second counts.

When leads run dry or witnesses grow uncooperative, officers experience a kind of vulnerability that can feel paralysing. This isn't mere frustration but a sense of moral defeat—a constant battle with the limitations of the system. They know every missing girl carries with her a community's pain, and often their own feelings of inadequacy. The question echoes: *Am I doing enough? Could I have done more?*

There is also a distinct loneliness. In such an emotionally demanding role, officers rarely have an outlet to express their fears, doubts, or sorrow. They may want to share their anguish but hold back, unsure if others would understand or if it might be seen as weakness. This emotional weight often goes unspoken.

A police officer's vulnerability is sometimes compounded by stereotypes or biases within the larger system, which can cloud judgment and delay responses. Too often, society dismisses certain cases, labelling girls as runaways or blaming their families—leaving officers fighting not only the case but also entrenched perceptions. Each time a missing girl isn't immediately prioritized, it stirs deep frustration.

Despite this, they carry on, often at great personal cost. Missing birthdays, forfeiting sleep, sidelining family events, they throw themselves into the mission. And yet, amidst helplessness and exhaustion, there remains a stubborn hope—a belief that their work can bring relief to families. Finding one girl, saving one life, can shift the balance of their inner struggles and reaffirm their purpose.

The need for police officers to evolve from responders to proactive changemakers speaks to a broader transformation in law enforcement. Traditionally, the role of the police has centred on reacting to crime, pursuing justice through arrests, and upholding order through enforcement. While these functions remain critical, there is a growing need for deeper engagement with societal issues, to prevent crime before it occurs and address the root causes that allow such issues to persist. In this evolved role, police officers are not merely custodians of public order; they become architects of social change, intervening at multiple levels to create safer and more just communities.

Sitting across from a victim, an officer feels the quiet yet unmistakable gravity of the moment settle over them. It is silent but heavy, like the calm before a storm. They know that each word spoken, each expression shown, can mean the difference between a victim feeling heard or dismissed. Emotions are high, both theirs and the victim's, and the urgency is clear: *I am here for you, and I will do everything within my power to help.*

The officer sees pain etched in the victim's face—a flicker of fear, shame, or perhaps a glimmer of hope—and recognizes the vulnerability of that moment. The victim may be carrying years of silence, hurt, or fear, and the officer becomes the first person they've dared to confide in. In that instant, the officer feels the weight of larger forces— social norms, biases, procedural limits, and the slow gears of justice—all pressing in. Yet they must show that here, now, they are not simply the face of an institution. They are someone ready to listen, to shoulder a portion of the burden, even if only for a few moments.

As the victim speaks, the officer's heart is conflicted. There is anger at a world that allows such suffering, at a system that sometimes fails to prevent or redress these crimes. Yet alongside this anger lies an almost fierce determination: *As long as I am here, I will not let this person down.* They know they cannot promise a perfect resolution—resources are limited, delays inevitable—but this knowledge only strengthens their resolve to do what they can in the moment.

They lean in closer, their voice steady yet gentle, their gestures small but significant—offering a glass of water, allowing silence when needed, connecting the victim with support networks. These actions silently say: *You are not just another case. You matter.*

When the meeting ends, the officer often feels a heartrending ache. There is satisfaction in having provided comfort, but it is tinged with frustration about the long road ahead. Even as they shake hands or give a reassuring nod, the weight remains: the responsibility to follow through, to keep pushing, to ensure the case is not lost among hundreds of others. Walking away, they replay the conversation, haunted by the question: *Could I have done more to ease their pain?*

Yet, despite these lingering doubts, the officer leaves knowing that in a world where answers often come slowly, their listening was perhaps the first step toward healing. And however small it may seem, they take pride in having been there for the victim, understanding that for those who are lost or hurting, even a single act of compassion can be the beginning of reclaiming their voice and their strength. The perception of the police is deeply rooted in societal narratives that have historically associated policing with force and control rather than empathy and protection. Though there have been years of reform and efforts to make the police more responsive, especially in sensitive matters involving women and children, the societal outlook remains skeptical. This is largely because perceptions are shaped not only by individual experiences but also by collective stories, news media, and past incidents that highlight gaps between law enforcement and public trust.

For the police, the challenge of earning this trust is multifaceted. On one side, they are seen as enforcers, upholding rules in a way that often feels impersonal or harsh to the public. On the other, they are expected to embody an empathetic, supportive role that goes beyond simply enforcing the law. The history of rigid hierarchical structures, corruption cases, and instances of misuse of power contribute to a societal expectation of bias or inefficiency, which can overshadow the reformed and sensitized approach modern police forces have adopted.

A truly trusting relationship has to be reciprocal. Just as the public expects the police to understand, support, and act equitably, the police need to sense respect and confidence from the public. This mutual trust requires sustained effort from both sides. Increasing transparency in police actions reinforces public confidence in the system, making it easier for society to believe in the integrity of the process. When investigations are seen as thorough, unbiased, and rooted in justice rather than political or social pressure, trust grows. Acts that call police accountability into question must be addressed promptly and fairly; doing so sends a powerful message that the force is committed not only to upholding the law but also to maintaining ethical standards.

Policing can no longer operate in isolation from the community. By involving community leaders, social workers, and local influencers, the police can build relationships that allow citizens to see them as part of the community rather than as an external controlling force. Positive interventions—stories of lives saved, victims assisted, and safety improved—must be highlighted. Too often these stories go untold, yet they are powerful tools for reshaping public perception. When people hear them, they are more likely to see the police as partners in justice and safety. Continuous training in cultural sensitivity, empathy, and communication also builds the skills officers need to engage positively with the public, helping to bridge gaps created by outdated stereotypes of the police as purely punitive figures.

Trust is a dual carriageway. While the onus often falls on the police to "earn" it, society also carries the responsibility of fostering a supportive environment that enables officers to perform effectively. Society must begin viewing police officers as allies rather than adversaries. Too often they are stereotyped as corrupt or indifferent, which shapes the public's approach to them. Recognizing that officers work under challenging, high-stress conditions fosters a spirit of partnership rather than opposition.

When police initiate reforms aimed at transparency, inclusivity, and justice, societal support is vital. Community meetings, awareness campaigns, and neighbourhood watch programmes offer opportunities for citizens to engage with such initiatives. Support signals a willingness to collaborate, encouraging officers to pursue change with public backing. Reforms take time; while it is right to hold police accountable, patience and understanding are equally necessary to ensure sustainable outcomes.

Constructive feedback also strengthens this relationship. Complaints of misconduct should be taken seriously, but society should also acknowledge instances where police go above and beyond. Positive reinforcement boosts morale, inspiring officers to continue serving with dedication. Public education on police procedures, rights, and limitations further prevents misunderstandings and allows for more informed, respectful engagement.

Equally important is recognition of police efforts. Acknowledging their work not only boosts morale but also humanizes officers in the eyes of the public. Police duties are demanding and often dangerous, and a simple expression of gratitude can motivate them to go beyond the call of duty. By involving police in community events and activities, society can create connections that transcend the transactional relationship of law enforcement, replacing fear or stigma with familiarity and trust.

Media and public discourse often highlight negative incidents, overlooking the routine yet impactful positive actions of the police. Balanced representation—acknowledging both successes and struggles—prevents one-sided narratives and builds a more complete picture of law enforcement.

The strength of justice lies in the bond of trust. When society stands with the police, they stand stronger for society. Citizens can support initiatives that advocate for better resources, training, and mental health support for officers. In doing so, they recognize that improved conditions for the police lead directly to better service for the community. A safe society is not built on enforcement alone but on the trust that society places in those who protect it.

Mutual trust empowers the police to serve effectively and allows society to become an active partner in shaping safer, more just communities. Trust is both a duty and a gift—the police earn it, and society gives it. It is the bridge that allows justice to walk with certainty. For the police to guard justice, society must guard faith in them. The courage of the police draws its strength from the trust of the people they protect.

At the heart of this shift of becoming a catalyst in the system, lies a commitment to community engagement. A police force that reaches beyond its jurisdictional duties to build trust within communities fosters an environment where people feel safe to voice their concerns and challenges. This sense of trust empowers citizens to report vulnerabilities openly, preventing minor issues from escalating into serious crimes. For instance, by closely engaging with local schools, neighbourhoods, and marginalized groups, officers can identify early indicators of issues such as human trafficking, domestic violence, and other social risks. This preventive approach is not only transformative in its capacity to protect but also aligns law enforcement with community values, thus humanizing police's image in society.

In becoming proactive changemakers, police officers also shoulder the responsibility of reshaping societal mindsets through education and sensitization. Officers who take the initiative to raise awareness on sensitive issues like gender-based violence, children's rights, and equally contribute to dismantling the stereotypes that inhibit justice and hinder progress. By educating the public, police officers foster a culture that encourages collective accountability, one where communities understand the impact of gender biases, learn to recognize the signs of abuse, and support victims in coming forward. This sensitization not only aids in crime prevention but also strengthens the social fabric, which often becomes fragmented in the absence of such consciousness.

Furthermore, proactive law enforcement involves a profound empathy for the experiences of vulnerable populations, particularly women and children, who face unique risks in society. By immersing themselves in the realities of these groups, police officers can offer a sense of reassurance and advocate for policies that address root causes rather than simply responding to symptoms. For instance, issues related to missing girls are often linked to systemic challenges such as poverty, lack of education, and social isolation. Officers who understand these intersections can advocate for cross-sector policies that bolster social safety nets, thus reducing vulnerabilities that can lead to crime.

The incorporation of data-driven approaches amplifies this vision by enabling officers to make informed decisions that target high-risk areas and patterns of criminal activity. Through predictive analysis, officers can strategically allocate resources and implement interventions in communities prone to crime, reducing the chances of offenses occurring. Data-backed policing, combined with an empathetic, engaged presence, creates a comprehensive strategy that addresses both immediate and systemic aspects of crime prevention.

Eventually, when police officers take on the mantle of changemakers, they transcend the conventional boundaries of their roles to cultivate a society resilient against crime. They shift from simply enforcing laws to actively nurturing environments that foster protection, accountability, and mutual reverence. This transformation redefines the role of law enforcement in a modern context, affirming that police officers, through sustained engagement and reform, can indeed be at the forefront of social progress. As changemakers, they not only protect the law but also become essential advocates for a society where justice is preemptive, inclusive, and rooted in a profound commitment to human dignity and equity. True policing is not just about catching criminals; it's about building trust and fostering community resilience.

The responsibility of addressing the disappearance of minor girls, or any crime, cannot fall solely on the police. While law enforcement is essential in investigating and resolving cases, genuine progress requires a deeply collaborative, community-driven approach. Tackling complex social issues demands a collective effort, one that brings together not only the police but also other stakeholders.

At a broader level, policymakers play an instrumental role by shaping protective laws, empowering communities, and enhancing coordination between agencies. A culture of vigilance, empathy, and shared responsibility can magnify the impact of police efforts, making them part of a stronger, interconnected framework against crime. If we hope to make real, lasting change, we must understand that safety is a collective responsibility—one achieved only through the united and active efforts of every part of society.

The historical perception of police as a force meant primarily to "control" society has its roots in colonial and authoritarian models, where the police were agents of state power tasked with suppressing dissent and maintaining order. Their relationship with society was often adversarial, with limited emphasis on collaboration. However, as societies have evolved and democratic values have gained prominence, there has been a significant shift toward viewing police not merely as enforcers of law but as protectors and collaborators within the community. This shift is perspicacious in socio-psychological terms, reflecting changes in how society views authority, trust, and partnership.

Redefining authority and power—from control to partnership—is central to this shift. Traditionally, police authority was a form of unilateral power, symbolising dominance over civilians to maintain order. In a collaborative model, this authority is redefined to underpin mutual responsibility, where police and citizens co-create a safe environment. This changes the power dynamic from a "top-down" approach to a "side-by-side" model, psychologically empowering communities to actively contribute to their safety. Shared decision-making fosters a more balanced perception of authority, where the police are seen less as authoritarian figures and more as community allies.

Collaborative policing humanizes officers, transforming them from "enforcers" to "protectors" in the eyes of the public. When police engage openly and empathetically with communities, it helps dismantle stereotypes that paint them as unapproachable or rigid. In this model, trust is mutual, requiring police to demonstrate accountability, transparency, and consistency. Trust becomes less about fear and more about mutual respect. This shift can help create a positive psychological association with law enforcement, strengthening its legitimacy and acceptance in society.

Emphasis on empathy and close engagement encourages officers to better understand the unique challenges and cultural dynamics within each community. This exposure cultivates sensitivity to the needs, struggles, and expectations of the people they serve. When police engage in active listening, they show the community that their voices are valued, helping bridge the gap between public and police, and fostering a shared sense of responsibility for public safety.

Moving from fear-based compliance to voluntary cooperation, collaborative policing encourages cooperation through respect and trust rather than fear of punishment. This psychological shift positions police as approachable, making people more willing to engage and share information, ultimately enhancing collective security. Collaborative policing is often accompanied by mechanisms such as community oversight, reporting channels, and feedback systems. When citizens see officers held accountable, trust deepens and resentment is replaced by a sense of shared purpose.

For police officers, this model redefines professional identity, emphasising the role of "public servant" over "law enforcer". This positively impacts morale and reduces the "us versus them" mentality that has historically distanced police from communities. Increasingly, officers are trained in softer skills such as conflict resolution, negotiation, and cultural sensitivity—skills essential for collaborative policing. Psychologically, this equips officers to handle diverse social situations with empathy and effectiveness.

Finally, collaborative policing reduces the "social distance" between police and the public, breaking down barriers and allowing genuine community-police integration. When officers participate in community events or lead outreach programmes, they become more than uniformed figures; they become neighbours, mentors, and role models. This integration fosters familiarity, reduces apprehension, and creates a friendlier, more cooperative atmosphere.

Influence on the community's sense of agency and responsibility comes from empowering communities. It invites community members to play an active role in ensuring their own safety, fostering a sense of agency. By strengthening social cohesion, communities feel they have a stake in law enforcement efforts and develop a collective identity centred around mutual support and cooperation. This can lead to reduced crime rates and increased solidarity, as people are more motivated to contribute positively to their environment.

By changing perceptions of justice and fairness, and through an enhanced perception of procedural justice, the police are seen as more accessible, approachable, and fair in their processes. When people feel their concerns are heard and addressed respectfully, it creates a sense of inclusivity. They are more likely to support solutions they have contributed to, increasing compliance with laws and regulations and reinforcing the idea that justice is a collective endeavour.

Community support can also alleviate some of the psychological burdens police face. Positive interactions with the community can reduce stress and burnout, as officers feel supported by the people they serve rather than constantly battling mistrust. Preventive measures, early interventions, and constructive dialogue help reduce adversarial encounters and confrontation.

Over time, this can help create a culture where law and order are upheld not by force but by a community's shared commitment to safety and justice. When police are seen as partners, communities evolve into stakeholders rather than subjects. This transformation helps develop a more resilient and proactive society, where both the police and the public actively work together to address the root causes of crime, leading to holistic and sustainable improvements.

The shift from a control-based model of policing to a collaborative, community-oriented approach is supported by various socio-psychological theories. Scholars across social psychology, criminology, and sociology have contributed to understanding how collaboration in policing impacts societal cohesion, trust in authority, and overall community well-being.

Procedural justice theory, primarily developed by scholars like Tom R. Tyler, suggests that people are more likely to comply with laws and cooperate with law enforcement when they feel that authorities are fair, transparent, and respectful. Rather than using coercive measures, building legitimacy through fair processes enhances people's perception of law enforcement. When police act transparently and fairly, communities are more likely to view them as legitimate and to follow rules voluntarily. This collaborative approach encourages compliance because people feel respected and valued, not coerced. The result is increased public trust, better cooperation with investigations, and a stronger sense of community. This also enhances police legitimacy, making their role as enforcers less necessary as communities engage more willingly in maintaining public order.

The social identity theory, developed by Henri Tajfel and John Turner, posits that people derive part of their identity from the groups to which they belong. If the police can foster a sense of shared identity with the community, citizens may view the police as part of "us" rather than "them," reducing conflict. Through collaborative efforts like community policing, the police can work to break down social barriers, creating a more inclusive identity that incorporates both officers and civilians. This reduces the "us vs. them" mentality and builds a more cooperative, cohesive relationship between police and the public. It also reduces social distance and fosters a collective commitment to community safety.

Collective efficacy, a concept explored by Robert J. Sampson, Stephen Raudenbush, and Felton Earls, refers to a community's shared belief in its ability to maintain social order and solve problems collectively. A strong sense of collective efficacy promotes informal social control, where communities work proactively to prevent crime. Collaborative policing strengthens collective efficacy by empowering communities to participate in their own safety and well-being. This community-driven effort reduces reliance on police intervention, leading to sustainable reductions in crime and a healthier, more resilient social dynamic. The broken windows theory, introduced by James Q. Wilson and George L. Kelling, argues that visible signs of disorder (like broken windows) can encourage further crime. Critics argue that harsh policing based on this theory led to over-policing in disadvantaged neighbourhoods, eroding trust. Recently, scholars have suggested an adaptation of the theory that emphasizes community empowerment and involvement rather than strict control. A collaborative approach addresses disorder not by aggressive policing but by involving the community in addressing issues like blight, truancy, and neighbourhood cleanliness. This approach empowers communities to take ownership, with police playing a supportive role rather than enforcing authority. Improved neighbourhood aesthetics and morale, reduction in minor crime without heavy-handed policing, and an enhanced sense of community ownership and pride.

Social Contract theory, rooted in the philosophical work of Thomas Hobbes, John Locke, and Jean-Jacques Rousseau, proposes that citizens agree to abide by laws in exchange for protection and social order. Modern interpretations suggest that for this contract to be effective, authorities must act with integrity and fairness, maintaining the public's trust. Collaborative policing reaffirms the social contract by ensuring that citizens' voices are part of the policing process. When police respect community needs and provide safety while valuing community input, it strengthens the implicit social contract.

Restorative justice, championed by scholars like Howard Zehr, advocates for a system that emphasizes repairing harm, restoring relationships, and involving community members in the justice process. Rather than focusing solely on punishment, restorative justice encourages accountability, healing, and community involvement. Collaborative policing allows for restorative practices in resolving minor offenses or community conflicts, where the police mediate rather than punish. Restorative circles and conflict resolution meetings can involve victims, offenders, and community members, focusing on understanding and repairing harm. Increased community healing, reduced recidivism, and a more supportive environment that focuses on restoration over retribution, making police community relationships more constructive and less punitive.

Humanistic psychology and empathy building, developed by figures like Carl Rogers and Abraham Maslow, emphasizes empathy, self-actualization, and the potential for growth. When applied to policing, humanistic principles encourage police to approach communities empathetically, recognizing each individual's unique context and experiences. Training in emotional intelligence and communication can help officers respond compassionately, especially in sensitive situations.

These theoretical underpinnings reveal that collaborative policing isn't merely a structural change, it's a cultural and psychological shift. By focusing on shared values, empathy, and community involvement, this approach aligns policing with modern democratic ideals, building a stronger, more cohesive society where police are allies and guardians, not controllers.

Now when it comes to crime against women, we need to discern that the position of women in society has been shaped by complex interplays of power, culture, and history. Traditionally, many societies have been structured around patriarchal norms, where men hold the majority of power in both public and private spheres, while women have often been confined to roles centered around domesticity and caregiving. This unequal power dynamic is deeply embedded in social institutions like family, education, religion, and the workplace, perpetuating systemic inequality. Sociologists argue that women's social position has historically been subordinate, with their contributions either devalued or made invisible by dominant ideologies. These ideologies often stem from patriarchal traditions that regard men as the breadwinners, decision-makers, and leaders, while women are expected to be obedient, nurturing, and confined to the private domain of home and family. For much of history, this gendered division of labour limited women's access to education, employment, and political power. However, as feminist sociologists such as Sylvia Walby have noted, gender inequality is not natural or inevitable but socially constructed through deeply entrenched power relations.

In modern sociological thought, there is a growing recognition that women have always played critical roles in society, though their contributions have often been stranded. Feminist theorists, including scholars like Betty Friedan and Bell hooks, emphasize the importance of recognizing women's agency and contributions across all sectors of life, from the domestic to the professional. They challenge the assumption that women are only valuable in nurturing roles and argue for the need to deconstruct the gender binaries that have historically constrained both women and men.

Women's desires, according to sociologists, reflect both personal aspirations and the struggle against societal constraints. Many women seek autonomy, the ability to pursue careers, education, and self-determination without being limited by gender expectations. Feminist sociologists highlight how women have historically been socialized to internalize societal expectations, which often conflict with their individual aspirations for independence and equality. Thus, a key sociological argument is that society needs to evolve to accommodate women's diverse desires, rather than imposing restrictive roles that limit their potential.

Today, women's position in society is in a state of flux, with notable progress but persistent inequalities. While women have made significant strides in areas such as education, employment, and political representation, gender inequality persists through wage gaps, underrepresentation in leadership roles, and societal norms that continue to place disproportionate expectations on women to balance professional and domestic responsibilities. Sociologists emphasize that this inequality is not just a matter of individual bias but is structurally reinforced through policies, media representations, and institutional practices. Moreover, sociologists argue that women's position must be understood through an intersectional lens, recognising that gender interacts with other forms of identity such as race, class, sexuality, and religion. For example, the experiences and challenges of women of colour or working-class women differ significantly from those of middle- or upper-class white women, leading to differentiated struggles for equality.

Ultimately, sociologists advocate for dismantling the structural barriers that perpetuate inequality. This includes addressing issues such as gender-based violence, unequal labour practices, and the socialization processes that start from birth, teaching girls to aspire to different futures than boys. This calls for a transformation of societal norms and institutions to create a more equitable society where women are seen and valued not for their adherence to traditional roles, but for their individual talents, aspirations, and humanity. The sociological perspective on women's position in society underscores that while progress has been made, deep-rooted structural inequalities remain. The challenge lies not only in recognizing women's contributions but in reshaping societal frameworks to ensure that women, in all their diversity, can participate fully and equally in all areas of life.

Sociologically, women's empowerment involves the redistribution of power within both the private and public spheres. At the household level, it seeks to dismantle the "domesticity trap," where women's roles are undervalued in terms of social and economic capital. At the societal level, it calls for the reallocation of political and economic power that has long been monopolized by men. This requires a reconceptualization of power itself, from something hierarchical and concentrated, to something shared and inclusive.

A woman may feel trapped in the shadow of her former self, a shell where her voice is lost and her identity has faded. Every day is a battle as she braces for the next wave of pain. She feels empty and broken, carrying a silent ache that no one else can see. Deep down, there is a gnawing sense of shame, as though she is to blame for the way she is treated. She feels embarrassed for not having left, for not standing up, yet powerless to make any other choice. A constant fear underlies her routine, with every word and action calculated to avoid triggering another episode of cruelty.

She feels isolated, cut off from the warmth and support of others. Even in a crowd, she feels entirely alone, as if living in a different world—invisible, forgotten. She fears that no one would understand her pain, or worse, that she would be judged if the truth were known. Inside, an overwhelming sadness weighs on her, sometimes making her wish for freedom, though despair whispers that she will never escape. Exhaustion consumes her, leaving her numb as sorrow, pain, and fear blur into a heavy silence. Yet, beneath it all, a fragile flicker of hope survives — the hope that one day someone will hear her, that she will find the strength to reclaim herself and leave the darkness behind.

Women, therefore, require empowerment not because they are inherently weaker or less capable than men, but because they are systemically disadvantaged by a society that has normalized male dominance and female subordination.

In this context, the question of why women cannot be treated equally without the need for empowerment points to the reality that equality cannot be assumed in a society built on unequal foundations. Sociologists argue that the idea of "equality" must be contextualized. Men and women do not start from the same social, economic, or cultural positions. Male privilege is deeply entrenched in societal structures, giving men unearned advantages, while women often must navigate landscapes shaped by gendered expectations, discrimination, and systemic barriers. Treating men and women "equally" without first addressing these power asymmetries would only perpetuate existing inequalities.

The notion of "extra power" required for women to achieve parity with men refers to the need for affirmative action, policy interventions, and social movements that actively seek to dismantle the systemic oppression of women. This is not about granting women undue privilege but about rectifying historical injustices and leveling the playing field. The focus of women's empowerment is on capacity-building, enabling women to have control over their own bodies, access to education, participation in governance, and economic independence, domains traditionally dominated by men.

Moreover, empowerment entails a collective dimension as well. Women's movements and feminist activism have been central to driving societal change, as they work to challenge the gendered division of labour, patriarchal laws, and cultural norms that legitimize male superiority. Empowerment, in this sense, is both a personal and political act that seeks to subvert the hegemonic power relations that marginalize women.

Women's empowerment is a multifaceted concept shaped by various theories and perspectives that highlight the sociological and psychological dimensions of women's experiences. These theories elucidate the mechanisms through which women can gain power, autonomy, and agency in their lives.

Feminist theory examines the social structures that perpetuate gender inequalities. It emphasizes the need for women to reclaim their rights and advocate for systemic changes that promote gender equality. Feminist scholars argue that empowerment is not merely about individual success but about collective action to dismantle oppressive structures.

Social constructionism posits that gender roles and identities are socially constructed through cultural norms and practices. Empowerment, therefore, involves deconstructing these socially imposed identities and challenging the narratives that restrict women's potential. By recognizing that societal expectations shape perceptions of gender, women can reclaim their identities and assert their agency.

Intersectionality, coined by Kimberlé Crenshaw, examines how various social identities—such as race, class, sexuality, and ability—intersect to create unique experiences of oppression and privilege. This theory underscores the importance of understanding the diverse contexts in which women live, emphasizing that empowerment must address multiple layers of discrimination. By acknowledging intersectionality, empowerment efforts can be more inclusive and effective in addressing the specific needs of marginalized women.

Empowerment theory, rooted in psychology, focuses on enhancing individual and collective power through skill development, self-efficacy, and confidence. This perspective highlights the importance of psychological resilience and the belief in one's ability to effect change, equipping women with the skills and knowledge necessary to assert their rights and navigate societal challenges.

Self-determination theory emphasizes the intrinsic motivation that drives individuals to pursue their goals and aspirations. Empowerment occurs when women are supported in their quest for autonomy, competence, and relatedness. By fostering environments that nurture self-determination, women can cultivate a sense of agency and empowerment, ultimately leading to greater personal and professional fulfilment.

Social learning theory, developed by Albert Bandura, posits that people learn behaviours and attitudes through observation and imitation. This theory underscores the role of role models and mentors in empowering women. By providing access to positive female role models and supportive networks, women can learn to navigate obstacles and develop the skills necessary for empowerment.

The synthesis of these sociological and psychological perspectives reveals that women's empowerment is a dynamic interplay of individual agency and societal structures. This comprehensive understanding underscores the need for targeted interventions that address the diverse challenges faced by women across different contexts, ultimately fostering an environment where empowerment can thrive.

Women's empowerment in India is a multifaceted issue that encompasses various perspectives, each shaped by cultural, social, economic, and political factors. These perspectives not only reflect the historical struggles of women but also inform their current status and prospects in contemporary society.

This explains why women hesitate to report crimes, particularly gender-based violence, to the police. These theories highlight the deeply embedded societal, psychological, and institutional barriers that deter women from seeking justice. Understanding these perspectives is crucial for addressing the issue globally and reforming systems to create safer spaces for women.

Globally, efforts to combat underreporting of crimes against women have varied. Several strategies have been employed in different countries to encourage women to report violence. Many countries, such as the UK, Australia, and Canada, have shifted toward a victim-centred approach, where law enforcement agencies are trained to handle sensitive cases with empathy and discretion. Specialized units, like "Family Violence Units" or "Women's Desks," are designed to cater to female victims, providing a safe environment where women can report crimes without fear of judgment.Some nations have implemented legal reforms to ensure women feel supported in coming forward. For example, India has enacted stringent laws against rape and domestic violence, while also offering anonymity to survivors. In Scandinavian countries, progressive legal frameworks include swift prosecution and protection orders to prevent retribution.

Globally, women's helplines, support centers, and crisis shelters offer confidential spaces where women can seek help before approaching the police. These services, available in countries like the US and Sweden, are crucial in providing women with the confidence and resources to navigate the reporting process.

Public awareness campaigns in countries like Canada and Australia aim to destigmatize victims of violence and encourage reporting. Media campaigns that focus on changing societal attitudes toward gender violence have shown promising results in breaking down cultural barriers to reporting.

Some countries have prioritized training their police forces to be more sensitive to gender-based violence. For example, South Africa has trained female police officers to handle rape and assault cases, making it easier for women to report crimes to someone they feel more comfortable with.

The pioneering efforts of different countries have been globally accepted and adopted by many. Despite these global efforts, the fight against underreporting remains complex and requires multifaceted solutions. It is essential to address the psychological, cultural, and systemic factors that silence women, while continuing to develop supportive environments where justice feels attainable.

Envisioning a world where a woman feels entirely free to think and express herself without hesitation is to dream of a society that has redefined its very core to uphold genuine equality, empathy, and respect for autonomy. In this ideal world, women are nurtured from an early age to recognize their inherent worth, fostering self-assurance and the freedom to communicate openly. Here, they could voice their thoughts, preferences, and boundaries, unhindered by societal judgments, fear of repercussions, or the constraints of traditional expectations.

Achieving such a world would mean dismantling long-entrenched stereotypes and gender biases, which restrict not only women but everyone. Education would play a foundational role, instilling values of mutual respect, empathy, and self-worth in boys and girls alike from a young age. Parents, teachers, mentors, and leaders would contribute by challenging limiting norms, celebrating individuality, and encouraging young people to embrace their distinct voices and perspectives. Women are not here to be beautiful, graceful, or quiet. They are here to be strong, confident, and free.

In such a society, the views of women would hold equal weight and be received with the same seriousness and respect as men's, with no implicit pressure to conform to gendered expectations. Workplaces, communities, and family structures would each embody and promote spaces where women's insights, ambitions, and critiques are valued, making it unremarkable yet meaningful for a woman to speak her mind, pursue her passions, and assert her boundaries.

A supportive legal and policy framework would be indispensable. Laws would proactively uphold women's right to speak, seek redress, and demand accountability in a society that respects personal choice and freedom. A robust legal framework would guarantee that a woman's opinions and preferences can be freely voiced, even when they push against conventional boundaries, without the fear of backlash or prejudice. As Malala Yousafzai says, "We realize the importance of our voices only when we are silenced".

While the creation of this world requires monumental cultural and systemic shifts, it's a vision worth striving for. Such a change would necessitate the collective evolution of cultural norms and individual mindsets, encouraging societies to value empathy, uphold individuality, and genuinely respect each person's voice. As we continue to progress in understanding and advocating for equality, every step taken to empower women to think and speak freely brings us closer to actualizing this imagined world. G.D.Anderson said, "Feminism isn't about making women strong. Women are already strong. It's about changing the way the world perceives that strength".

To envision a truly free and safe world for women, the role of men is not only supportive but transformative. This transformation begins with sensitizing young men and boys, as they are in a unique position to challenge and dismantle the stereotypes, privileges, and biases that sustain gender-based inequality and violence. Instead of placing the burden of safety on women, asking them to modify their behaviour, dress, or ambitions, men should be at the forefront of fostering a culture that respects women's autonomy and dignity.

The empowerment of a woman is not only her personal journey but also a shared societal responsibility, where the role of a man can be pivotal in creating spaces where her potential can flourish without fear or limitation. When men step into this role with respect, understanding, and partnership, they contribute to breaking down the barriers of patriarchy that have historically held women back. Empowerment, then, is not merely an act of giving but an act of standing alongside, ensuring that women are heard, respected, and supported in every step they take.

Take, for instance, the story of a young girl with a dream to study engineering in a village where girls are expected to marry young and look after households. Her father, a farmer himself, knows that many in his community may question why a girl needs to study so much. But he believes in his daughter's potential, defying his own social conditioning and breaking the mould. Every morning, he walks her to the bus stop, shielding her from sneering comments and dismissive looks. He sits with her late into the night under the dim light of a kerosene lamp, helping her solve equations he doesn't fully understand, but he tries his best to encourage her.

When she faces self-doubt, he lifts her spirits, reminding her of her capabilities and telling her stories of women he admires. His constant support instils in her the courage to overcome her challenges. She grows up not feeling limited by society's boundaries but strengthened by her father's belief in her potential. She completes her studies and becomes an engineer, not only transforming her own life but inspiring other girls in her village.

In this journey, the father's role goes beyond mere support. His involvement is a quiet yet powerful message that men and women are allies in each other's empowerment. By standing with her, he sets an example that ripples outward, teaching others that a man's belief in a woman's strength can be the very foundation of her empowerment.

Men can act as allies by actively opposing gender-based violence and discriminatory practices, advocating for women's rights, and promoting gender equality. This involves speaking out against sexist remarks, standing against harassment, and challenging attitudes that belittle or devalue women. As allies, men must respect and amplify women's voices, understanding that creating a safe world is not about protecting women as one would a vulnerable entity but empowering them as equal individuals.

To bring about this shift, sensitization must start early. Young boys should be taught to understand and respect boundaries, to recognize the autonomy of others, and to reject stereotypical gender roles that depict women as submissive or secondary. Education systems, families, and society at large should foster qualities like empathy, emotional intelligence, and respect for all individuals, breaking away from the toxic norms of masculinity that equate dominance with strength. Schools can incorporate curriculum modules on gender equality, emotional intelligence, and respect for diversity, encouraging boys to view their female peers as equals.

Sensitization efforts should also focus on redefining masculinity. Too often, masculinity is associated with dominance, aggression, and control, which leads to viewing women as "others" or as "belonging" to men in some way. By promoting a vision of masculinity rooted in respect, responsibility, and empathy, society can cultivate a generation of men who perceive women as equal partners rather than as entities to control or protect. This reframing can lead to a more supportive environment where men feel accountable for contributing to a safer society.

Men hold significant power in various domains—from workplaces to social settings—to set standards for what is acceptable. They should take proactive steps to create spaces where women feel safe and respected, whether this is by establishing zero-tolerance policies against harassment or by setting respectful, inclusive social norms. Men can lead by example, demonstrating that creating safe spaces is a shared responsibility that benefits everyone.

Family plays a central role in shaping young minds. If boys see their fathers and male figures sharing household responsibilities, respecting their spouses, and treating women as equals, they are more likely to internalize these values. Fathers, in particular, play a powerful role in teaching their sons that respect for women begins at home. This includes encouraging and celebrating the achievements of female family members, thereby setting a tone that men and women are not limited by traditional roles.

A key responsibility for men is to counteract narratives that shift the blame for harassment or assault onto women. Men should refuse to accept or perpetuate attitudes that question women's choices, instead recognizing that a safe society holds perpetrators accountable, not victims. This includes using their voices to advocate for fair representation of women in media and culture, challenging portrayals that objectify or trivialize women.

Men, especially those in positions of influence, can act as mentors to younger boys and men, guiding them toward values of equality and respect. They can also influence their peers by openly discussing the need for a shift in how society perceives gender roles, demonstrating that these values are integral to personal and social success. Peer networks and friendships offer powerful platforms to reinforce positive behaviour and discourage toxic, sexist, or violent tendencies.

In essence, building a free and safe world for women requires men to actively participate as agents of change, taking responsibility for creating a culture that values gender equality. Instead of placing the responsibility solely on women to navigate safety and respect, men must embrace their role as integral contributors to a fair, just, and inclusive society. Through genuine partnership and equal commitment, men and women can together dismantle the deep-seated biases that hinder progress, ultimately ensuring that freedom and safety are not privileges, but rights accessible to all.

Building a world that is genuinely safe and secure for women involves an interconnected approach that brings together the insights of scholars, social activists, psychologists, criminologists, and policymakers. It is not only about establishing a physically secure environment but about creating a society where women's autonomy and dignity are upheld, where they feel equally valued, and where systems actively work to dismantle structures that lead to gender-based violence and discrimination. This means equality in access to resources, education, and opportunities, and a social system that removes barriers preventing women from participating fully and freely.

Scholars of social and economic justice argue that policy shifts are crucial. Laws must guarantee equal pay, equal opportunities in education and employment, and support systems for women balancing multiple roles. Affirmative action policies in workplaces, educational institutions, and political structures can ensure that women's voices and perspectives are represented. A world where cultural norms do not limit women's aspirations or stigmatize them based on their choices. Sociologists such as Erving Goffman and Pierre Bourdieu propose that change happens when society collectively revises its perceptions. Education plays a pivotal role here, rethinking how we socialize children to understand gender roles. By teaching both boys and girls about consent, respect, and empathy from a young age, we can build a foundation of mutual respect.

A world where women's mental health is acknowledged and prioritized. In such a society, emotional well-being would be as crucial as physical safety. Psychologists highlight the need for safe spaces and counselling services for women, particularly those affected by violence or trauma. This can involve creating community support networks and ensuring access to mental health resources. Additionally, campaigns that address toxic masculinity can prevent violence at its roots, fostering a healthier emotional environment for both men and women.

A world where systems are responsive, protective, and compassionate when addressing violence against women. Criminologists and legal scholars emphasize the importance of responsive legal systems that not only punish offenders but provide adequate support to survivors. Reforms in policing, such as specialized training in gender sensitivity, the establishment of dedicated units to address gender-based violence, and stricter sentencing for offenders, create a deterrent effect.

A world where women have financial independence, eliminating reliance that can often lead to abuse and exploitation. Scholars of economics advocate for policies that encourage female entrepreneurship, microloans, and vocational training. By empowering women economically, we enable them to make autonomous choices about their lives and leave unsafe situations more easily.

A world where public spaces are designed with women's safety in mind—well-lit streets, safe public transportation, and responsive emergency services. Urban planners and architects have increasingly focused on "gender-sensitive" design, which considers the safety needs of women. Ensuring that transport is safe and accessible, incorporating more public lighting, and designing inclusive community spaces can significantly reduce risks.

A world where women are equally represented in leadership and governance. Research shows that when women are involved in decision-making, policies become more inclusive and considerate of women's issues. Having more women in politics, the judiciary, and corporate leadership can help shape policies that address the root causes of inequality and violence against women.

Lastly, we must see this effort as an ongoing commitment. Societal change is gradual, and every generation must pass on the values of respect, equality, and security to sustain this vision. By understanding and implementing these theories, we do not just build a safer world for women but create a society where human dignity is fundamental, and every individual has the freedom to live without fear.

In today's world, sustainability in the pursuit of equality and safety for all is especially challenging due to rapid globalization, technological advancements, and shifting political landscapes. Economic inequality has intensified; while some regions thrive with increased access to resources and innovation, others struggle with limited infrastructure and opportunities. This gap is stark in issues like climate change, where wealthier nations and corporations, despite contributing the most to global emissions, can often afford to shield themselves from the worst effects, leaving vulnerable communities—particularly in developing countries—disproportionately exposed.

Social biases persist, impacting diverse communities worldwide, with marginalized groups frequently denied the same level of safety and opportunities. Racial and gender discrimination continues to manifest in employment, education, healthcare, and policing, creating systemic obstacles for historically disadvantaged populations.

Additionally, as digital technologies rapidly evolve, they create both potential and risk; while digital tools could bridge gaps in access and equity, the digital divide grows wider, with millions lacking access to essential technology, keeping them from economic participation and critical information.

Global political tensions and populism also make cooperation difficult. While international cooperation is essential for addressing global issues like poverty, migration, and environmental degradation, many countries are increasingly focused on nationalism, which limits collaborative solutions. When governments prioritize short-term economic gains over collective safety and equality, sustainability becomes a secondary concern. This contemporary context makes it evident that while there is widespread recognition of the need for a safe, equitable world, the path to sustaining such a world is obstructed by structural inequalities, biases, and the often-conflicting interests of economic development, environmental sustainability, and social justice.

The theoretical arc of this thought follows the principles of sustainable development intersecting with social justice theories, along with frameworks from structural inequality and systems theory. At its core, the notion is rooted in sustainable development, as defined by the UN Sustainable Development Goals (SDGs). This framework emphasizes that true sustainability must encompass not only environmental preservation but also social inclusivity and economic equity. The primary objective is to create systems that meet present needs without compromising future generations' ability to thrive. Social justice theories argue that fairness and equality are essential for any society to thrive. The thought aligns with theorists like John Rawls, who emphasize that social and economic inequalities must be arranged so that they are of the greatest benefit to the least advantaged members of society. This builds on the idea that a safe and equal world isn't possible without redistributive measures that account for historical and structural disadvantages. Structural inequality theories, such as those proposed by Pierre Bourdieu and Iris Marion Young, frame the systemic barriers that prevent equality and safety in society. They highlight that economic, social, and cultural capital is unevenly distributed, often reinforcing cycles of privilege for some groups and disenfranchisement for others. This framework helps explain why achieving equality in safety and opportunity is challenging when established systems perpetuate these disparities. Systems theory brings attention to how issues like economic inequality, social bias, and environmental degradation are interconnected and cannot be resolved in isolation. According to this perspective, change in one part of the system affects all others, often in unpredictable ways. This interconnectedness explains why a push for economic growth might lead to environmental harm, or how social biases can undermine.

Envisioning a world entirely free of stereotypes or preconceived notions is compelling, though it brings complex challenges. Stereotypes often arise as mental shortcuts that help people make sense of the world by categorizing experiences and individuals based on prior observations. While this simplifies processing information, it also limits understanding by creating rigid expectations.

If we consider a world without stereotypes, it would require people to approach every interaction, person, and situation without any form of pre-judgment. This would mean that individuals would have to rely on direct, personal experiences and individual character assessments rather than broad generalizations. Such a world would be rooted in openness and curiosity, where people would feel more valued for their uniqueness, and diverse ways of thinking and being could flourish.

However, stereotypes are so deeply embedded in culture, socialization, and even language that eradicating them entirely would demand substantial social, psychological, and structural repositioning. Education systems would need to emphasize critical thinking and self-awareness from a young age, teaching individuals to question assumptions and remain open to a multitude of perspectives. Additionally, media, literature, and cultural narratives would need to reflect a more balanced portrayal of diversity to counter stereotype formation.

Without stereotypes, society might achieve a more equitable landscape. People's life choices—such as career paths, relationships, and self-expression—could be less constrained by societal expectations. Yet, some argue that stereotypes serve a functional role in building cultural coherence and social identity. In their absence, individuals might face greater pressure to define and understand identities with fewer societal "guides". Nonetheless, the potential for empathy, tolerance, and personal freedom would likely outweigh this, creating a world where individuals engage with one another through mutual respect and understanding rather than assumption.

Ultimately, while achieving a stereotype-free world might be impractical, efforts to reduce their influence could allow society to come closer to this ideal, fostering a world where individuals are seen and valued for their true selves.

Stereotypes often operate subconsciously, so the first step is awareness. Educational programmes and campaigns can help people recognize when they're relying on stereotypes and understand their harmful impact. Schools and workplaces can incorporate discussions about biases and stereotypes, fostering environments that value open-mindedness and individuality. Teaching critical thinking and media literacy from a young age helps people question and deconstruct stereotypes rather than accept them at face value.

Negative stereotypes often fade when people have genuine, personal experiences with individuals who defy these biases. When people engage with others outside their social groups, they see the richness of individuality that stereotypes mask. Policies that promote diversity and inclusivity in schools, communities, and workplaces encourage interactions across different backgrounds and foster understanding.

Media is one of the most influential tools in shaping perceptions. By promoting diverse and accurate representations of people and communities, media can help challenge stereotypes. Movies, books, and television shows that showcase multidimensional portrayals—avoiding one-sided caricatures—go a long way in shifting mindsets. Storytelling is equally powerful in challenging stereotypes. Sharing real-life stories, especially those that highlight resilience, achievements, and positive contributions of people from stereotyped groups, helps counter limiting narratives and opens new perspectives.

Language reflects and reinforces stereotypes, so revisiting the words we use is essential. Terms and phrases that perpetuate negative stereotypes should be consciously replaced with neutral, respectful language. Social norms around what is "acceptable" or "expected" for certain groups can also be questioned and redefined. For example, challenging the notion that certain jobs are better suited for one gender or ethnicity can lead to more inclusive work environments.

Empathy-building exercises and workshops can promote understanding by encouraging people to consider others' perspectives. When people empathize, they are less likely to see others through the lens of stereotypes. Self-reflection also helps individuals recognize and challenge their biases. Asking questions like, "Why do I feel this way about this person?" or "Is this belief based on experience or assumption?" can help dismantle stereotypes within themselves.

Institutional support is crucial to break down stereotypes ingrained in laws, policies, and organizational structures. Bias training, equitable hiring practices, and anti-discrimination policies can create environments that value diversity and hold people accountable for perpetuating stereotypes. Policies aimed at reducing inequality—such as equal access to education, healthcare, and job opportunities—also help weaken stereotypes by giving everyone the chance to succeed and break out of predefined roles.

Societies evolve through stories that challenge old beliefs and present new possibilities. When individuals, families, and communities openly discuss examples of people breaking stereotypes, it creates positive role models for others. New narratives—such as those celebrating women in science, men in caregiving roles, or minorities in leadership—gradually normalize diverse paths and weaken stereotypes over time. By combining individual, social, and institutional changes, we can dismantle stereotypes that limit growth and progress. This approach does not erase them overnight, but steadily weakens their hold, advancing us toward a society where people's actions, talents, and character define them more than outdated perceptions.

A minor girl carries a heavy burden in her heart, a weight that words cannot easily lift. Something has been done to her—something unjust and violating—and while the law demands punishment for the wrong, she feels frozen in fear. She is gripped by a silence so profound it renders her voice a mere whisper within.

She knows what happened to her was wrong, that she deserves justice. And yet, she cannot bring herself to speak. The words get caught in her throat, tangled in shame, confusion, and a deeply rooted fear of disbelief or judgment. How would her family react? Could they understand her pain, or would they, too, be overwhelmed by it?

In her mind, she replays the events again and again, but each time the fear grows stronger, and the idea of telling anyone grows more distant. She feels lost in a world that suddenly seems harsher, more unforgiving than ever before. She is a small figure adrift in a vast, uncharted ocean of emotions—guilt, anger, despair, and a profound loneliness that presses on her spirit.

This reveals the inner landscape of a young girl whose innocence has been shattered, yet whose heart holds back from seeking solace or justice. It is as if she exists in a realm beyond words, where fear is her only companion and silence becomes a shield. But even in this silence, there is an unspoken plea—a faint hope that someone, somewhere, might understand her pain and help her find her voice again.

Do we, as a society, have the sensitivity to perceive this pain? These questions need to be answered. This void needs to be filled.

The dilemma of returning home for a girl who has left her family is a complex emotional battleground, filled with conflicting feelings, fears, and desires.

She sits alone, feeling the weight of her decision pressing on her shoulders, heavy and unrelenting. She misses the warmth of home, the comforting sounds of her family, the familiar scent of her mother's cooking, and the laughter echoing through the walls. A deep ache stirs within her, a longing for the security she once had but didn't realize until she left. She wants nothing more than to go back, to feel that safety once more.

But each time she imagines walking through that door, a surge of fear stops her. She remembers the voices of neighbours gossiping, the stern, unforgiving look she fears seeing in her father's eyes, and the possible anger and disappointment on her mother's face. How could she return after what she has done? The shame of her choices, the fear of judgment, and the worry that she will forever be seen as the girl who defied everyone's expectations all combine to form an invisible wall, keeping her away.

She feels unworthy, like she has lost her place in the family, like her very presence would bring disgrace upon them. In her mind, she replays everything she might hear upon her return, questions about where she was, what she did, and, most painfully, why she left. She's terrified that no one will understand, no one will see her desperation, her loneliness, and the pain she felt that drove her to run.

Every time she gathers the courage to return, a wave of doubt crashes over her. She wonders if she can bear the judgment, the whispers, the anger, and the blame. She wants to believe her family will understand, that they will welcome her back with open arms, but she fears that her return might be met with shame rather than love, with punishment rather than understanding.

And so, she remains stuck, caught between two worlds, one she ran from, and one she does not know. She longs to come back, to feel her mother's embrace, to hear her father's voice softened with forgiveness, to see her family again, but the fear keeps her in place. She is lost, a girl without a home, haunted by the hope of returning and the despair that she might never belong again.

At the core of her dilemma is an innate longing for the safety and familiarity of home. After facing the harsh realities of the outside world, where she may have encountered loneliness, danger, and emotional upheaval, the comforts of home, like warmth, security, and love, become even more pronounced. She remembers moments of joy, laughter, and protection that she once took for granted. This nostalgia creates a strong pull to return, but the fear of how her family will react complicates this desire.

Alongside fear, there's a heavy burden of shame and guilt. She might grapple with the belief that leaving was a betrayal of her family's trust and values. This can manifest in self-loathing and feelings of being unworthy of love. The guilt may also be compounded by worries about the impact of her departure on her family, how they might have suffered due to her absence. This emotional weight can further entrench her reluctance to return, as she feels undeserving of a warm welcome. Ultimately, the dilemma of returning home is an emotional labyrinth. It involves navigating a landscape filled with fear, regret, longing, and the search for belonging. For a minor girl caught in this turmoil, the path back can feel both necessary and impossibly daunting, as she balances her desire for safety and love against her fears of judgment and rejection.

Building a world that welcomes missing girls back, without judgment or prejudice, requires a transformation in how society perceives and values each human life.

To embrace missing girls with an open heart, we must cultivate compassion and empathy in our communities. This means shifting the narrative from judgment to understanding, from questioning motives to providing a safe space. Recognizing that each of these girls has faced unique struggles, and their journey may involve trauma, loss, or betrayal, should guide our responses to them. A compassionate society is one that sees each girl as more than her circumstances, embracing her for her intrinsic human dignity. When a missing girl returns, society tends to label her based on why she left or what she may have experienced. By dismantling these harmful stereotypes and stigmas, we can create an environment that does not see a returning girl as a subject of suspicion but rather as someone in need of acceptance. Society must redefine its value system to place the individual above societal norms, recognizing her experience without attaching shame or blame. Support systems, ranging from family and friends to community organizations and state institutions, play a vital role in creating a welcoming environment. This would mean training professionals, from social workers to law enforcement officers, to handle return cases with sensitivity, and implementing policies that prioritize the rehabilitation and reintegration of these girls. Accessible mental health resources, educational opportunities, and vocational training programmes can be foundational in helping girls rebuild their lives.

Legal frameworks must also evolve to protect and respect the rights of girls who return, allowing them to reintegrate without discrimination. Reforming laws to prevent honour-based discrimination or mistreatment, ensuring privacy and protection from media sensationalism, and enabling them to reclaim their identity with dignity are essential steps. Additionally, creating pathways for societal recognition of past injustices and offering reparative measures can validate their worth and establish a just foundation. It's often said that "it takes a village," and in this context, a community-based approach to reintegration is paramount. When communities take ownership of the welfare and safety of missing girls, they become invested in supporting them through open hearts.

Public narratives around missing girls often sensationalize their struggles, which only deepens societal prejudices. Instead, promoting stories of resilience, healing, and personal growth can inspire hope and encourage acceptance. By shifting public discourse from victimhood to empowerment, we can reshape how society views these girls, showing that they are individuals capable of immense strength, deserving of a second chance to grow and contribute. In this world, the gates would remain open because society as a whole would see every return not as an act to be scrutinized but as a testament to resilience and the importance of community support. In making this possible, we create a society that values human life above preconceived notions of right and wrong, a society that, in its acceptance, rebuilds lives and strengthens its collective humanity. The issue of a missing minor girl transcends the simplistic notion of locating a lost individual; it serves as a profound reflection of societal failures, psychological complexities, and systemic inadequacies that warrant deep examination. Understanding this issue requires us to navigate a entanglement of interconnected dimensions that encompass not only the immediate act of disappearance but also the myriad factors that contribute to and stem from such events.

At its core, the disappearance of a minor girl signals a broader societal crisis, one that highlights how individual lives are entangled in a web of cultural, familial, and systemic narratives. When a girl goes missing, the focus is often placed on the physical act of locating her. However, this perspective overlooks the emotional and psychological ramifications that ripple through families and communities. The anguish experienced by the family is profound and multifaceted, characterized by feelings of helplessness, fear, and guilt. This emotional landscape is often neglected in the urgency of the search, yet it is critical to understanding the full impact of the disappearance.

The act of a girl going missing disrupts not only the family unit but also the broader community dynamics. It raises alarm, triggers fear, and can lead to a collective sense of vulnerability that affects community cohesion and trust. The phenomenon of missing girls is deeply rooted in the societal constructs surrounding gender and power. The narrative surrounding these cases often reflects entrenched patriarchal values that define how girls are perceived and treated. In many cultures, girls are viewed as property or as individuals whose worth is tied to their behaviour and adherence to societal norms.

When a girl goes missing, it often exposes the controlling dynamics that govern her life, highlighting societal tendencies to blame or shame rather than understand the circumstances leading to her disappearance. The stigmatization of missing girls often results in their voices being marginalized. The societal impulse to impose narratives that fit conventional roles, such as viewing them solely as runaways, minimizes the real threats they face, such as abuse or exploitation, thus hindering comprehensive understanding and action.

The search for a missing girl typically involves various institutional responses that reveal significant systemic flaws. These inefficiencies complicate the recovery process and reflect broader societal neglect regarding issues affecting minors. Law enforcement agencies may lack the necessary training, resources, or protocols to effectively handle cases of missing minors. This leads to delays, missed leads, and ultimately, the potential for irreversible harm to the girl. The lack of a standardized, sensitive approach to such cases underscores a systemic disregard for the complexities involved.

The absence of cohesive support structures, such as mental health services, community programmes, and educational initiatives, can exacerbate the trauma experienced by both the girl and her family. When these systems fail to coordinate effectively, they leave vulnerable individuals without the necessary safety nets, highlighting a critical gap in societal responsibility.

The process of reuniting a missing girl with her family and society involves more than simply bringing her home; it encompasses a host of challenges that demand a nuanced understanding of her experiences during her absence. Upon her return, the girl often faces significant emotional and psychological barriers. The trauma she may have endured can complicate her re-acclimatization to her previous life, making it essential to address not only her immediate safety but also her long-term psychological well-being.

The family may undergo its own transformations during the period of separation. Resentments, guilt, and fear can emerge, complicating the reintegration process. Understanding these dynamics is critical for fostering healthy family relationships post-disappearance.

Ultimately, the issue of a missing minor girl necessitates a collective reckoning with the societal frameworks that contribute to such disappearances. It challenges us to confront uncomfortable truths about how we view and treat vulnerable populations. Addressing the issue requires more than just reactive measures; it demands proactive cultural shifts that redefine societal norms surrounding gender, safety, and agency. This involves fostering environments where girls feel empowered to express their needs and concerns without fear of reprisal or judgment.

Society must engage in meaningful dialogue around the factors leading to missing minors. This involves empowering communities to take ownership of the safety and well-being of all their members, fostering a collective ethos of care and vigilance.

In conclusion, the disappearance of a minor girl is not simply an issue of finding something that has been lost; it is an intricate tapestry of societal dysfunction, emotional turmoil, and systemic failure that requires comprehensive understanding and action. To address this crisis, society must unravel the multifaceted narratives surrounding missing girls, recognizing the profound implications for individuals and communities alike. By moving beyond the search for a lost individual, we can begin to engage with the underlying issues that contribute to these tragedies, ultimately working toward a more compassionate and effective response that values the dignity and humanity of every child.

As we reach the final pages of this journey, we must remember that behind each statistic, each story, lies an individual with dreams, potential, and dignity that cannot be diminished. This book has explored the deep-rooted issues that lead girls to leave their homes, the societal influences and personal challenges that pull them into uncertainty, and the crucial steps we as a society, as law enforcers, and as individuals can take to bring them back to safety and dignity.

But hope springs eternal. It is within our reach to build a world where girls don't feel the need to leave, where family homes are spaces of security and acceptance, and communities become their first line of support. We must foster environments where young girls can express themselves freely, have access to resources that nurture their ambitions, and be equipped with the awareness to recognize their own value. Prevention begins here, in empowering families to shed old stereotypes and nurturing spaces where girls' voices are heard, respected, and amplified.

For those who have already endured the difficult journey, our responsibility is not simply to bring them home but to help them find a new home within themselves. Rehabilitation should be more than reintegration; it should be a process of healing and empowerment. Each girl found and returned is a testament to resilience, and we owe it to her to provide not only support but also pathways to education, skill-building, and mental wellness. Let us make every effort to transform their homecoming into a powerful new beginning, a step toward dreams they might have believed lost.

In closing, let us all rise as changemakers, bridging gaps, building safer communities, and nurturing the innate strength within these girls. Our commitment to change today will be their hope for tomorrow. Together, we can create a society where girls feel empowered to stay, grow, and thrive—a society where they are seen not just as victims, but as individuals capable of shaping their own destinies.

As we arrive at the end of this exploration, one truth stands clear: each missing girl is more than a file in a police station or a story in a community. She is a life, a dream, a possibility. Behind every case, there is a unique world of hopes, fears, and unspoken struggles. When a girl disappears, an entire universe trembles. But where there is loss, there must also be light, and where there is hardship, there is always a path forward.

Throughout this journey, we have seen the silent but potent forces that push these young souls away from the warmth of home. The reasons are known: a blend of social pressures, misunderstandings, fears, and sometimes even a desperate search for love and acceptance. But just as these factors compel them to leave, there are just as many reasons to create environments that invite them to stay. Prevention begins when every home becomes a sanctuary of respect and understanding, where girls can breathe freely, express themselves without fear, and grow without constraint.

It is not only about stopping a girl from leaving but about creating spaces where she wouldn't want to leave in the first place. Families must become her allies, society her support, and authorities her advocates. If we hope to see fewer of these cases, we must collectively redefine what it means to belong, to be safe, and to be valued.

And for those who do return, our duty transcends simply bringing them back. Rehabilitation is not about filling a void but about nurturing a soul. These girls come back to us with invisible scars, with dreams that have been dimmed, and hearts that carry a weight we may never fully understand. Our role is to help them rediscover their strength, to open doors to education and skill-building that reaffirm their worth and potential, and to create avenues of mental and emotional support that mend what life has fractured. This return must become a rebirth, a step toward a life where they are no longer bound by what happened but liberated by what can be.

As caretakers of society, it falls on us to see these young women as more than just survivors — to recognize the fire within them, a resilience that defies the darkest challenges. They are not only returning; they are rising. And in honouring their courage, we transform their journeys from one of pain to one of triumph.

Let us hold this vision close, a world where young girls feel cherished, where they do not feel the need to run but instead are encouraged to dream and to soar. Let us commit to being the society they deserve, one that sees them, hears them, and stands with them. Together, we can create a future where they feel safe to stay, to grow, and to become everything they were meant to be. This is our duty, our mission, and our hope. Let it guide us.

Let us build a world where no girl feels the need to run away from home, where her dreams find roots, and her voice finds strength. For every girl we bring back, let us give her not just safety, but wings to rise above, to heal, to hope, and to shine as the light she was always meant to be. As we close the pages of this book, we are left not only with the haunting stories of the girls who vanished but also with a call to action for each of us. Behind every statistic lies a life full of dreams, aspirations, and loved ones left in agony. These stories, though diverse in their circumstances, share a common thread, a reminder of the vulnerabilities faced by young girls in our society.

The cases we've explored reveal systemic failures, societal indifference, and the urgent need for reform. They challenge us to confront the uncomfortable truths about gender-based violence, societal norms, and the often-invisible barriers that prevent justice from being served. Each girl represents not just a case file, but a potential future extinguished too soon.

It is imperative that we foster a culture of vigilance and support, where communities come together to protect their most vulnerable members. Awareness campaigns, educational programmes, and stronger law enforcement responses are crucial in preventing future tragedies. We must advocate for policies that ensure safety, empower women, and hold perpetrators accountable.

Let us remember that change begins with us, our voices, our actions, and our commitment to justice. By sharing these stories, we honour the lives of those who have gone missing, ensuring they are not forgotten. Together, we can strive to create a world where every girl feels safe, valued, and free to pursue her dreams without fear.

In the end, *She Goes Missing* may serve not just as a reflection of a grim reality, but as a beacon of hope, a reminder that through awareness, compassion, and action, we can make a difference. Let us work tirelessly to ensure that no girl ever goes missing again!

References

- Aassve, A., Billari, F. C., & Ongaro, F. (2003). The impact of income and employment status on leaving home: Evidence from the Italian ECHP sample. *Labour: Review of Labour Economics and Industrial Relations*, 15(3), 501–529. https://doi.org/10.1111/1467-9914.00175
- African Population and Health Research Center. (2009). *Nairobi Urban Health & Demographic Surveillance System: Summary indicators*. Retrieved from http://www.aphrc.org/insidepage/page.php?app=stats_nhdss&pop8=8
- Afridi, F., Dinkelman, T., & Mahajan, T. (2018). Why are fewer married women joining the workforce in rural India? A decomposition analysis over two decades. *Journal of Population Economics*, 31, 783–818.
- Afridi, F., Mukhopadhyay, A., & Sahoo, S. (2016). Female labour force participation and child education in India: Evidence from the National Rural Employment Guarantee Scheme. *IZA Journal of Labor and Development*, 5, 1–27.
- Ahearn, M. (2004). Literacy, power and agency:

love letters and development in Nepal. *Language and Education*, 18(4), 305–316.

- Ainsworth-Darnell, J. W., & Downey, D. B. (1998). Assessing the oppositional culture explanation for racial/ethnic differences in school performance. *American Sociological Review*, 63(4), 536–553.

- Alfano, M. (2017). Daughters, dowries, deliveries: the effect of marital payments on fertility choices in India. *Journal of Development Economics*, 125, 89–104.

- Allgood-Merten, B., Lewinsohn, P., & Hops, H. (1990). Sex differences and adolescent depression. *Journal of Abnormal Psychology*, 99, 5–63.

- Allensworth, E., Nomi, T., Montgomery, N., & Lee, V. E. (2009). College preparatory curriculum for all: Academic consequences of requiring Algebra and English I for ninth graders in Chicago. *Educational Evaluation and Policy Analysis*, 31(4), 367–391. https://doi.org/10.3102/0162373709343471

- Amuyunzu-Nyamongo, M. K., & Magadi, M. A. (2006). Sexual privacy and early sexual debut in Nairobi informal settlements. *Community, Work and Family*, 9(2), 143–158.

- Anderson, B. (1983). *Imagined communities: Reflections on the origin and spread of nationalism.* London: Verso.

- Anderson, S., & Genicot, G. (2015). Suicide and property rights in India. *Journal of Development Economics*, 114, 64–78.

- Anderson, S. (2012). *Sherwood Anderson: Collected stories: Winesburg, Ohio / The Triumph of the Egg / Horses and Men / Death in the Woods / Uncollected stories.* Library of America.

- Anderson, S., & Ray, D. (2012). The age distribution of missing women in India. *Economic & Political Weekly*, 46(47), 187–195.
- Anderson, E. (2011). Updating the outcome. *Gender & Society*, 25(2), 250–268. https://doi.org/10.1177/0891243210396872
- Antonio, A. L. (2004). The influence of friendship groups on intellectual self-confidence and educational aspirations in college. *Journal of Higher Education*, 75(4), 446–472.
- Ariès, P. (1965). *Centuries of childhood: A social history of family life*. Vintage Books.
- Ariès, P. (1973). *Centuries of childhood*. Harmondsworth, UK: Penguin.
- Arnett, J. (2000). Emerging adulthood: A theory of development from the late teens through the early twenties. *American Psychologist*, 55(5), 469–480.
- An, L., Mertig, A. G., & Liu, J. G. (2003). Adolescents leaving parental home: Psychosocial correlates and implications for conservation. *Population and Environment*, 24(5), 415–444. https://doi.org/10.1023/A:1023694924954
- Allport, G. W. (1954). *The nature of prejudice*. Cambridge, MA: Addison-Wesley.
- Aquilino, W. S. (1991). Family structure and home-leaving: A further specification of the relationship. *Journal of Marriage and the Family*, 53(4), 999–1010. https://doi.org/10.2307/353003
- Applbaum, K. D. (1995). Marriage with the proper stranger: Arranged marriage in metropolitan Japan. *Ethnology*, 34(1), 37–51.
- Asarnow, J. R., Carlson, G., & Guthrie, D. (1987). Coping strategies, self-perceptions, hopelessness,

and perceived family environments in depressed and suicidal children. *Journal of Consulting and Clinical Psychology*, 55, 361–366.

- Astin, H. S. (1975). Sex differences in mathematical and scientific precocity. *The Journal of Special Education*, 9(1), 79–91.

- Augoustinos, M., & Walker, L. (1995). *Social cognition*. Thousand Oaks, CA: Sage.

- Avison, W., & McAlpine, D. (1992). Gender differences in symptoms of depression among adolescents. *Journal of Health and Social Behavior*, 33, 77–96.

- Avery, R., Goldscheider, F. K., & Speare, A. (1992). Feathered nest/gilded cage: Parental income and leaving home in the transition to adulthood. *Demography*, 29(3), 375–388.

- Azzarito, L. (2009). The panopticon of physical education: Pretty, active and ideally white. *Physical Education and Sport Pedagogy*, 14(1), 19–39. https://doi.org/10.1080/17408980701712106

- Azzarito, L., & Katzew, A. (2010). Performing identities in physical education: (En)gendering fluid selves. *Research Quarterly for Exercise and Sport*, 81(1), 25–37. https://doi.org/10.1080/02701367.2010.10599625

- Aassve, A., Billari, F. C., & Ongaro, F. (2003). The impact of income and employment status on leaving home: Evidence from the Italian ECHP sample. *Labour: Review of Labour Economics and Industrial Relations*, 15(3), 501–529. https://doi.org/10.1111/1467-9914.00175

- African Population and Health Research Center. (2009). *Nairobi Urban Health & Demographic*

Surveillance System: Summary indicators. Retrieved from http://www.aphrc.org/insidepage/page. php?app=stats_nhdss&pop8=8

- Afridi, F., Dinkelman, T., & Mahajan, T. (2018). Why are fewer married women joining the workforce in rural India? A decomposition analysis over two decades. *Journal of Population Economics*, 31, 783–818.

- Afridi, F., Mukhopadhyay, A., & Sahoo, S. (2016). Female labour force participation and child education in India: Evidence from the National Rural Employment Guarantee Scheme. *IZA Journal of Labor and Development*, 5, 1–27.

- Azzarito, L., Solmon, M. A., & Harrison, L., Jr. (2006). 'If I had a choice, I would': A feminist poststructuralist perspective on girls in physical education. *Research Quarterly for Exercise and Sport*, 77(2), 222–239.

- Bain, S. (2012). Comment posted on *John Whitwell: A Personal Site of Professional Interest*.

- Bain, L. L. (1990). A critical analysis of the hidden curriculum in physical education. In D. Kirk & R. Tinning (Eds.), *Physical education, curriculum, and culture: Critical issues in the contemporary crisis* (pp. –). London: The Falmer Press.

- Bakeman, R., & Quera, V. (2011). *Sequential analysis and observational methods for the behavioral sciences*. Cambridge University Press.

- Barber, B. L., Eccles, J. S., & Stone, M. R. (2001). Whatever happened to the jock, the brain, and the princess? *Journal of Adolescent Research*, 16(5), 429–455. https://doi.org/10.1177/0743558401165002

- Barton, S., Gonzalez, R., & Tomlinson, P. (2012). *Therapeutic residential care for children and young people: An attachment- and trauma-informed model for practice.*London & Philadelphia: Jessica Kingsley Publishers.
- Baxi, P. (2014). *Public secrets of law: Rape trials in India*. New Delhi: Oxford University Press.
- Beaman, L., Chattopadhyay, R., Duflo, E., Pande, R., & Topalova, P. (2009). Powerful women: Does exposure reduce bias? *Quarterly Journal of Economics*, 124(4), 1497–1540.
- Beaman, L., Duflo, E., Pande, R., & Topalova, P. (2012). Female leadership raises aspirations and educational attainment of girls. *Science*, 335(6068), 582–586.
- Bearman, P. S., Moody, J., & Stovel, K. (2004). Chains of affection: The structure of adolescent romantic and sexual networks. *American Journal of Sociology*, 110(1), 44–91.
- Bebbington, P. (1985). Three cognitive theories of depression. *Psychological Medicine*, 15, 759–769.
- Beck, A. T., Rush, A. J., Shaw, B., & Emery, G. (1979). *Cognitive therapy of depression*. New York: Guilford.
- Becker, J. (1979). Vulnerable self-esteem as a predisposing factor in depressive disorders. In R. Depue (Ed.), *The psychobiology of the depressive disorders: Implications for the effects of stress* (pp. 317–334). New York: Academic Press.
- Beckett, L. (2004). Editorial: Health, the body, and identity work in health and physical education. *Sport, Education and Society*, 9(2), 171–173. https://doi.org/10.1080/1357332042000233921

- Behm-Morawitz, E., & Mastro, D. (2009). The effects of the sexualization of female video game characters on gender stereotyping and female self-concept. *Sex Roles*, 61(11), 808–823. https://doi.org/10.1007/s11199-009-9683-8
- Beilock, S. L., Gunderson, E. A., Ramirez, G., & Levine, S. C. (2010). Female teachers' math anxiety affects girls' math achievement. *Proceedings of the National Academy of Sciences*, 107(5), 1860–1863. https://doi.org/10.1073/pnas.0910967107
- Billari, F. C., & Liefbroer, A. C. (2007). Should I stay or should I go? The impact of age norms on leaving home. *Demography*, 44(1), 181–198.
- Blumer, H. (1986). *Symbolic interactionism: Perspective and method*. Berkeley, CA: University of California Press.
- Borgers, N., de Leeuw, E., & Hox, J. (2000). Children as respondents in survey research: Cognitive development and response quality. *Bulletin de Méthodologie Sociologique*, 66(1), 60–75. doi: 10.1177/075910630006600106
- Bourdieu, P. (1984). *Distinction: A social critique of the judgement of taste*. Cambridge, MA: Harvard University Press.
- Bourdieu, P. (2000). Cultural reproduction and social reproduction. In R. Arum & I. R. Beattie (Eds.), *The structure of schooling: Readings in the sociology of education* (pp. 55–68). Mountain View, CA: Mayfield Publishing.
- Bernhardt, A., Field, E., Pande, R., & Rigol, N. (2019). Household matters: Revisiting the returns to capital among female microentrepreneurs. *American Economic Review Insights*, 1(2), 141–160.

- Bernhardt, E., Gähler, M., & Goldscheider, F. (2005). Childhood family structure and routes out of the parental home in Sweden. *Acta Sociologica*, 48(2), 99–115.

- Benefo, K. D. (2004). Are partner and relationship characteristics associated with condom use in Zambian nonmarital relationships? *International Family Planning Perspectives*, 30(3), 118–127.

- Becker, P., & Clark, W. (2001). Introduction. In P. Becker & W. Clark (Eds.), *Little tools of knowledge: Historical essays on academic and bureaucratic practices* (pp. 1–34). Ann Arbor: University of Michigan Press.

- Benveniste, E. (1971). Active and middle voice in the verb. In E. Benveniste (Ed.), *Problems in general linguistics* (pp. 45–52). Coral Gables, FL: University of Miami Press.

- Bertrand-Dansereau, A., & Clark, S. (2016). Pragmatic tradition or romantic aspiration? The causes of impulsive marriage and early divorce among women in rural Malawi. *Demographic Research*, 35, 47–80. doi: 10.4054/DemRes.2016.35.3

- Bettelheim, B. (1986). *Documentary Horizon* [Video]. Part 1: https://www.youtube.com/watch?v=IEI7Q/Vtk-Ms&t=235 ; Part 2: https://www.dailymotion.com/video/x7n0igf

- Billari, F. C., & Ongaro, F. (1999). Lasciare la famiglia di origine: Quando e perché? [Leaving family of origin: When and why?] In P. D. Sandre, A. Pinnelli, & A. Santini (Eds.), *Nuzialità e fecondità in trasformazione: Percorsi e fattori del cambiamento* (pp. 327–346). Bologna, Italy: Il Mulino.

- Birkeland, M. S., Melkevik, O., Holsen, I., & Wold, B. (2012). Trajectories of global self-esteem during adolescence. *Journal of Adolescence*, 35, 43–54.
- Black, M. (2000). *Growing up alone: The hidden cost of poverty*. United Nations Children's Fund. Retrieved from http://cfsc.trunky.net/_uploads/Publications/141.growing_up_alone_hidden_cost_poverty.pdf
- Bloch, R., & Rao, V. (2002). Terror as a bargaining instrument: A case study of dowry violence in rural India. *American Economic Review*, 92(4), 1029–1043.
- Bustamante, D. O. (1999). Family structure problems, child mistreatment, street children and drug use: A community-based approach. In *Prevention of street migration: Resource pack*. University College Cork.
- Boaten, A. B. (2008). Street children: Experiences from the streets of Accra. *Research Journal of International Studies*, 8, 76–84.
- Casa Alianza. (2008). *Worldwide statistics*. Retrieved December 30, 2019, from www.hultonfoundation.org/press/16-pdf3.pdf
- Boserup, E. (1970). *Women's role in economic development*. George Allen and Unwin.
- Bosson, J. K., Vandello, J., & Buckner, C. (2019). *The psychology of sex and gender*. Thousand Oaks, CA: Sage.
- Boyden, J., Pankhurst, A., & Tafere, Y. (2012). Child protection and harmful traditional practices: Female early marriage and genital modification in Ethiopia. *Development in Practice*, 22, 510–522. https://doi.org/10.1080/09614524.2012.672957

- Bramham, P. (2003). Boys, masculinities and PE. *Sport, Education and Society*, 8(1), 57–70. doi: 10.1080/1357332032000050060
- Brass, N., McKellar, North, E., & Ryan, A. (2019). Early adolescents' adjustment at school: A fresh look at grade and gender differences. *Journal of Early Adolescence*, 39(5), 689–716.
- Brewer, M. B. (1988). A dual process model of impression formation. In T. Srull & R. Wyer (Eds.), *Advances in social cognition* (pp. 1–36). Hillsdale, NJ: Lawrence Erlbaum.
- Brinkman, D., Overholser, J., & Klier, D. (1994). Emotional distress in adolescent psychiatric inpatients: Direct and indirect measures. *Journal of Personality Assessment*, 62, 472–484.
- Briggs, J. L. (1970). *Never in anger: Portrait of an Eskimo family*. Cambridge, MA: Harvard University Press.
- Brint, S., Cantwell, A., & Hanneman, R. (2008). The two cultures of undergraduate academic engagement. *Research in Higher Education*, 49(5), 383–402. doi: 10.1007/s11162-008-9090-y
- Bronfenbrenner, U. (1977). Toward an experimental ecology of human development. *American Psychologist*, 32(7), 513–531. doi: 10.1037/0003-066X.32.7.513
- Brown, D. (2005). An economy of gendered practices? Learning to teach physical education from the perspective of Pierre Bourdieu's embodied sociology. *Sport, Education and Society*, 10(1), 3–23. doi: 10.1080/135733205298785
- Brown, D., & Evans, J. (2004). Reproducing gender? Intergenerational links and the male PE teacher as

a cultural conduit in teaching physical education. *Journal of Teaching in Physical Education*, 23(1), 48–70.

- Bronfenbrenner, U. (1986). Ecology of the family as a context for human development: Research perspectives. *Developmental Psychology*, 22(6), 723–742. doi: 10.1037/0012-1649.22.6.723

- Brown, B. B., Eicher, S. A., & Petrie, S. (1986). The importance of peer group ("crowd") affiliation in adolescence. *Journal of Adolescence*, 9(1), 73–96.

- Bryk, A. S., & Schneider, B. (2002). *Trust in schools: A core resource for improvement*. New York: Russell Sage Foundation.

- Buchmann, C., & DiPrete, T. A. (2006). The growing female advantage in college completion: The role of family background and academic achievement. *American Sociological Review*, 71(4), 515–541.

- Bühler-Niederberger, D. (2010). Childhood sociology in ten countries. *Current Sociology*, 58(2), 369–384. doi: 10.1177/0011392109354250

- Brule, R. (2020). Reform, representation, and resistance: The politics of property rights enforcement. *Journal of Politics*, 82(4), 1390–1405.

- Burdsey, D. (2008). *British Asians and football: Culture, identity, exclusion*. New York: Routledge.

- Busch, H., & Hofer, J. (2011). Identity, prosocial behavior, and generative concern in German and Cameroonian Nso adolescents. *Journal of Adolescence*, 34(4), 629–638. doi: 10.1016/j.adolescence.2010.09.009

- Bussey, K. (2011). Gender identity development. In S. J. Schwartz, K. Luyckx, & V. L. Vignoles

(Eds.), *Handbook of identity theory and research* (pp. 603–628). New York: Springer.

- Butler, A. C. (2005). Gender differences in the prevalence of same-sex sexual partnering: 1988–2002. *Social Forces*, 84(1), 421–449.

- Byrne, D. (2005). *Social exclusion*. New York: McGraw-Hill Education.

- Bryman, A. (2004). *Social research methods*. New York, NY: Oxford University Press.

- Calarco, J. M. (2011). "I need help!" Social class and children's help-seeking in elementary school. *American Sociological Review*, 76(6), 862–882. doi: 10.1177/0003122411427177

- Calvi, R., Hochn-Velasco, L., & Mantovanelli, F. G. (2022). The Protestant legacy: Missions, gender, and human capital in India. *Journal of Human Resources*, 57(6), 1946–1980.

- Calvi, R., & Keskar, A. (2023). Til dowry do us part: Bargaining and violence in Indian families. *Review of Economics and Statistics*, forthcoming. https://doi.org/10.1162/rest_a_01399

- Cammerota, J., & Fine, M. (2008). Youth participatory action research: A pedagogy for transformational resistance. In J. Cammerota & M. Fine (Eds.), *Revolutionizing education: Youth participatory action research* (pp. 1–12). London: Routledge.

- Carlisle Duncan, M. (2001). The sociology of ability and disability in physical activity. *Sociology of Sport Journal*, 18, 1–4.

- Carney, C., McGehee, D., Harland, K., Weiss, M., & Raby, M. (2015, March). Using naturalistic driving data to assess the prevalence of environmental factors and driver behaviors in teen driver crashes. AAA Foundation for Traffic Safety. Retrieved from https://www.aaafoundation.org/sites/default/files/2015TeenCrashCausationReport.pdf

- Carrington, B. (2007). Merely identity: Cultural identity and the politics of sport. *Sociology of Sport Journal*, 24(1), 49–66.
- Carranza, E. (2014). Soil endowments, female labor force participation, and the demographic deficit of women in India. *American Economic Journal: Applied Economics*, 6(4), 197–225.
- Carroll, J. L. (2016). *Sexuality now: Embracing diversity* (5th ed.). Boston, MA: Cengage Learning.
- Carswell, G., & De Neve, G. (2013). Women and the crossroads: Implementation of employment guarantee scheme in rural Tamil Nadu. *Economic and Political Weekly*, 48(52), 82–93.
- Caspi, A., Lynam, D., Moffitt, T. E., & Silva, P. A. (1993). Unraveling girls' delinquency: Biological, dispositional, and contextual contributions to adolescent misbehavior. *Developmental Psychology*, 29(1), 19–30.
- Castilla, C. (2018). Political role models and child marriage in India. *Review of Development Economics*, 22(4), 1409–1431.
- Castilla, C. (2019). What's yours is mine, and what's mine is mine: Field experiment on income concealing between spouses in India. *Journal of Development Economics*, 137, 125–140.
- Carter, P. (2003). 'Black' cultural capital, status positioning, and schooling conflicts for low-income African American youth. *Social Problems*, 50(1), 136–155.

- Catsambis, S. (1994). The path to math: Gender and racial-ethnic differences in mathematics participation from middle school to high school. *Sociology of Education*, 67(3), 199–215.
- Caughy, M. O. B., Nettles, S. M., O'Campo, P. J., & Lohrfink, K. F. (2006). Neighborhood matters: Racial socialization of African American children. *Child Development*, 77(5), 1220–1236. doi: 10.1111/j.1467-8624.2006.00930.x
- Chein, J., Albert, D., O'Brien, L., Uckert, K., & Steinberg, L. (2011). Peers increase adolescent risk taking by enhancing activity in the brain's reward circuitry. *Developmental Science*, 14(2), F1–F10. doi: 10.1111/j.1467-7687.2010.01035.x
- Chen, B., Vansteenkiste, M., Beyers, W., Soenens, B., & Van Petegem, S. (2013). Autonomy in family decision making for Chinese adolescents: Disentangling the dual meaning of autonomy. *Journal of Cross-Cultural Psychology*, 44, 1184–1209.
- Chang, W., Diaz-Martin, L., Gopalan, A., Guarnieri, E., Jayachandran, S., & Walsh, C. (2020). What works to enhance women's agency: Cross-cutting lessons from experimental and quasi-experimental studies. *J-PAL Working Paper*.
- Chattopadhyay, R., & Duflo, E. (2004). Women as policy makers: Evidence from a randomized policy experiment in India. *Econometrica*, 72(5), 1409–1443.
- Chin, Y. M. (2012). Male backlash, bargaining, or exposure reduction? Women's working status and physical spousal violence in India. *Journal of Population Economics*, 25, 175–200.

- Chirico, F. (2018). Stop violence and crime against children. *Journal of Health and Social Sciences*, 3(2), 105–108.
- Chamberlain, G. (2014a, March 21). India's tea firms urged to act on slave trafficking after girls freed. *The Guardian*. Retrieved from http://www.theguardian.com/world/2014/mar/01/india-tea-firms-urged-tackle-slave-traffic-plantations
- Chamberlain, G. (2014b, March 2). The tea pickers sold into slavery. *The Guardian*. Retrieved from http://www.theguardian.com/global-development/2014/mar/02/tea-workers-sold-into-slavery
- Chuta, N., & Morrow, V. (2015). Youth trajectories through work and marriage in rural Ethiopia. Oxford, UK: University of Oxford, Young Lives.
- Cillessen, A., & Borch, C. (2008). Analyzing social networks in adolescence. In N. Card, J. Selig, & T. Little (Eds.), *Modeling dyadic and interdependent data in the developmental and behavioral sciences* (pp. 61–86). New York: Routledge.
- Clarke, J., Hall, S., Jefferson, T., & Roberts, B. (1975). Subcultures, cultures and class: A theoretical overview. In S. Hall & T. Jefferson (Eds.), *Resistance through rituals: Youth subcultures in post-war Britain* (pp. 9–74). London: Routledge. (Reprinted 2000)
- Cole, J. (2011). A cultural dialectics of generational change. *Review of Research in Education*, 35(1), 60–88. doi: 10.3102/0091732X10391371
- Coman, W., & Devaney, C. (2011). Reflecting on outcomes for looked-after children: An ecological perspective. *Child Care in Practice*, 17(1), 37–53. Routledge.

- Conticini, A., & Hulme, D. (2006). Escaping violence, seeking freedom: Why children in Bangladesh migrate to the street. *Global Poverty Research Group, Working Paper Series*.
- Connolly, J., Craig, W., Goldberg, A., & Pepler, D. (2004). Mixed-gender groups, dating, and romantic relationships in early adolescence. *Journal of Research on Adolescence*, 14, 185–207.
- Connolly, J., Furman, W., & Konarski, R. (2000). The role of peers in the emergence of heterosexual romantic relationships in adolescence. *Child Development*, 71, 1395–1408.
- Cook-Sather, A. (2002). 'Authorizing students' perspectives: Towards trust, dialogue, and change in education'. *Educational Researcher*, 31(4), 3–14. doi: 10.3102/0013189X031004003
- Cook-Sather, A. (2006). *Education is translation*. Philadelphia: University of Pennsylvania Press.
- Cook-Sather, A. (2007). Translating researchers: Re-imagining the work of investigating students' experiences in school. In D. Thiessen & A. Cook-Sather (Eds.), *International handbook of student experience in elementary and secondary school* (pp. 829–871). Dordrecht, The Netherlands: Springer.
- Corsaro, W. A. (2003). *We're friends, right?: Inside kids' culture*. Washington, D.C.: Joseph Henry Press.
- Corsaro, W. A. (2011). *The sociology of childhood* (3rd ed.). Thousand Oaks: Pine Forge Press.
- Costa, F. M., Jessor, R., Turbin, M. S., Dong, Q., Zhang, H., & Wang, C. (2005). The role of social contexts in adolescence: Context protection and context risk in the United States and China. *Applied*

Developmental Science, 9(2), 67–85. doi:10.1207/s1532480xads0902_3

- Costigan, C. L., Cauce, A. M., & Etchinson, K. (2007). Changes in African American mother-daughter relationships during adolescence: Conflict, autonomy, and warmth. In B. J. R. Leadbeater & N. Way (Eds.), *Urban girls revisited: Building strengths* (pp. 177–201). New York, NY: New York University Press.

- Côtè, J. E. (2006). Emerging adulthood as an institutionalized moratorium: Risks and benefits to identity formation. In J. J. Arnett & J. T. Tanner (Eds.), *Emerging adults in America: Coming of age in the 21st century* (pp. 85–116). Washington, DC: American Psychological Association.

- Crain, W. (2005). *Theories of development: Concepts and applications* (5th ed.). New Jersey: Pearson.

- Creswell, J. W. (2008). *Research design: Qualitative, quantitative, and mixed methods approaches*. London, UK: SAGE Publications.

- Crooks, K. L., & Baur, K. (2007). *Our sexuality* (10th ed.). Belmont, CA: Wadsworth.

- Crosnoe, R., & Benner, A. D. (2015). Children at school. In M. H. Bornstein, T. Leventhal, & R. M. Lerner (Eds.), *Handbook of child psychology and developmental science: Ecological settings and processes* (pp. 268–304). Hoboken, NJ: John Wiley & Sons Inc.

- Crosnoe, R. (2000). Friendships in childhood and adolescence: The life course and new directions. *Social Psychology Quarterly*, 63(4), 377–391.

- Crosnoe, R., & Schneider, B. (2010). Social capital, information, and socioeconomic disparities in math course work. *American Journal of Education*, 117(1), 79–107.

- Csíkszentmihályi, M., & Larson, R. (1987). Validity and reliability of the experience sampling method. *Journal of Nervous and Mental Disease*, 175(9), 526–536. doi: 10.1097/00005053-198709000-00004

- Cvencek, D., Meltzoff, A. N., & Greenwald, A. G. (2011). Math-gender stereotypes in elementary school children. *Child Development*, 82(3), 766–779. doi: 10.1111/j.1467-8624.2010.01529.x

- Cuddy, A. J. C., Fiske, S. T., & Glick, P. (2007). The BLAS map: Behaviors from intergroup affect and stereotypes. *Journal of Personality and Social Psychology*, 92, 631–648.

- Davis, R. H. (1999). *Lives of Indian images*. Princeton, NJ: Princeton University Press.

- Davis, H., & Unruh, W. R. (1981). The development of the self-schema in adult depression. *Journal of Abnormal Psychology*, 90, 125–133.

- Dean, J., & Jayachandran, S. (2019). Changing family attitudes to promote female employment. *AEA Papers and Proceedings*, 109, 138–142.

- Deininger, K., Jin, S., Nagarajan, H., & Xia, F. (2014). Does female reservation affect long-term political outcomes? Evidence from rural India. *Journal of Development Studies*, 51(1), 32–49.

- Deininger, K., Goyal, A., & Nagaranjan, H. (2013). Women inheritance rights and intergenerational transmission of resources in India. *Journal of Human Resources*, 48(1), 114–141.

- Department for Education. (2014). *Statutory guidance on children who run away or go missing from home or care*. UK Gov Crown Copyright. https://

assets.publishing.service.gov.uk/government/
uploads/system/uploads/attachment_data/
file/307867/Statutory_Guidance_Missing_from_
care_3.pdf

- De Jong, J. G., Liefbroer, A. C., & Beekink, E. (1991). The effect of parental resources on patterns of leaving home among young adults in the Netherlands. *European Review of Sociology*, 7, 55–71.
- De Wit, D. J., Karioja, K., Rye, B. J., & Shain, M. (2011). Perceptions of declining classmate and teacher support following the transition to high school: Potential correlates of increasing student mental health difficulties. *Psychology in the Schools*, 48, 556–572.
- Dishion, T. J., & Tipsord, J. M. (2011). Peer contagion in child and adolescent social and emotional development. *Annual Review of Psychology*, 62, 189–214.
- Dobbs, D. (2012). Beautiful brains. *National Geographic*, 220(4), 36.
- Dolgin, K. G. (2011). *The adolescent: Development, relationships, and culture* (13th ed.). Boston, MA: Pearson.
- Dodoo, F. N., Zulu, E. M., & Ezch, A. C. (2007). Urban-rural differences in the socioeconomic deprivation–sexual behavior link in Kenya. *Social Science & Medicine*, 64, 1019–1031.
- Domina, T. (2005). Leveling the home advantage: Assessing the effectiveness of parental involvement in elementary school. *Sociology of Education*, 78(3), 233–249. doi: 10.1177/003804070507800303
- Donald, R. H., Hendershott, P. H., & Kim, D. (1993). The impact of real rents and wages on

household formation. *Review of Economics and Statistics*, 75, 284–293.

- Dowling, F. (2011). Getting in touch with our feelings: The emotional geographies of gender relations in PETE. *Sport, Education and Society*, 13(3), 247–266. doi: 10.1080/13573320802200560
- Dowling, F., & Karhus, S. (2008). An analysis of the ideological work of the discourses of 'fair play' and moral education in perpetuating inequitable gender practices in PETE. *Physical Education and Sport Pedagogy*, 16(2), 197–211. doi: 10.1080/17408989.2010.532781
- Dusek, J., & Flaherty, J. (1981). The development of the self-concept during the adolescent years. *Monographs of the Society for Research in Child Development*, 46(4), 1–61
- Durães, R. S. D. S., Folquitto, C. T. F., & Serafim, A. D. P. (2020). Cognitive-behavioral therapy combined with mindfulness for a case of severe sleep bruxism and social anxiety in an elderly woman: A single case study for 6-month follow-up. *International Journal of Psychosocial Rehabilitation*, 24(5), 1145–1155
- Du Bois, W. E. B. (1903). *The Souls of Black Folk* (1994 ed., Vol. 54). Mineola, NY: Dover Publications
- Duchesne, S., Larose, S., & Feng, B. (2019). Achievement goals and engagement with academic work in early high school: Does seeking help from teachers matter? *Journal of Early Adolescence*, 39(2), 222–252
- Dudovitz, R. N., Chung, P. J., Elliott, M. N., Davies, S. L., Tortolero, S., ... Baumler, E. (2015). Relationship of age for grade and pubertal stage to

early initiation of substance use. *Preventing Chronic Disease*, 12, 150234. doi: 10.5888/pcd12.150234

- Dyer, R. (1993). *The Matter of Images*. London: Routledge

- Dyson, T., & Moore, M. (1983). On kinship structure, female autonomy, and demographic behaviour in India. *Population and Development Review*, 9(1), 35–60

- Dyson, J. (2014). *Working Childhoods: Youth, Agency and the Environment in India*. Cambridge, UK: Cambridge University Press

- Eccles, J. S. (1987). Gender roles and women's achievement-related decisions. *Psychology of Women Quarterly*, 11(2), 135–172. doi: 10.1111/j.1471-6402.1987.tb00781.x

- Eccles, J. S. (1994). Understanding women's educational and occupational choices: Applying the Eccles et al. model of achievement-related choices. *Psychology of Women Quarterly*, 18(4), 585–609. doi: 10.1111/j.1471-6402.1994.tb01049.x

- Eccles, J. S. (2005). Subjective task value and the Eccles et al. model of achievement-related choices. In A. J. Elliot (Ed.), *Handbook of competence and motivation* (pp. 105–121). New York: Guilford Press

- Eccles, J. S., & Rosner, R. W. (2015). School and community influences on human development. In M. H. Bornstein & M. E. Lamb (Eds.), *Developmental Science* (7th ed.). New York: Psychology Press

- Erikson, E. H. (1963). *Childhood and Society* (2nd ed.). New York: Norton

- Ermisch, J. (1999). Prices, parents, and young people's household formation. *Journal of Urban Economics*, 45, 47–71

- Erulkar, A. S., Mekbih, T., Simie, N., & Gulema, T. (2007). Migration and vulnerability among adolescents in slum areas of Addis Ababa, Ethiopia. *Journal of Youth Studies*, 9, 361–374. doi: 10.1080/13676260600805697

- Ellen, I. G., & Turner, M. A. (1997). Does neighborhood matter? Assessing recent evidence. *Housing Policy Debate*, 8(4), 833–866. doi: 10.1080/10511482.1997.9521280

- Emerson, R. M., Fretz, R. I., & Shaw, L. L. (1995). *Writing ethnographic fieldnotes*. Chicago: University of Chicago Press

- Elkind, D. (1967). Egocentrism in adolescence. *Child Development*, 38, 1025–1034

- Eveleth, P., & Tanner, J. (1990). *Worldwide variation in human growth* (2nd ed.). New York: Cambridge University Press

- Farland-Smith, D. (2009). Exploring middle school girls' science identities: Examining attitudes and perceptions of scientists when working "side-by-side" with scientists. *School Science and Mathematics*, 109(7), 415–427. doi: 10.1111/j.1949-8594.2009.tb17872.x

- Feldman, A. F., & Matjasko, J. L. (2005). The role of school-based extracurricular activities in adolescent development: A comprehensive review and future directions. *Review of Educational Research*, 75(2), 159–210. doi: 10.3102/00346543075002159

- Fine, G. A., & Kleinman, S. (1979). Rethinking subculture: An interactionist analysis. *American Journal of Sociology*, 85(1), 1–20

- Ferguson, K. M. (2009). Exploring family environmental characteristics and multiple abuse experiences among homeless youth. *Journal of Interpersonal Violence*, 24, 1875–1891. https://doi.org/10.1177/0886260508325490

- Fiegenberg, B., Field, E., & Pande, R. (2013). The economic returns to social interaction: Experimental evidence from microfinance. *Review of Economic Studies*, 80(4), 1459–1483

- Fiegenberg, B., Field, E., Pande, R., Rigol, N., & Sarkar, S. (2014). Do group dynamics influence social capital gains among microfinance clients? Evidence from a randomized experiment in urban India. *Journal of Policy Analysis and Management*, 33(4), 932–949

- Field, E., Jayachandran, S., Pande, R., & Rigol, N. (2016). Friendship at work: Can peer effects catalyse female entrepreneurship? *American Economic Journal: Economic Policy*, 8(2), 125–153

- Field, E., Pande, R., Papp, J., & Rigol, N. (2013). Does the classic microfinance model discourage entrepreneurship among the poor? Experimental evidence from India. *American Economic Review*, 103(6), 2196–2226

- Field, E., Pande, R., Rigol, N., Schaner, S., & Moore, C. T. (2021). On her own account: How strengthening women's financial control impacts labor supply and gender norms. *American Economic Review*, 111(7), 2342–2375

- Finkelhor, D. (1984). *Child sexual abuse: New theory and research*. New York: Free Press

- Finkelhor, D., & Drauba-Leatherman, J. (1994). Children as victims of violence: A national survey. *Pediatrics*, 94, 413–420

- Finkelhor, D. (1993). Epidemiological factors in the clinical identification of child sexual abuse. *Child Abuse & Neglect*, 17, 67–70

- Fiske, S. T., & Neuberg, S. L. (1990). A continuum model of impression formation, from category-based to individuating processes: Influence of information and motivation on attention and interpretation. In M. P. Zanna (Ed.), *Advances in Experimental Social Psychology* (pp. 1–74). New York: Academic Press

- Fisette, J. L. (2011). Exploring how girls navigate their embodied identities in physical education. *Physical Education and Sport Pedagogy*, 16(2), 179–196

- Fisette, J. L. (2013). "Are you listening?": Adolescent girls voice how they negotiate self-identified barriers to their success and survival in physical education. *Physical Education and Sport Pedagogy*, 18(2), 184–203

- Fisette, J. L., & Walton, T. A. (in press for print publication; December 2011, electronic publication). "If you really knew me"…I am empowered through action. *Sport, Education and Society*. doi:10.1080/13573322.2011.643297

- Fisette, J. L., & Walton, T. A. (2013). Empowering high school girls as media consumers/producers: Engaging in activist research through visual methods. In L. Azzarito & D. Kirk (Eds.), *Pedagogies, Physical Culture and Visual Methods* (pp. 30–46). Routledge

- Fleming, P. J., Silverman, J., Ghule, M., Ritter, J., Battala, M., Velhal, G., Nair, S., Dasgupta, A., Donta, B., Saggurti, N., & Raj, A. (2018). Can a gender equity and family planning intervention for men change their gender ideology? Results from the CHARM intervention in rural India. *Studies in Family Planning*, 49(1), 41–56

- Fleming, J., & Courtney, B. (1984). The dimensionality of self-esteem: II. Hierarchical facet model for revised measurement scales. *Journal of Personality and Social Psychology*, 46, 404–421

- Flanagan, C., & Levine, P. (2010). Civic Engagement and the Transition to Adulthood. *The Future of Children*, 20(1), 159–179
- Flanagan, C. A., Bowes, J. M., Jonsson, B., Csapo, B., & Sheblanova, E. (1998). Ties that Bind: Correlates of Adolescents' Civic Commitments in Seven Countries. *Journal of Social Issues*, 54(3), 457–475. doi: 10.1111/j.1540-4560.1998.tb01230.x
- Foucault, M. (2003). *Abnormal: Lectures at the College de France, 1974–1975* (Vol. 2). London: Macmillan
- Foucault, M. (1979). *Discipline and Punish: The Birth of the Prison* (A. Sheridan, Trans.). New York: Vintage
- Foucault, M., Martin, L. H., Gutman, H., & Hutton, P. H. (1988). *Technologies of the self: A seminar with Michel Foucault*. Amherst, MA: University of Massachusetts Press
- Fowler, F. J. (2009). *Survey research methods*. Sage Publications
- Frank, K. A., Muller, C., Schiller, K. S., Riegle-Crumb, C., Mueller, A. S., Crosnoe, R., & Pearson, J. (2008). The Social Dynamics of Mathematics Course taking in High School. *The American Journal of Sociology*, 113(6), 1645–1696. doi: 10.1086/587153
- Frankenberg, E., Lee, C., & Orfield, G. (2003). *A Multiracial Society with Segregated Schools: Are We Losing the Dream?* Civil Rights Project
- Forsberg, L., & Tebelius, U. (2011). The riding school as a site for gender identity

construction among Swedish teenage girls. *World Leisure Journal*, 53(1), 42–56. doi: 10.1080/04419057.2011.552218

- Friedlmeier, W., Corapci, F., & Cole, P. M. (2011). Emotion socialization in cross-cultural perspective. *Social and Personality Psychology Compass*, 5(7), 410–427. doi: 10.1111/j.1751-9004.2011.00362.x
- Friedman, J., Asnis, G., Boeck, M., & DiFiore, J. (1987). Prevalence of specific suicidal behaviors in a high school sample. *American Journal of Psychiatry*, 144, 1203–1206
- Fricke, T., Thornton, A., & Dahal, D. R. (1998). Netting in Nepal: Social change, the life course, and bride service in Sangila. *Human Ecology*, 26(2), 213–237
- Furman, W., & Shaffer, L. (2003). The role of romantic relationships in adolescent development. In P. Florsheim (Ed.), *Adolescent romantic relations and sexual behavior: Theory, research, and practical implications* (pp. 3–22). Mahwah, NJ: Erlbaum
- Gair, S., & Moloney, S. (2013). Broadening notions of 'missing persons' to increase social inclusion, public empathy and healing: Considering the case of children missing through adoption. *Journal of Social Inclusion*, 4(1), 90–109
- Gardner, F., Ward, S., Burton, J., & Wilson, C. (2003). The role of mother-child joint play in the early development of children's conduct problems: A longitudinal observational study. *Social Development*, 12(3), 361–378. doi: 10.1111/1467-9507.00238
- Gaskins, S., & Miller, P. J. (2009). The cultural roles of emotions in pretend play. In *Transactions

at Play (pp. 5–21). Lanham, MD: University Press of America

- Garcia, A. R., Metraux, S., Chen, C., Park, J., Culhane, D., & Furstenberg, F. (2018). Patterns of multisystem service use and school dropout among seventh-, eighth-, and ninth-grade students. *Journal of Early Adolescence*, 38(8), 1041–1073.

- Garrison, C., Jackson, K., Addy, C., & McKeown, R. (1991). Suicidal behaviors in young adolescents. *American Journal of Epidemiology*, 133, 1005–1014

- Geertz, C. (1973). *The Interpretation of Cultures: Selected Essays*. New York: Basic Books.

- Geertz, C. (1973). Thick Description: Toward an Interpretive Idea of Culture. In *The Interpretation of Cultures: Selected Essays* (pp. 3–30). New York: Basic Books.

- George, S., & Adiga, S. (2017). *Caste among Muslims: Ethnographic account from a Karnataka village*. Institute for Social and Economic Change.

- Ghimire, A., & Samuels, F. (2014). *Change and continuity in social norms and practices around marriage and education in Nepal*. Overnicas Development Institute.

- Giddens, A. (1984). *The constitution of society: Outline of the theory of structuration*. Cambridge, UK: Polity Press.

- Giddens, A., & Sutton, P. W. (2017). *Sociology*. Polity Press.

- Giedd, J. N. (2015). The amazing teen brain. *Scientific American*, 312(6), 32–37.

- Griffin, N., Chassin, L., & Young, D. (1981). Measurement of global self-concept versus multiple role-specific self-concepts in adolescents. *Adolescence*, 16, 549–556.

- Goldstein, D. E. (2004). *Once upon a virus: AIDS legends and vernacular risk perception*. Logan, USA: Utah State University Press.
- Goldscheider, F., & Goldscheider, C. (1993). *Leaving Home Before Marriage: Ethnicity, Familism, and Generational Relationships*. Madison: University of Wisconsin Press.
- Goldenberg, C., Gallimore, R., Reese, L., & Garnier, H. (2001). Cause or Effect? A longitudinal study of immigrant Latino parents' aspirations and expectations, and their children's school performance. *American Educational Research Journal*, 38(3), 547–582. doi: 10.3102/00028312038003547
- Goldrick-Rab, S. (2006). Following their every move: An investigation of social-class differences in college pathways. *Sociology of Education*, 79(1), 61.
- Gore, M. S. (1965). *The traditional Indian family: Comparative family systems*. Houghton Mifflin.
- Graneheim, U. H., & Lundman, B. (2004). Qualitative content analysis in nursing research: Concepts, procedures, and measures to achieve trustworthiness. *Nurse Education Today*, 24, 105–112. https://doi.org/10.1016/j.nedt.2003.10.001
- Graber, J. A. (2013). Pubertal timing and the development of psychopathology in adolescence and beyond. *Hormones and Behavior*, 64, 262–289.
- Grotevant, H. (1987). Toward a process model of identity formation. *Journal of Adolescent Research*, 2, 203–222.
- Grusec, J. E. (2011). Socialization processes in the family: Social and emotional development. *Annual*

Review of Psychology, 62, 243–269. doi: 10.1146/annurev.psych.121208.131650

- Guérin, I. (2013). Bonded labour, agrarian changes and capitalism: Emerging patterns in South India. *Journal of Agrarian Change*, 13(3), 405–423.
- Gurney, P. (1986). Self-esteem in the classroom. *School Psychology International*, 7, 199–209.
- Hagborg, W. (1993). The Rosenberg Self-Esteem Scale and Harter's Self-Perception Profile for Adolescents: A concurrent validity study. *Psychology in the Schools*, 30, 132–136.
- Hagan, J., & Dinovitzer, R. (1999). Collateral consequences of imprisonment for children, communities, and prisoners. *Crime and Justice*, 26, 121–162.
- Hakyemez, S. (2017). Torture, heroism, and the ordinary in Prison No. 5, Turkey. *Anthropological Quarterly*, 90(1), 107–138.
- Hagerman, M. A. (2010). "I like being interviewed!": Kids' perspectives on participating in social research. *Sociological Studies of Children and Youth*, 13, 61–105.
- Hall, G. S. (1904). *Adolescence: Its psychology and its relations to physiology, anthropology, sociology, sex, crime, religion, and education.* New York: Appleton.
- Hall, S., & Jefferson, T. (1976). *Resistance through rituals: Youth subcultures in post-war Britain.* New York: Holmes & Meyer.
- Hallinan, M. T. (2006). *School sector and student outcomes.* Notre Dame, IN: University of Notre Dame Press.
- Hall, S. (1997). The spectacle of the "Other." In S. Hall (Ed.), *Representation: Cultural representations*

and signifying practices (pp. 223–290). Thousand Oaks, CA: Sage.

- Hall, S. (1996). Introduction: Who needs identity? In S. Hall & P. Du Gay (Eds.), *Questions of cultural identity* (pp. 1–18). London: Sage.
- Hanawalt, B. A. (1995). *Growing up in medieval London: The experience of childhood in history*. New York: Oxford University Press.
- Handel, G., Cahill, S., & Elkin, F. (2007). *Children and society: The sociology of children and childhood socialization*. New York: Oxford University Press.
- Harper, J., & Marshall, E. (1991). Adolescents' problems and their relationship to self-esteem. *Adolescence*, 26, 799–808.
- Harter, S. (1990). Developmental differences in the nature of self-representations: Implications for the understanding, assessment, and treatment of maladaptive behaviors. *Cognitive Therapy and Research*, 14, 113–142.
- Harter, S. (2006). The self. In N. Eisenberg (Ed.), *Handbook of child psychology: Vol. 3 Social, emotional, and personality development* (6th ed., pp. 505–570). Hoboken, NJ: Wiley.
- Harter, S. (2012). Emerging self-processes during childhood and adolescence. In M. R. Leary & J. P. Tangney (Eds.), *Handbook of self and identity* (2nd ed., pp. 680–715). New York: Guilford.
- Hartup, W. W. (1996). The company they keep: Friendships and their developmental significance. *Child Development*, 67(1), 1–13.
- Harrison, L., Jr., Harrison, C., & Moore, L. N. (2002). African American racial identity in sport.

Sport, Education and Society, 7(2), 121–133. https:// doi.org/10.1080/1357332022000018823

- Hamilton, D. L., & Trolier, T. K. (1986). Stereotypes and stereotyping: An overview of the cognitive approach. In J. F. Dovidio & S. L. Gaertner (Eds.), *Prejudice, discrimination and racism* (pp. 127–163). Orlando, FL: Academic Press.
- Hart, K. (2010). The economy and morality of elopement in rural western Turkey. *Ethnologia Europaea*, 40(1), 58–76.
- Heath, R., & Tan, X. (2020). Intrahousehold bargaining, female autonomy, and labor supply: Theory and evidence from India. *Journal of the European Economic Association*, 18(4), 1928–1968.
- Herman, J. L. (1992). *Trauma and recovery*. New York: Basic Books.
- Hickey, C. (2008). Physical education, sport and hyper-masculinity in schools. *Sport, Education and Society*, 13(2), 147–161. https://doi. org/10.1080/13573320801957061
- Hinton, P. R. (2000). *Stereotypes, cognition and culture*. Hove, UK: Psychology Press.
- Hihara, S., Umemura, T., & Sugimura, K. (2019). Considering the negatively formed identity: Relationships between negative identity and problematic psychosocial beliefs. *Journal of Adolescence*, 70, 24–32.
- Hill, C., & Kearl, H. (2011). *Crossing the line: Sexual harassment at school*. Washington, DC: American Association of University Women (AAUW).
- Hilliard, L. J., & Liben, L. S. (2010). Differing levels of gender salience in preschool classrooms: Effects on children's gender attitudes and intergroup bias.

Child Development, 81(6), 1787–1798. https://doi. org/10.1111/j.1467-8624.2010.01510.x

- Hirschfield, P., & Gasper, J. (2011). The relationship between school engagement and delinquency in late childhood and early adolescence. *Journal of Youth and Adolescence, 40*(1), 3–22. https://doi. org/10.1007/s10964-010-9579-5

- Hoffmann, V., Rao, V., Surendra, V., & Datta, U. (2017). Relief from usury: Impact of a community-based microcredit program in rural India. *World Bank Policy Research Working Paper No. 8021.*

- Holdsworth, C. (2000). Leaving home in Britain and Spain. *European Sociological Review, 16*(2), 201–222.

- Holmes, L. (2008). *Living in limbo: The experiences of, and impacts on, the families of missing people.* London: Missing People Charity.

- Hu, L., & Schlosser, A. (2015). Prenatal sex selection and girls' well-being: Evidence from India. *The Economic Journal, 125*(587), 1227–1261.

- Horton, P. B., & Hunt, C. L. (1984). *Sociology.* New York: McGraw-Hill Inc.

- Huang, C., & Brittain, I. (2006). Negotiating identities through disability sport. *Sociology of Sport Journal, 23*, 352–375.

- Hudson, J. I., Hiripi, E., Pope, H. G., & Kessler, R. C. (2007). The prevalence and correlates of eating disorders in the National Comorbidity Survey Replication. *Biological Psychiatry, 61*(3), 348–358.

- Hughes, D., Rodriguez, J., Smith, E. P., Johnson, D. J., Stevenson, H. C., & Spicer, P. (2006). Parents' ethnic-racial socialization practices: A review of research and directions for future study.

Developmental Psychology, 42(5), 747–770. https://doi.org/10.1037/0012-1649.42.5.747

- Hull, M. (2012). *Government of paper: The materiality of bureaucracy in urban Pakistan.* Berkeley, CA: University of California Press.
- Hunter, E. C., Katz, L. F., Shortt, J. W., Davis, B., Leve, C., Allen, N. B., & Sheeber, L. B. (2011). How do I feel about feelings? Emotion socialization in families of depressed and healthy adolescents. *Journal of Youth and Adolescence, 40*(4), 428–441. https://doi.org/10.1007/s10964-010-9545-2
- Hussain, A., & Afzal, H. (2013). Exploring the issue of 'run-away women' in Pakistan: A call for social and legal change. *Journal of Law and Social Research, 4,* 59–72.
- Hyde, J. S., & DeLamater, J. D. (2008). *Understanding human sexuality* (10th ed.). Boston, MA: McGraw-Hill.
- Ibrahim, A. (2013). "Who is a bigger terrorist than the police?" Photography as a politics of encounter in Delhi's Batla House. *South Asian Popular Culture, 11*(2), 133–144.
- Inamdar, S., Siomopoulos, G., Osborn, M., & Bianchi, E. (1979). Phenomenology associated with depressed moods in adolescents. *American Journal of Psychiatry, 136,* 156–159.
- Iqbal, M. W. (2008). Street children: An overlooked issue in Pakistan. *Child Abuse Review, 17*(3), 201–209.
- Jacobs, J. E., Davis-Kean, P., Bleeker, M. M., Eccles, J. S., & Malanchuk, O. (2005). "I can, but I don't want to": The impact of parents, interests, and activities on gender differences in math. In A. M.

Gallagher & J. C. Kaufman (Eds.), *Gender differences in mathematics: An integrative psychological approach* (pp. 246–263). New York, NY: Cambridge University Press.

- James, A., Jenks, C., & Prout, A. (2005). Theorizing childhood. In C. Jenks (Ed.), *Childhood: Critical concepts in sociology* (Vol. 1, pp. 138–160). London: Taylor & Francis.

- Jassal, N. (2020). Gender, law enforcement, and access to justice: Evidence from all-women police stations in India. *American Political Science Review*, *114*(4), 1035–1054.

- Dignan, J. (2005). *Understanding victims and restorative justice*. Maidenhead, Berkshire, UK: Open University Press. *Current Issues in Criminal Justice*, *18*(3), 501–502.

- Jejeebhoy, S., Santhya, K. G., Acharya, R., Francis Zavier, A. J., Pandey, N., Singh, S. K., Saxena, K., Rampal, S., Basu, S., Gogor, A., Joshi, M., & Ojha, S. (2017). Empowering women and addressing violence against them through self-help groups (SHGs). *Population Council Report*.

- Jeanes, R. (2011). "I'm into high heels and make up but I still love football": Exploring gender identity and football participation with preadolescent girls. *Soccer & Society*, *12*(3), 402–420. https://doi.org/10.1080/14660970.2011.568107

- Jensen, R., & Oster, E. (2009). The power of TV: Cable television and women's status in India. *Quarterly Journal of Economics*, *124*(3), 1057–1094.

- Jessor, R. (1991). Risk behavior in adolescence: A psychosocial framework for understanding and action. *Journal of Adolescent Health*, *12*(8), 597–605.

- Jessor, R., Turbin, M. S., Costa, F. M., Dong, Q., Zhang, H., & Wang, C. (2003). Adolescent problem behavior in China and the United States: A cross-national study of psychosocial protective factors. *Journal of Research on Adolescence, 13*(3), 329–360. https://doi.org/10.1111/1532-7795.1303004

- Jones, O. (2012). *Chavs: The demonization of the working class.* London & New York: Verso.

- Jodl, K. M., Michael, A., Malanchuk, O., Eccles, J. S., & Sameroff, A. (2001). Parents' roles in shaping early adolescents' occupational aspirations. *Child Development, 72*(4), 1247–1265. https://doi.org/10.1111/1467-8624.00345

- Juang, L. P., Silbereisen, R. K., & Wiesner, M. (1999). Predictors of leaving home in young adults raised in Germany: A replication of a 1991 study. *Journal of Marriage and the Family, 61*(2), 505–515. https://doi.org/10.2307/353765

- Juang, L. P., & Silbereisen, R. K. (2002). The relationship between adolescent academic capability beliefs, parenting, and school grades. *Journal of Adolescence, 25*(1), 3–18. https://doi.org/10.1006/jado.2001.0445

- Kaiser, E., & Sinanan, A. N. (2019). Survival and resilience of female street children experiencing sexual violence in Bangladesh: A qualitative study. *Journal of Child Sexual Abuse.* https://doi.org/10.1080/10538712.2019.1685615

- Kahneman, D. (2011). *Thinking, fast and slow.* New York, NY: Farrar, Straus and Giroux.

- Kandel, D., & Davies, M. (1982). Epidemiology of depressive mood in adolescents: An empirical study. *Archives of General Psychiatry, 39*, 1205–1212.

- Katz-Wise, S. L., & Hyde, J. S. (2012). Victimization experiences of lesbian, gay, and bisexual individuals: A meta-analysis. *Journal of Sex Research*, 49(2–3), 142–167. https://doi.org/10.10 80/00224499.2011.637247
- Kazdin, A., French, N., Unis, A., Esveldt-Dawson, K., & Sherick, A. (1983). Hopelessness, depression, and suicidal intent among psychiatrically disturbed inpatient children. *Journal of Consulting and Clinical Psychology*, *51*, 504–510.
- Kazdin, A., Rodgers, A., & Colbus, D. (1986). The Hopelessness Scale for Children: Psychometric characteristics and concurrent validity. *Journal of Consulting and Clinical Psychology*, *54*, 241–245.
- Keijsers, L., Branje, S., Hawk, S. T., Schwartz, S. J., Frijns, T., Koot, H. M., & Meeus, W. (2012). Forbidden friends as forbidden fruit: Parental supervision of friendships, contact with deviant peers, and adolescent delinquency. *Child Development*, *83*(2), 651–666. https://doi. org/10.1111/j.1467-8624.2011.01701.x
- Keniston, K., & Cottle, T. J. (1972). Youth: A "new" stage of life. In *The prospect of youth. Contexts for sociological inquiry* (pp. 631–654). Boston, MA: Little and Brown.
- Kelly, D. M., Pomerantz, S., & Currie, D. H. (2008). "You can break so many more rules": The identity work and play of become skater girls. In M. D. Giardina & M. K. Donnelly (Eds.), *Youth culture and sport: Identity, power, and politics* (pp. 113–125). New York, NY: Taylor and Francis.
- Kett, J. F. (1977). *Rites of passage: Adolescence in America, 1790 to the present*. New York, NY: Basic Books.

- King, C., Naylor, M., Segal, H., Evans, T., & Shain, B. (1993). Global self-worth, specific self-perceptions of competence, and depression in adolescents. *Journal of the American Academy of Child & Adolescent Psychiatry, 32,* 745–752.
- King, M. (2007). The sociology of childhood as scientific communication. *Childhood, 14*(2), 193–213. https://doi.org/10.1177/0907568207078327
- Klasen, S., & Pieters, J. (2015). What explains the stagnation of female labor force participation in urban India? *World Bank Economic Review, 29*(3), 449–478.
- Knoppers, A., & McDonald, M. (2010). Scholarship on gender and sport in *Sex Roles* and beyond. *Sex Roles, 63,* 311–323. https://doi.org/10.1007/s11199-010-9841-z
- Koc, I. (2007). The timing of leaving the parental home and its relationship with other life course events in Turkey. *Marriage and Family Review, 42*(1), 15–22.
- Kotila, L., & Lönnqvist, J. (1988). Adolescent suicide attempts: Sex differences predicting suicide. *Acta Psychiatrica Scandinavica, 77,* 264–270.
- Kuate-Defo, B. (2006). Multilevel modeling of influences on transitions to adulthood in developing countries with special reference to Cameroon. In C. B. Lloyd, J. R. Behrman, N. P. Stromquist, & B. Cohen (Eds.), *The changing transitions to adulthood in developing countries: Selected studies* (pp. 367–423). Washington, DC: The National Academies Press.
- Kolsky, E. (2010). "The body evidencing the crime": Rape on trial in colonial India, 1860–1947. *Gender & History, 22*(1), 109–130.

- Kreager, D. A. (2004). Strangers in the halls: Isolation and delinquency in school networks. *Social Forces, 83*(1), 351–390.
- Kurtz-Costes, B., DeFreitas, S. C., Halle, T. G., & Kinlaw, C. R. (2011). Gender and racial favouritism in Black and White preschool girls. *British Journal of Developmental Psychology, 29*(2), 270–287. https://doi.org/10.1111/j.2044-835X.2010.02018.x
- Kurtz, P. D., Jarvis, S. V., & Kurtz, G. L. (1991). Problems of homeless youths: Empirical findings and human services issues. *Social Work, 36*, 311–314.
- L'Engle, K. L., Brown, J. D., & Kenneavy, K. (2006). The mass media are an important context for adolescents' sexual behavior. *Journal of Adolescent Health, 38*(3), 186–192. https://doi.org/10.1016/j.jadohealth.2005.03.020
- Laferrère, A. (2005). Leaving the nest: The interaction of parental income and family environment (Working Paper No. 2005-01). Centre de Recherche en Economie et Statistique. Retrieved from http://EconPapers.repec.org/RePEc/crs/wpaper/2005-01
- Lancy, D. F. (2007). Accounting for variability in mother-child play. *American Anthropologist, 109*(2), 273–284. https://doi.org/10.1525/aa.2007.109.2.273
- Laithangbam, L. (2014, July 16). Child trafficking in Manipur a cause for concern. *The Hindu*. Retrieved from http://www.thehindu.com/news/national/other-states/child-trafficking-in-manipur-a-cause-for-concern/article6216760.ece
- Landefeld, T. (2010). Minorities in science mentoring and diversity (Vol. 4, pp. 19–43). New York, NY: Springer.

- Lareau, A., & Horvat, E. M. (1999). Moments of social inclusion and exclusion: Race, class, and cultural capital in family-school relationships. *Sociology of Education*, 72(1), 37–53.
- Larson, R., & Ham, M. (1993). Stress and "storm and stress" in early adolescence: The relationship of negative events with dysphoric affect. *Journal of Early Adolescence*, 29, 130–140.
- Lawson, H. A. (2005). Empowering people, facilitating community development, and contributing to sustainable development: The social work of sport, exercise, and physical education programs. *Sport, Education and Society*, 10(1), 135–160. https://doi.org/10.1080/1357332052000308800
- Lawson, R. (1995). The challenge of new poverty: Lessons from Europe and North America. In K. Funken & P. Cooper (Eds.), *Old and new poverty: The challenge for reform* (pp. 5–28). Rivers Oram Press.
- Leaper, C. (2011). Research in developmental psychology on gender and relationships: Reflections on the past and looking into the future. *British Journal of Developmental Psychology*, 29(2), 347–356. https://doi.org/10.1111/j.2044-835X.2011.02035.x
- Lee, J. D. (1998). Which kids can "become" scientists? Effects of gender, self-concepts, and perceptions of scientists. *Social Psychology Quarterly*, 61(3), 199–219. https://doi.org/10.2307/2787108
- Leventhal, T., & Brooks-Gunn, J. (2000). The neighborhoods they live in: The effects of neighborhood residence on child and adolescent outcomes. *Psychological Bulletin*, 126(2), 309–337.

- LeVine, R. A. (2003). *Childhood socialization: Comparative studies of parenting, learning, and educational change.*Hong Kong, China: University of Hong Kong.
- Leventhal, K. S., Gillham, J., DeMaria, L., Andrew, G., Peabody, J., & Leventhal, S. (2015). Building psychosocial assets and well-being among adolescent girls: A randomized controlled trial. *Journal of Adolescence, 45,* 284–295.
- Leslie, A. W., & Peters, H. E. (1996). Economic incentives for financial and residential independence. *Demography, 33*(1), 82–97.
- Lloyd, C. B. (Ed.). (2005). *Growing up global: The changing transitions to adulthood in developing countries.* Washington, DC: The National Academies Press.
- Lippmann, W. (1965 [1922]). *Public opinion.* London: Free Press/Collier Macmillan.
- Lister, R. (2004). The third way's social investment state. In J. Lewis & R. Surender (Eds.), *Welfare state change: Towards a third way* (pp. 157–181). Oxford: Oxford Scholarship Online.
- Li, Y., & Lerner, R. M. (2011). Trajectories of school engagement during adolescence: Implications for grades, depression, delinquency, and substance use. *Developmental Psychology, 47*(1), 233–247. https://doi.org/10.1037/a0021307
- Liechty, M. (2003). *Suitably modern: Making middle-class culture in a new consumer society.* Princeton, NJ: Princeton University Press.
- Littlefield, M. B. (2008). The media as a system of racialization. *American Behavioral Scientist, 51*(5), 675–685. https://doi.org/10.1177/0002764207307747

- Lockyer, S., & Pickering, M. (2009). *Beyond a joke: The limits of humour*. New York, NY: Palgrave Macmillan.
- Luciano, M., & Collins, P. F. (2012). Incentive motivation, cognitive control, and the adolescent brain: Is it time for a paradigm shift? *Child Development Perspectives*, 6(4), 394–399.
- Luke, N., & Munshi, K. (2011). Women as agents of change: Female income and mobility in India. *Journal of Development Economics*, 94(1), 1–17.
- Lutfey, K., & Mortimer, J. (2006). Development and socialization through the adult life course. In J. Delamater (Ed.), *Handbook of Social Psychology* (pp. 183–202). Springer US.
- Macrae, C. N., & Bodenhausen, G. V. (2000). Social cognition: Thinking categorically about others. *Annual Review of Psychology*, 51, 93–120.
- Maccoby, E. E. (1990). Gender and relationships: A developmental account. *American Psychologist*, 45(4), 513–520. https://doi.org/10.1037/0003-066X.45.4.513
- Mamidi, S. C., & Mamidi, B. B. (2015). Building helplines and caring for missing children: A community project. In V. Pulla & B. B. Mamidi (Eds.), *Some aspects of community empowerment and resilience* (pp. 206–225). New Delhi: Allied Publishers.
- Manral, K. (2013, February 5). Nobody's missing children. *Tehelka.com*. Retrieved from http://www.tehelka.com/nobodys-missing-children/
- Mannheim, K. (1952). *The problem of generations: Essays on the sociology of knowledge* (p. 278). New York: Oxford University Press.

- Marcia, J. E. (1966). Development and validation of ego-identity status. *Journal of Personality and Social Psychology*, 3(5), 551–558. https://doi.org/10.1037/h0023281
- Martin, K. A. (2009). Normalizing heterosexuality: Mothers' assumptions, talk, and strategies with young children. *American Sociological Review*, 74(2), 190–207. https://doi.org/10.1177/000312240907400202
- Martin, P. R., & Bateson, P. (1993). *Measuring behaviour: An introductory guide*. Cambridge University Press.
- Marcia, J. (2010). Life transitions and stress in the context of psychosocial development. In T. W. Miller (Ed.), *Handbook of stressful transitions across the lifespan* (Part 1, pp. 19–34). New York, NY: Springer Science & Business Media.
- Marton, P., Connolly, J., Kutcher, S., & Korenblum, M. (1993). Cognitive social skills and social self-appraisal in depressed adolescents. *Journal of the American Academy of Child and Adolescent Psychiatry*, 32, 739–744.
- Marton, P., Golombek, H., Stein, B., & Korenblum, M. (1988). The relation of personality functions and adaptive skills to self-esteem in early adolescence. *Journal of Youth and Adolescence*, 17, 393–401.
- Marttunen, M., Aro, H., Henriksson, M., & Lonnqvist, J. (1991). Mental disorders in adolescent suicide: DSM-III-R Axes I and II diagnoses in suicides among 13-to 19-year-olds in Finland. *Archives of General Psychiatry*, 48, 834–839.
- Marsh, H. W., & Kleitman, S. (2005). Consequences of employment during high school: Character

building, subversion of academic goals, or a threshold? *American Educational Research Journal*, *42*, 331–369.

- Matthews, S. H. (2007). A window on the 'new' sociology of childhood. *Sociology Compass*, *1*(1), 322–334. https://doi.org/10.1111/j.1751-9020.2007.00001.x

- McAdams, D. P. (2013). Self and identity. In R. Biswas-Diener & E. Diener (Eds.), *Noba textbook series: Psychology*. Champaign, IL: DEF Publishers. Retrieved from: https://nobaproject.com

- McCauley, E., Mitchell, J., Burke, P., & Moss, S. (1988). Cognitive attributes of depression in children and adolescents. *Journal of Consulting and Clinical Psychology*, *56*, 903–908.

- McClintock, M., & Herdt, G. (1996). Rethinking puberty: The development of sexual attraction. *Current Directions in Psychological Science*, *5*, 178–183.

- McKelway, M. (2021). Women's agency and women's employment: How women's sense of agency affects their labor supply. Working Paper, Stanford University.

- McCormack, M. (2010). The declining significance of homohysteria for male students in three sixth forms in the south of England. *British Educational Research Journal*, *37*(2), 337–353. https://doi.org/10.1080/01411921003653357

- McCormack, M. (2011). Hierarchy without hegemony: Locating boys in an inclusive school setting. *Sociological Perspectives*, *54*(1), 83–102.

- McFarland, D. A. (2004). Resistance as a social drama: A study of change-oriented encounters.

American Journal of Sociology, 109(6), 1249–1318. https://doi.org/10.1086/381913

- McGhee Hassrick, E., & Schneider, B. (2009). Parent surveillance in schools: A question of social class. *American Journal of Education, 115*(2), 195–225.

- McPherson, M., Smith-Lovin, L., & Cook, J. M. (2001). Birds of a feather: Homophily in social networks. *Annual Review of Sociology, 27*, 415–444.

- McRobbie, A. (1999). *In the culture society: Art, fashion, and popular music.* Routledge.

- Mead, M. (1928). *Coming of age in Samoa.* Oxford, England: Morrow.

- Verwoerd, M., & Lopes, C. (2015). Sexualized violence in the national debate: Cross-border observations on India and South Africa.

- Merton, D. (1997). The meaning of meanness: Popularity, competition, and conflict among junior high girls. *Sociology of Education, 70*, 175–191.

- Marsden, M. (2007). Love and elopement in northern Pakistan. *Journal of the Royal Anthropological Institute, 13*, 91–108. https://doi.org/10.1111/j.1467-9655.2007.00415.x

- Marshall, M. N. (1996). Sampling for qualitative research. *Family Practice, 13*, 522–526. https://doi.org/10.1093/fampra/13.6.522

- Martinez, R. J. (2006). Understanding runaway teens. *Journal of Child and Adolescent Psychiatric Nursing, 19*, 77–88. https://doi.org/10.1111/j.1744-6171.2006.00049.x

- Maxwell, J. A. (2013). *Qualitative research design: An interactive approach.* Thousand Oaks, CA: SAGE Publications.

- Maxwell, B. E. (1992). Hostility, depression, and self-esteem among troubled and homeless adolescents in crisis. *Journal of Youth and Adolescence, 21*, 139–150.
- Mekonnen, B. M., & Aspen, H. (2009). Early marriage and the campaign against it in Ethiopia. In S. Ege, H. Aspen, B. Teferra, & S. Bekele (Eds.), *Proceedings of the 16th International Conference of Ethiopian Studies*, Trondheim, Norway.
- Mickelson, R. A. (1989). Why does Jane read and write so well? The anomaly of women's achievement. *Sociology of Education, 62*(1), 47–63.
- Miller, B. C., Benson, B., & Galbraith, K. A. (2001). Family relationships and adolescent pregnancy risk: A research synthesis. *Developmental Review, 21*(1), 1–38. https://doi.org/10.1006/drev.2000.0513
- Miller, K. E., Farrell, M. P., Barnes, G. M., Melnick, M. J., & Sabo, D. (2005). Gender/racial differences in jock identity, dating, and adolescent sexual risk. *Journal of Youth and Adolescence, 34*(2), 123–136. https://doi.org/10.1007/s10964-005-3211-0
- Missing People. (2021). Children's views on being reported missing from care. *Missing People: Registered charity in England and Wales, and in Scotland.* Retrieved from: https://www.missingpeople.org.uk/childrens-views-on-being-reported-missing-from-care
- Mjaaland, T. (2013). At the frontiers of change? Women and girls' pursuit of education in northwestern Tigray, Ethiopia (Doctoral dissertation). University of Bergen, Norway. Retrieved from Bora Home.
- Molla, R. S. (2018). Pastoral care in the living web for at-risk children in Ethiopia. *Journal of Pastoral*

Theology, 28, 189–202. https://doi.org/10.1080/10 649867.2018.1547957

- Morris, A. S., Silk, J. S., Morris, M. D. S., Steinberg, L., Aucoin, K. J., & Keyes, A. W. (2011). The influence of mother-child emotion regulation strategies on children's expression of anger and sadness. *Developmental Psychology, 47*(1), 213–225. https://doi.org/10.1037/a0021021
- Muller, C. (1998). Gender differences in parental involvement and adolescents' mathematics achievement. *Sociology of Education, 71*(4), 336–356.
- Moskowitz, A., Stein, J. A., & Lightfoot, M. (2013). The mediating roles of stress and maladaptive behavior on self-harm and suicide attempts among runaway and homeless youth. *Journal of Youth and Adolescence, 42*, 1015–1027. https://doi.org/10.1007/s10964-012-9793-4
- Murphy-Graham, E., & Leal, G. (2015). Child marriage, agency, and schooling in rural Honduras. *Comparative Education Review, 59*(1), 24–49.
- Murray, S. (2008). Pathologizing "fatness": Medical authority and popular culture. *Sociology of Sport Journal, 25*, 7–21.
- Murray, C. A. (1999). *The underclass revisited.* American Enterprise Institute.
- Mulder, C. H. (2000, September). Leaving home in the Netherlands: When and in which housing. Paper presented at *Leaving Home: A European Focus*, Rostock, Germany.
- National Commission for Protection of Child Rights (NCPCR). (2013). *Status of children in 14–18 years: Review of policy, programme and legislative*

framework, 2012–2013. Retrieved from http://neper.gov.in/view_file.php?fid=466

- National Crime Records Bureau. (2011). *Crime in India.* Retrieved from http://nerts.nic.in/
- National Science Foundation, National Center for Science and Engineering Statistics. (2011). Special tabulations of U.S. Department of Education, National Center for Education Statistics, Integrated Postsecondary Education Data System, Completions Survey, 2001–09. *Table 5-1: Bachelor's degrees, by sex and field: 2001–09.* Arlington, VA: National Science Foundation.
- Nelson, A., & Spears Brown, C. (2019). Too pretty for homework: Sexualized gender stereotypes predict academic attitudes for gender-typical early adolescent girls. *Journal of Early Adolescence, 39*(4), 603–617.
- Nelson, W. M., Politano, P. M., Finch, A. J., Wendel, N., & Mayhall, C. (1987). Children's Depression Inventory: Normative data and utility with emotionally disturbed children. *Journal of the American Academy of Child & Adolescent Psychiatry, 26,* 43–48.
- Overholser, J. C. (1993). Idiographic, quantitative assessment of self-esteem. *Personality and Individual Differences, 14,* 639–646.
- Neugarten, B. L. (1974). Age groups in American society and the rise of the young-old. *The Annals of the American Academy of Political and Social Science, 415*(1), 187–198. https://doi.org/10.1177/000271627441500114
- Niu, S., & Tienda, M. (2012). High school economic composition and college persistence. *Research in*

Higher Education, 1–33. https://doi.org/10.1007/s11162-012-9265-4

- Nowell, L. S., Norris, J. M., White, D. E., & Moules, N. J. (2017). Thematic analysis: Striving to meet the trustworthiness criteria. *International Journal of Qualitative Methods, 16*, 1–13. https://doi.org/10.1177/1609406917733847

- Oberman, M. (1994). Turning girls into women: Reevaluating modern statutory rape law. *Journal of Criminal Law & Criminology, 85*(1), 15–79.

- O'Brien, K. S., Hunter, J. A., & Banks, M. M. (2007). Implicit anti-fat bias in physical educators: Physical attributes, ideology and socialization. *International Journal of Obesity, 31*(2), 308–314. https://doi.org/10.1038/sj.ijo.0803398

- Oliver, K. L. (1999). Adolescent girls' body-narratives: Learning to desire and create a "fashionable" image. *Teachers College Record, 101*, 220–246. https://doi.org/10.1111/0161-4681.00039

- Oliver, K. L., & Lalik, R. (2001). The body as curriculum: Learning with adolescent girls. *Journal of Curriculum Studies, 33*(3), 303–333. https://doi.org/10.1080/00220270010006046

- Oliver, K. L., & Lalik, R. (2004). 'The beauty walk': Interrogating whiteness as the norm for beauty within one school's hidden curriculum. In J. Evans, B. Davies, & J. Wright (Eds.), *Body knowledge and control: Studies in the sociology of physical education and health* (pp. 115–129). New York: Routledge.

- Overholser, J. C., Miller, I., & Norman, W. (1987). The course of depressive symptoms in suicidal versus non-suicidal depressed inpatients. *Journal of Nervous and Mental Disease, 175*, 450–456.

- Paechter, C. (2003). Power, bodies, and identity: How different forms of physical education construct varying masculinities and femininities in secondary schools. *Sex Education, 3*(1), 47–59. https://doi.org/10.1080/1468181032000052153
- Pankhurst, A., Tiumelissan, A., & Chuta, N. (2016). The interplay between community, household, and child level influences on trajectories to early marriage in Ethiopia: Evidence from Young Lives. Oxford, UK: University of Oxford, Oxford Department of International Development (ODID).
- Parr, H., & Fyle, N. (2013). Missing geographies. *Progress in Human Geography, 37*(5), 615–638.
- Parr, H., & Stevenson, O. (2015). 'No news today': Talk of witnessing with families of missing people. *Cultural Geographies, 22*(2), 297–315.
- Parr, H., Stevenson, O., Fyfe, N., & Woolnough, P. (2015). Living absence: The strange geographies of missing people. *Environment and Planning D: Society and Space, 33*(1), 191–208.
- Parsons, T. (1951). *The social system*. London: Routledge.
- Pascoe, C. (2007). *Dude, you're a fag: Masculinity and sexuality in high school*. Berkeley, CA: University of California Press.
- Pearson, J., Muller, C., & Wilkinson, L. (2007). Adolescent same-sex attraction and academic outcomes: The role of school attachment and engagement. *Social Problems, 54*(4), 523–542.
- Pepler, D. J., & Craig, W. M. (1995). A peek behind the fence: Naturalistic observations of aggressive children with remote audiovisual recording.

Developmental Psychology, 31(4), 548–553. https://doi.org/10.1037/0012-1649.31.4.548

- Perez-Felkner, L. (2009). *Cultivating college dreams: Social pathways to educational attainment* (Doctoral dissertation). The University of Chicago, Chicago.
- Peled, E., & Cohavi, A. (2009). The meaning of running away for girls. *Child Abuse & Neglect, 33*, 739–749. https://doi.org/10.1016/j.chiabu.2007.04.018
- Pelaez, S. (2012). *Se la robaron (Elopement) in central Mexico: An ethnographic case study from Santiago Tlacotepec*(Master's thesis). University of Texas-Pan American.
- Perkins, T. E. (1979). Rethinking stereotypes. In M. Barrett, P. Corrigan, A. Kohn, & J. Wolff (Eds.), *Ideology and cultural production* (pp. [page numbers if available]). London: Croom Helm.
- PEW Research Center. (2022). *How Indians view gender roles in families and society.*
- Phillips, A. (2009, February 12). In praise of difficult children. *London Review of Books, 31*(3). Retrieved from https://www.irb.co.uk/the-paper/31/n03/adamphillips/in-praise-of-difficult-children
- Phinney, J. S. (1989). Stages of ethnic identity development in minority group adolescents. *Journal of Early Adolescence, 9*, 34–49.
- Phinney, J. S. (1992). The Multi-group Ethnic Identity Measure: A new scale for use with adolescents and young adults from diverse groups. *Journal of Adolescent Research, 7*, 156–176.
- Phinney, J. S. (2006). Ethnic identity exploration. In J. J. Arnett & J. L. Tanner (Eds.), *Emerging adults in America: Coming of age in the 21st Century* (pp. 117–

134). Washington, DC: American Psychological Association.

- Piaget, J. (2000). Piaget's theory. In *Childhood cognitive development: The essential readings* (pp. 33–47). Malden, MA: Blackwell Publishing.
- Pickering, M. (2001). *Stereotyping: The politics of representation*. New York: Palgrave Macmillan.
- Pickering, M. (2004). Bigotry. In E. Cashmore (Ed.), *Encyclopaedia of Race and Ethnic Studies* (pp. 53–57). New York: Routledge.
- Pickering, M. (2004). Racial stereotypes. In G. Taylor & S. Spencer (Eds.), *Perspectives on social identity* (pp. 91–106). New York: Routledge.
- Pickering, M. (2014). Stereotypes. In S. Attardo (Ed.), *Encyclopedia of humor studies* (Vol. 2, pp. 737–741). Los Angeles, CA: Sage.
- Pietromonaco, P. (1985). The influence of affect on self-perception in depression. *Social Cognition, 3*, 121–134.
- Pollock, L. A. (1983). *Forgotten children: Parent-child relations from 1500 to 1900*. New York: Cambridge University Press.
- Pong, S.-L., Hao, L., & Gardner, E. (2005). The roles of parenting styles and social capital in the school performance of immigrant Asian and Hispanic adolescents. *Social Science Quarterly, 86*(4), 928–950. https://doi.org/10.1111/j.0038-4941.2005.00364.x
- Porter, S., & Umbach, P. (2006). College major choice: An analysis of person-environment fit. *Research in Higher Education, 47*(4), 429–449. https://doi.org/10.1007/s11162-005-9002-3

- Portes, A., & Rumbaut, R. G. (2001). *Legacies: The story of the immigrant second generation*. Berkeley, CA: University of California Press.
- Portes, A., & Rumbaut, R. G. (2012). *Children of immigrants longitudinal study (CILS), 1991–2006* [Data set]. Inter-university Consortium for Political and Social Research (ICPSR). http://dx.doi.org/10.3886/ICPSR20520.v2
- Powell, A. J., Hlavka, H. R., & Mulla, S. (2017). Intersectionality and credibility in child sexual assault trials. *Gender & Society, 31*(4), 457–480.
- Prillaman, S. A. (2023). Strength in numbers: How women's groups close India's political gender gap. *American Journal of Political Science, 67*(2), 390–410.
- Rosenberg, M. (1985). Self-concept and psychological well-being in adolescence. In R. Leahy (Ed.), *The development of the self* (pp. 205–246). New York: Academic Press.
- Pufall, P. B., & Unsworth, R. P. (2004). *Rethinking childhood*. New Brunswick, NJ: Rutgers University Press.
- Pulla, V. (2016). Unprecedented move. *Space and Culture, India, 4*(2), 1–2.
- Queller, S., & Smith, E. (2002). Subtyping versus bookkeeping in stereotype learning and change: Connectionist simulations and empirical findings. *Journal of Personality and Social Psychology, 82,* 300–313.
- Rayner, G. (2015, July 9). Madeleine McCann latest: Are police any closer to knowing the truth? *The Telegraph*. Retrieved from http://www.telegraph.co.uk/news/2016/03/16/madeleine-

mccann-latest-are-police-any-closer-to-knowing-the-tru/

- Rees, G., & Lee, J. (2005). *Still running II*. London: The Children's Society.
- Raval, V., Raval, P. H., & Raj, S. P. (2010). Damned if they flee, doomed if they don't: Narratives of runaway adolescent females from rural India. *Journal of Family Violence, 25,* 755–764. https://doi.org/10.1007/s10896-010-9333-5
- Rew, L., Taylor-Seehafer, M., & Thomas, N. Y. (2001). Correlates of resilience in homeless adolescents. *Journal of Nursing Scholarship, 13,* 33–40.
- Ream, R. K. (2005). Toward understanding how social capital mediates the impact of mobility on Mexican American achievement. *Social Forces, 84,* 201–224.
- Reynolds, J. R., & Johnson, M. K. (2011). Change in the stratification of educational expectations and their realization. *Social Forces, 90*(1), 85–109. https://doi.org/10.1093/sf/90.1.85
- Riegle-Crumb, C., Farkas, G., & Muller, C. (2006). The role of gender and friendship in advanced course taking. *Sociology of Education, 79*(3), 206–228. https://doi.org/10.1177/003804070607900302
- Rivas-Drake, D., & Mooney, M. (2009). Neither colorblind nor oppositional: Perceived minority status and trajectories of academic adjustment among Latinos in elite higher education. *Developmental Psychology, 45*(3), 642–651. https://doi.org/10.1037/a0014135
- Riggins, S. H. (Ed.). (1997). *The language and politics of exclusion*. Thousand Oaks, CA: Sage.

- Richardson, D., Poudel, M., & Laurie, N. (2009). Sexual trafficking in Nepal: Constructing citizenship and livelihoods. *Gender, Place & Culture, 16*(3), 259–278.

- Robson, R. (1990). Lavender bruises: Intra-lesbian violence, law and lesbian legal theory. *Golden Gate University Law Review, 20*(3), 567–591.

- Robbins, D., & Alessi, N. (1985). Depressive symptoms and suicidal behavior in adolescents. *American Journal of Psychiatry, 142,* 588–592.

- Roediger, D. (2008). *How race survived US history: From settlement and slavery to the Obama phenomenon.* New York: Verso.

- Rogoff, B. (2003). *The cultural nature of human development.* New York: Oxford University Press.

- Rosen, D. M. (2007). Child soldiers, international humanitarian law, and the globalization of childhood. *American Anthropologist, 109*(2), 296–306. https://doi.org/10.1525/aa.2007.109.2.296

- Rosenfeld, M. J., & Kim, B.-S. (2005). The independence of young adults and the rise of interracial and same-sex unions. *American Sociological Review, 70*(4), 541–562. https://doi.org/10.1177/000312240507000401

- Ronholt, H. (2002). 'It's only the sissies...': Analysis of teaching and learning processes in physical education: A contribution to the hidden curriculum. *Sport, Education and Society, 7*(1), 25–36. https://doi.org/10.1080/13573320120113558

- Rosenblum, D. (2015). Unintended consequences of women's inheritance rights on female mortality in India. *Economic Development and Cultural Change, 63*(2), 223–248.

- Rosenbaum, J. (2006). Reborn a virgin: Adolescents' retracting of virginity pledges and sexual histories. *American Journal of Public Health, 96*(6), 1098–1103.
- Rosenberg, M. M. (1986). Self-concept from middle childhood through adolescence. In J. Suls & A. Greenwald (Eds.), *Psychological perspectives on the self, Vol. 3* (pp. 107–136). Hillsdale, NJ: Lawrence Erlbaum.
- Rosenberg, M., Schooler, C., & Schoenbach, C. (1989). Self-esteem and adolescent problems: Modeling reciprocal effects. *American Sociological Review, 54*, 1004–1018.
- Ruble, D. N., Taylor, L. J., Cyphers, L., Greulich, F. K., Lurye, L. E., & Shrout, P. E. (2007). The role of gender constancy in early gender development. *Child Development, 78*(4), 1121–1136. https://doi.org/10.1111/j.1467-8624.2007.01056.x
- Rusconi, A. (2000, September). Paper presented at the 7th Workshop of the European Research Network on Transition in Youth, Antwerp, Belgium.
- Rubenstein, J., Heeren, T., Housman, D., Rubin, C., & Stechler, G. (1989). Suicidal behavior in "normal" adolescents: Risk and protective factors. *Journal of Adolescence, 59*, 59–71.
- Russell, S. T., Clarke, T. J., & Clary, J. (2009). Are teens "post-gay"? Contemporary adolescents' sexual identity labels. *Journal of Youth and Adolescence, 38*, 884–890.
- Rutter, M. (1987). Psychosocial resilience and protective mechanisms. *American Journal of Orthopsychiatry, 57*, 316–331.
- Ryan, A. M., Shim, S. S., & Makara, K. A. (2013). Changes in academic adjustment and relational self-

worth across the transition to middle school. *Journal of Youth and Adolescence, 42,* 1372–1384.

- Sabean, D. W. (2001). Peasant voices and bureaucratic texts: Narrative structure in early modern German protocols. In P. Becker & W. Clark (Eds.), *Little tools of knowledge: Historical essays on academic and bureaucratic practices* (pp. 67–94). Ann Arbor: The University of Michigan Press.

- Sadker, M. (2004). Gender equity in the classroom: The unfinished agenda. In M. Kimmel (Ed.), *The gendered society reader* (2nd ed.). New York: Oxford University Press.

- Ullman, S. E. (1996). Social reactions, coping strategies, and self-blame attributions in adjustment to sexual assault. Retrieved from https://citeseerx.ist.psu.edu/viewdoc/download?doi=10.1.1.873.8072&rep=rep1&type=pdf

- Sabates, R., Harris, A. L., & Staff, J. (2011). Ambition gone awry: The long-term socioeconomic consequences of misaligned and uncertain ambitions in adolescence. *Social Science Quarterly, 92*(4), 959–977. https://doi.org/10.1111/j.1540-6237.2011.00799.x

- Sampson, R. J., Morenoff, J. D., & Felton, E. (1999). Beyond social capital: Spatial dynamics of collective efficacy for children. *American Sociological Review, 64*(5), 633–660.

- Sampson, R. J., Morenoff, J. D., & Gannon-Rowley, T. (2002). Assessing neighborhood effects: Social processes and new directions in research. *Annual Review of Sociology, 28,* 443–478. https://doi.org/10.1146/annurev.soc.28.110601.141114

- Schilt, K. (2003). "I'll resist with every inch and every breath." *Youth & Society, 35*(1), 71–97. https://doi.org/10.1177/0044118X03254566
- Schneider, B. L. (1997). *Sloan study of youth and social development, 1992–1997 [United States]*. ICPSR04551-v1. Retrieved from http://www.icpsr.umich.edu/icpsrweb/ICPSR/studies/04551/detail
- Schmalz, D. L., & Kerstetter, D. L. (2006). Girlie girls and manly men: Children's stigma consciousness of gender in sports and physical activities. *Journal of Leisure Research, 38*(4), 536–557.
- Schaffner, L. (1999). *Teenage runaways: Broken hearts and "bad attitudes"*. London, UK: Routledge.
- Schneider, B. L., Ford, T., & Perez-Felkner, L. (2010). Social networks and the education of children and youth. In P. Peterson, E. Baker, & B. McGaw (Eds.), *International encyclopedia of education* (pp. 705–711). Oxford: Elsevier.
- Schoen, R. F. (2015). Educated girls, absent grooms, and runaway brides: Narrating social change in rural Bangladesh. *Forum Qualitative Sozialforschung / Forum Qualitative Social Research, 16*(1), Article 2178. https://doi.org/10.17169/fqs-16.1.2178
- Schwartz, P. D., Maynard, A. M., & Uzelac, S. M. (2008). Adolescent egocentrism: A contemporary view. *Adolescence, 43*, 441–447.
- Seifert, K. (2012). *Educational psychology*. Retrieved from http://cnx.org/content/col11302/1.2
- Sewell, W. H., & Hauser, R. M. (1975). *Education, occupation, and earnings: Achievement in the early career*. New York: Academic Press.

- Sharp, N. (2015). Keeping it from the community: Sofer communities, 156–166. https://doi.org/10.1108/SC-03-2015-0007

- Shin, H., & Ryan, A. M. (2014). Early adolescent friendships and academic adjustment: Examining selection and influence processes with longitudinal social network analysis. *Developmental Psychology*, *50*(11), 2462–2472.

- Shomaker, L. B., & Furman, W. (2009). Parent-adolescent relationship qualities, internal working models, and attachment styles as predictors of adolescents' interactions with friends. *Journal of Social and Personal Relationships*, *26*(4), 579–603.

- Sinclair, S., & Carlsson, R. (2013). What will I be when I grow up? The impact of gender identity threat on adolescents' occupational preferences. *Journal of Adolescence*, *36*(3), 465–474.

- Simon, C., & Starks, B. (2002). Racial differences in the effects of significant others on students' educational expectations. *Sociology of Education*, *75*(4), 306–327. https://doi.org/10.2307/3090281

- Small, M. L. (2002). Culture, cohorts, and social organization theory: Understanding local participation in a Latino housing project. *American Journal of Sociology*, *108*(1), 1–54.

- Small, M. L. (2009). *Unanticipated gains: Origins of network inequality in everyday life*. New York: Oxford University Press.

- Smith, R. C. (2002). Gender, ethnicity, and race in school and work outcomes of second-generation Mexican-Americans. In M. M. Suarez-Orozco & M. M. Paez (Eds.), *Latinos: Remaking America* (pp. 110–125). Berkeley: University of California Press.

- Smucker, M. R., Craighead, W. E., Craighead, L. W., & Green, B. J. (1986). Normative and reliability data for the Children's Depression Inventory. *Journal of Abnormal Child Psychology, 14*, 25–39.
- Sloan, K. A. (2005). *Runaway daughters: Seduction, elopement, and humor in nineteenth-century Mexico.* Albuquerque: University of New Mexico Press.
- Sonnert, G. (2009). Parents who influence their children to become scientists. *Social Studies of Science, 39*(6), 927–941. https://doi.org/10.1177/0306312709335843
- Spenner, K. I., Buchmann, C., & Landerman, L. R. (2005). The Black-White achievement gap in the first college year: Evidence from a new longitudinal case study. In D. P. Baker & A. W. Wiseman (Eds.), *The impact of comparative education research on institutional theory* (pp. 345–377). Oxford, UK: Elsevier Science.
- Spinrad, T. L., Eisenberg, N., Gaertner, B., Popp, T., Smith, C. L., Kupfer, A., ... Hofer, C. (2007). Relations of maternal socialization and toddlers' effortful control to children's adjustment and social competence. *Developmental Psychology, 43*(5), 1170–1186. https://doi.org/10.1037/0012-1649.43.5.1170
- Spirito, A., Williams, C., Stark, L., & Hart, K. (1988). The Hopelessness Scale for Children: Psychometric properties with normal and emotionally disturbed adolescents. *Journal of Abnormal Child Psychology, 16*, 445–458.
- Stake, J. E., & Nickens, S. D. (2005). Adolescent girls' and boys' science peer relationships and perceptions of the possible self as scientist. *Sex

Roles, 52(1), 1–11. https://doi.org/10.1007/s11199-005-1189-4

- Stanton-Salazar, R. D., & Spina, S. U. (2000). The network orientations of highly resilient urban minority youth: A network-analytic account of minority socialization and its educational implications. *The Urban Review*, 32(3), 227–261.
- Staller, K. M. (2003). Constructing the runaway youth problem: Boy adventures to girl prostitutes, 1960–197. *Journal of Communication*, 53, 330–346. https://doi.org/10.1111/j.1460-2466.2003.tb02594.x
- Stark, L., Landis, D., Thomson, B., & Potts, A. (2016). Navigating support, resilience, and care: Exploring the impact of informal social networks on the rehabilitation and care of young female survivors of sexual violence in northern Uganda. *Peace and Conflict: Journal of Peace Psychology*, 22, 217–225. http://dx.doi.org/10.1037/pac0000162
- Steinberg, L., Icenogle, G., Shulman, E. P., et al. (2018). Around the world, adolescence is a time of heightened sensation seeking and immature self-regulation. *Developmental Science*, 21, e12532. https://doi.org/10.1111/desc.12532
- Steele, C. M. (2003). Stereotype threat and African-American student achievement. In C. Steele, T. Perry, & A. G. Hillard, III (Eds.), *Young, gifted, and Black: Promoting high achievement among African-American students* (pp. 109–130). Boston: Beacon Press.
- Steele, C. M., Spencer, S. J., & Aronson, J. (2002). Contending with group image: The psychology of stereotype and social identity threat. *Advances in Experimental Social Psychology*, 34, 379–440.

- Stevenson, H. C., & Arrington, E. G. (2009). Racial/ethnic socialization mediates perceived racism and the racial identity of African American adolescents. *Cultural Diversity and Ethnic Minority Psychology, 15*(2), 125–136. https://doi.org/10.1037/a0015500
- Stöckbenau, K., Heise, L., Wamoyi, J., & Bobrova, N. (2016). Revisiting the understanding of "transactional sex" in sub-Saharan Africa: A review and synthesis of the literature. *Social Science & Medicine, 168,* 186–197. http://dx.doi.org/10.1016/j.socscimed.2016.09.023
- Strayer, F. F., & Santos, A. J. (1996). Affiliative structures in preschool peer groups. *Social Development, 5*(2), 117–130. https://doi.org/10.1111/j.1467-9507.1996.tb00075.x
- Strober, M. (1985). Depressive illness in adolescence. *Psychiatry Annals, 15,* 375–378.
- St. Louis, B. (2003). Sport, genetics, and the 'natural athlete': The resurgence of racial science. *Body & Society, 9*(2), 75–95. https://doi.org/10.1177/1357034X030092004
- Strauss, A., & Corbin, J. (1998). *Basics of qualitative research: Techniques and procedures for developing grounded theory.* Thousand Oaks, CA: Sage.
- Stabile, C. A. (2006). *White victims, Black villains: Gender, race, and crime news in US culture.* New York: Routledge.
- Stretfeld, S. (1990, April 24). For Bruno Bettelheim, a place to die. *The Washington Post.* https://www.washingtonpost.com/archive/lifestyle/1990/04/24/for-bruno-bettelheim-a-place-to-die/5fa1f843-be85-4eae-966b-0d5abe7b8fb9/

- Smeaton, E. (2005). *Living on the edge: The experiences of detached young runaways*. London: The Children's Society.

- Smaje, C. (1997). Not just a social construct: Theorising race and ethnicity. *Sociology, 31*(2), 307–327. https://doi.org/10.1177/0038038597031002007

- Smith, F. R., & De Coster, J. (1998). Knowledge acquisition, accessibility, and use in person and stereotyping: Simulation with a recurrent connectionist network. *Journal of Personality and Social Psychology, 74*, 21–35.

- Sorell, G. T., & Montgomery, M. J. (2001). Feminist perspectives on the relevance of Erikson's theory for contemporary identity development research. *Identity: An International Journal of Theory and Research, 2*, 97–128.

- Syed, M., & Azmitia, M. (2009). Longitudinal trajectories of ethnic identity during the college years. *Journal of Research on Adolescence, 19*, 601–624. https://doi.org/10.1111/j.1532-7795.2009.00609.x

- Syed, M., & Juang, L. P. (2014). Ethnic identity, identity coherence, and psychological functioning: Testing basic assumptions of the developmental model. *Cultural Diversity and Ethnic Minority Psychology, 20*(2), 176–190. https://doi.org/10.1037/a0035330

- Sylva, K., Melhuish, E., Sammons, P., Siraj-Blatchford, L., & Taggart, B. (Eds.) (2010). *Early childhood matters: Evidence from the effective pre-school and primary education project*. London: Routledge.

- Szwedo, D. E., Mikami, A. Y., & Allen, J. P. (2012). Social networking site use predicts changes in young adults' psychological adjustment. *Journal of Research on Adolescence, n/a–n/a.* https://doi.org/10.1111/j.1532-7795.2012.00788.x
- Tadele, G., & Kifle, W. (2012). Chapter 2: Ethiopia. In J. J. Arnett (Ed.), *Adolescent psychology around the world* (pp. 15–27). New York, NY: Psychology Press.
- Tajfel, H. (1981). *Human groups and social categories.* Cambridge: Cambridge University Press.
- Tartamella, L., Herscher, E., & Woolston, C. (2004). *Generation extra large: Rescuing our children from the obesity epidemic.* New York: Basic Books.
- Taub, R. P., Taylor, D. G., & Dunham, J. D. (1984). *Paths of neighborhood change: Race and crime in urban America.* Chicago: University of Chicago Press.
- Taylor, J., Gilligan, C., & Sullivan, A. (1995). *Between voice and silence: Women and girls, race and relationship.* Cambridge, MA: Harvard University Press.
- Taylor, T., & Doherty, A. (2005). Adolescent sport, recreation and physical education: Experiences of recent arrivals to Canada. *Sport, Education and Society, 10*(2), 211–238. https://doi.org/10.1080/13573320500111770
- Terefe, W., Desta, A., Alemayehu, M., Asmelash, A., Kifle, H., & Gebre, F. (2015). *Report on baseline assessment on harmful traditional practices in five woredas of North West and Western Zones of Tigray.* Mekelle: Mums for Mums, Tigray Women's Affairs and Mekelle University. Funded by Civil Society Support Program (CSSP).

- Thelwall, M. (2008). Social networks, gender, and friending: An analysis of MySpace member profiles. *Journal of the American Society for Information Science and Technology*, 59(8), 1321–1330. https://doi.org/10.1002/asi.20835

- Thomas, Y., Hermitte, M.-A., & Napoli, P. (2011). *Les opérations du droit*. Paris: EHESS.

- Thomas, W. I., & Znaniecki, F. (1918). *The Polish peasant in Europe and America*. Chicago: University of Chicago Press.

- Thornberry, T. P., Lizotte, A. J., Krohn, M. D., Farnworth, M., & Jang, S. J. (1994). Delinquent peers, beliefs, and delinquent behavior: A longitudinal test of interactional theory. *Criminology*, 32(1), 47–83. https://doi.org/10.1111/j.1745-9125.1994.tb01146.x

- Thomas, R. M. (1979). *Comparing theories of child development*. Santa Barbara, CA: Wadsworth.

- Thorne, B., & Luria, Z. (1986). Sexuality and gender in children's daily worlds. *Social Problems*, 33(3), 176–190.

- Tolman, D. L., & McClelland, S. I. (2011). Normative sexuality development in adolescence: A decade in review, 2000–2009. *Journal of Research on Adolescence*, 21(1), 242–255. https://doi.org/10.1111/j.1532-7795.2010.00726.x

- Thornton, A., & Lin, H. S. (1994). *Social change and the family in Taiwan*. Chicago: University of Chicago Press.

- Tinning, R. (2004). Rethinking the preparation of HPE teachers: Ruminations on knowledge, identity, and ways of thinking. *Asia-Pacific Journal of Teacher Education, 32*(3), 241–253. https://doi.org/10.1080/1359866042000295406

• Trotter, R. T. (2012). Qualitative research sample design and sample size: Resolving and unresolved issues and inferential imperative. *Preventive Medicine, 55,* 398–400. https://doi.org/10.1016/j.ypmed.2012.07.003

• Troxel, W. M., Rodriquez, A., Seelam, R., Tucker, J., Shih, R., & D'Amico. (2019). Associations of longitudinal sleep trajectories with risky sexual behavior during late adolescence. *Health Psychology.* Retrieved from https://psycnet.apa.org/doiLanding?doi=10.1037%2Fhea0000753

• Islam, T. (2013, July). Interview by I. Watson, Institute of Research for Social Science (IRISS), UK. *Residential Childcare in Bangladesh* [Episode 40]. [No longer available].

• Tyler, K., Whitbeck, L. B., Hoyt, D. R., & Cauce, A. M. (2001). The effects of a high-risk environment on the sexual victimization of homeless and runaway youth. *Violence and Victims, 16*(4), 441–455.

• Umana-Taylor, A. (2003). Ethnic identity and self-esteem: Examining the roles of social context. *Journal of Adolescence, 27,* 139–146.

• UNESCO. (2018). *Street children*. [Cited 30 December 2019]. Available from: http://www.unesco.org/new/en/social-and-human-sciences/themes/fight-against-discrimination/education-of-children-in-need/street-children/

• UNODCCP. (2009). *Rapid situation assessment of street children in Cairo and Alexandria.* [Cited 31 December 2019]. Available from: https://www.

unodc.org/documents/egypt/egypt_street_children_report.pdf

- United Nations Population Fund (UNFPA). (2008). *Report on Activities Undertaken on "Stop Early Marriage Campaign"*. Addis Ababa, Ethiopia: UNFPA.
- Van der Kolk, B. (2014). *The body keeps the score: Brain, mind, and body in the healing of trauma*. New York: Viking.
- Van Blerk, L. (2007). AIDS, mobility and commercial sex in Ethiopia: Implications for policy. *AIDS Care, 12*, 79–86. https://doi.org/10.1080/09540120600805091
- Van Rooy, D., Van Overwalle, F., Vanhoomissen, T., Labiousc, C., & French, R. (2003). A recurrent connectionist model of group. *Psychological Review, 3*, 536–563.
- Vismann, C. (2008). *Files: Law and media technology* (G. Winthrop-Young, Trans.). Stanford: Stanford University Press.
- Wade, T. D., Keski-Rahkonen, A., & Hudson, J. I. (2011). Epidemiology of eating disorders. In *Textbook of Psychiatric Epidemiology* (3rd ed., pp. 343–360).
- Wagg, S. (1992). I blame the parents: Childhood and politics in modern Britain. *Sociology Review*, 10–15.
- Walker, J. A. (2012). Early marriage in Africa: Trends, harmful effects, and interventions. *African Journal of Reproductive Health, 16*(2), 231–240.
- Wang, M.-T., Willett, J. B., & Eccles, J. S. (2011). The assessment of school engagement: Examining dimensionality and measurement

invariance by gender and race/ethnicity. *Journal of School Psychology, 49*(4), 465–480. https://doi.org/10.1016/j.jsp.2011.04.001

- Ward, L. M. (2003). Understanding the role of entertainment media in the sexual socialization of American youth: A review of empirical research. *Developmental Review, 23*(3), 347–388. https://doi.org/10.1016/s0273-2297(03)00013-3

- Ward, C. L., & Seager, J. R. (2010). South African street children: A survey and recommendations for services. *Development Southern Africa, 21*(1), 85–100.

- Wilson, A., & Krane, R. (1980). Change in self-esteem and its effects on symptoms of depression. *Cognitive Therapy and Research, 4*, 419–421.

- Weaver, S. (2011). *The rhetoric of racist humour.* Burlington, VT: Ashgate.

- Weber, M. (1968). *Economy and society: An outline of interpretive sociology* (E. Fischoff, Trans.). New York: Bedminster Press.

- Weintraub, K. (2016). Young and sleep deprived. *Monitor on Psychology, 47*(2), 46–50.

- Weir, K. (2015). Marijuana and the developing brain. *Monitor on Psychology, 46*(10), 49–52.

- Weir, K. (2016). The risks of earlier puberty. *Monitor on Psychology, 47*(3), 41–44.

- Wellard, I., Pickard, A., & Bailey, R. (2007). "A shock of electricity just sort of goes through my body": Physical activity and embodied reflexive practices in young female ballet dancers. *Gender and Education, 19*(1), 79–91. https://doi.org/10.1080/09540250601087793

- Wigger, I. (2010). "Black shame"—the campaign against "racial degeneration" and female degradation in interwar Europe. *Race & Class*, *51*(3), 33–46.
- Winnicott, D. W. (1963). Communicating and not communicating: Leading to a study of certain opposites. In D. W. Winnicott (1990), *The maturational processes and the facilitating environment* (pp. [specific pages if needed]). London & New York: Karnac.
- Willis, P. E. (1977). *Learning to labor: How working class kids get working class jobs*. New York: Columbia University Press.
- Wilson, W. J. (1996). *When work disappears* (1997 ed.). New York: Vintage Books.
- Winkler, E. N. (2010). "I learn being black from everywhere I go": Color blindness, travel, and the formation of racial attitudes among African American adolescents. In *Children and Youth Speak for Themselves* (Sociological Studies of Children and Youth, 13), 423–453.
- Wood, D., Kurtz-Costes, B., & Copping, K. E. (2011). Gender differences in motivational pathways to college for middle-class African American youths. *Developmental Psychology*, *47*(4), 961–968. https://doi.org/10.1037/a0023745
- World Economic Forum. (2022). *Global Gender Gap Report 2022*.
- Workman, M., & Beer, J. (1989). Self-esteem, depression, and alcohol dependency among high school students. *Psychological Reports*, *65*, 451–455.
- Wrench, A., & Garrett, R. (2012). Identity work: Stories told in learning to teach physical education.

Sport, Education and Society, 17(1), 1–19. https://doi.org/10.1080/13573322.2011.607909

- Yardley, J. (2012, April 5). Maid's cries cast light on child labor in India. *The New York Times*. Retrieved from http://india.blogs.nytimes.com/2012/04/05/maids-cries-cast-light-on-child-labor-in-india/?_r=0
- Yau, J. C., & Reich, S. M. (2018). "It's just a lot of work": Adolescents' self-presentation norms and practices on Facebook and Instagram. *Journal of Research on Adolescence, 29*(1), 196–209.
- Yinger, J. M. (1960). Contraculture and subculture. *American Sociological Review, 25*(5), 625–635.
- Youniss, J., McLellan, J. A., & Yates, M. (1999). Religion, community service, and identity in American youth. *Journal of Adolescence, 22*(2), 243–253.
- Zelizer, V. A. R. (1994). *Pricing the priceless child: The changing social value of children*. Princeton, NJ: Princeton University Press.
- Zhou, M. (1997). Growing up American: The challenge confronting immigrant children and children of immigrants. *Annual Review of Sociology, 23*(1), 63–95. https://doi.org/10.1146/annurev.soc.23.1.63
- Zimmer, R. W., Gill, B., Booker, K., Lavertu, S., Sass, T. R., & Witte, J. (2009). *Charter schools in eight states: Effects on achievement, attainment, integration, and competition*. Santa Monica, CA: RAND.